HOW TO
REPAIR & RESTORE
BODYWORK

David H. Jacobs, Jr.

Motorbooks International
Publishers & Wholesalers ®

First published in 1991 by Motorbooks International Publishers & Wholesalers, P O Box 2, 729 Prospect Avenue, Osceola, WI 54020 USA

Motorbooks International books are also available at discounts in bulk quantity for industrial or sales-promotional use. For details write to Special Sales Manager at the Publisher's address

Library of Congress Cataloging-in-Publication Data
Jacobs, David H.
  How to repair and restore bodywork / David H. Jacobs, Jr.
    p.   cm.
  Includes index.
  ISBN 0-87938-514-6
  1. Automobiles–Bodies–Maintenance and repair I. Title.
TL255.J33 1991
629.26–dc20   90-24613

On the front cover: Dan Mycon of Newlook Autobody in Kirkland, Washington, begins work on the crumpled rear end of a Toyota MR2.
On the back cover: From repairs of minor parking lot dents to major restoration bodywork using lead filler—this book will show you how. *The Eastwood Company*

Printed and bound in the United States of America

Contents

Acknowledgments

To write a book about autobody work that professes to be consistent with the methods and techniques used by professional autobody technicians, one has to recognize and interpret the talents of specialists in the field. This book could not have been written without help from a few of these talented professionals. Therefore, I want to thank them for their helpful assistance throughout the course of this endeavor.

First, I want to thank Dan Mycon, owner of Newlook Autobody in Kirkland, Washington. He is a real "car guy" who gets involved with all of the projects at his shop because he simply likes cars and loves the autobody repair business. He let me hang around his shop for days on end to photograph repairs in progress and he answered more questions than I care to number.

Mike Kane is Newlook's premier bodyman. His patience is second to none. In the middle of intricate jobs, Mike would never hesitate to fully explain the techniques involved or the reasons why he did certain things a particular way. I appreciate his knowledge of the autobody business and want to thank him for sharing some of it with me.

Terry Vanhee has been painting automobiles for a long time. At Newlook, he is regarded as a professional in every sense of the word. Like Kane, he took plenty of time out of his busy schedule to fully explain what painters look for in quality autobody repairs.

Dennis Laursen painted cars for twenty years until retiring from that profession to become a sales rep for Bel-Tech Auto Paint of Bellevue, Washington. His insight into the autobody arena from a veteran painter's and now a supply jobber's standpoint helped to drive home points of safety and the need to use respirators and safety equipment all the time.

Mike Link and Doug Burrous have a lot of experience working on cars. I want to thank them for sharing their "learned the hard way" lessons with me. Link was right when he said, "While working on intricate door panels and other car parts, you need three tiny hands with a light bulb on one finger, an eye on another and a set of vise grips on each."

Jim Poluch, sales executive for The Eastwood Company, provided lots of special autobody tools and equipment for this project. Along with that, he made sure copies of The Eastwood Company's *Restoration News* were delivered, which featured lots of in-depth information regarding autobody restoration techniques and prescribed methods.

Adam and Matt Jacobs proved to be great helpers during photography sessions by writing down information about every picture taken with special notes on unique operations. Thanks also go to Janna Jacobs for barking up the side of her car so Kane could fix it in front of the camera. She was also quite helpful during editing tasks.

Finally, I want to thank Tim Parker, Barbara Harold, Michael Dregni, Greg Field and Mary LaBarre of Motorbooks International. Their continued support and editorial assistance helped to make this project an enjoyable and worthwhile experience.

4

Introduction

Automobiles are manufactured with thousands of different parts combined to serve integral functions for maximum operational performance and passenger comfort. The kinds of material used for these parts include steel, glass, aluminum, plastic, fiberglass and rubber. Each individual part is secured in place by screws, bolts, clips, rivets, welds or adhesives. Because they are individual parts assembled together to make single units, they can be dismantled for repair or replacement in case of collision damage or deterioration.

Since motorized vehicles are combinations of separate pieces, any damaged car or truck could conceivably be repaired with new parts to reach acceptable driving standards no matter the degree of damage. However, one has to consider the cost involved in buying new parts and the labor fees required for professionals to install them. These dollar amounts are what insurance adjustors must consider when deciding whether to pay for repairs or simply "total" a vehicle. When costs of repairs outweigh an automobile's actual worth, insurance companies generally choose to replace the car with another one of equal value, the least expensive option.

Professional autobody technicians are in the business of repairing wrecked vehicles. A lot of their time is spent removing broken parts to replace them with new ones. The rest is concentrated on dent repair and alignment requirements. Some enterprising individuals specialize in restoring automobiles totaled by insurance companies. Because their time is essentially their own, they can afford to leisurely repair or replace damaged parts in hopes that the sale of their reconditioned vehicle will compensate for the hours they put into repairs.

With the interest in automobiles of all kinds skyrocketing throughout the world, a number of new companies have been formed that offer replacement parts for just about any make or model ever made. Plenty of catalogs from car parts specialty stores are readily available that offer enthusiastic auto restorers myriad items like floor pans, quarter panels, weather stripping, molding clips, decals, emblems, window trim and just about anything else you can imagine. Where some parts for older cars are no longer available from manufacturers, creative companies have been able to develop reproduction methods that conform to exacting standards.

Years ago, a television commercial focused around a new car ashtray advertised to cost the same as a new car. The sales pitch was directed toward the ashtray's quality of construction, its style and usability. At the ad's end, an announcer was eager to explain that along with the purchase of this fine ashtray, you would receive a complete, brand new automobile absolutely free. Not only that, but the car would fit perfectly around the ashtray and match its color scheme to boot.

Now, since it appears evident that every part of every car can eventually be replaced, it seems possible, although impractical, that you could build a new car around a lone surviving ashtray. The labor and parts replacement costs would be astronomical, but nevertheless, it could be done. Therefore, an individual autobody repair person needs to decide the feasibility of repairs when damage to a car is considerable. The vehicle's intrinsic value has to be weighed against realistic part replacement costs and labor commitments.

To effect major repairs to cars and trucks that have suffered extensive body or chassis damage, professional technicians rely on the performance of expensive technical equipment. Frame and suspension repairs must be made according to exact specifications in order for vehicles to perform safely. In addition, governmental regulations require specific repair procedures to ensure passenger safety. Major frame, chassis and suspension repairs cannot be made by backyard mechanics using chains and come-alongs. They must be done by knowledgeable experts who have attended certified training schools and are up to date on the latest repair methods, techniques and recognized standards.

On the other hand, there are a lot of "body only" repairs that can be successfully achieved by do-it-yourself auto enthusiasts with minimal assortments of body shop equipment and mechanic's tools. The purpose of this book is to show you how to fix minor to moderate autobody collision problems correctly, using methods and techniques consistent with those of professional autobody technicians. Along the way, you will also learn how to assess hidden damage, remove and replace all kinds of body pieces, repair dings and dents, prepare areas for paint and find replacement parts.

Information provided in the following chapters will show you how minor to moderate collision repairs are managed. Upon completion of your project, you should not only realize a substantial dollar savings, but also reap rewards through the personal satisfaction of knowing that your job was well done.

Safety during autobody repair endeavors is always a major concern. You are urged to follow all safety recommendations featured throughout this text. Completion of any body repair project is supposed to carry with it a certain amount of enjoyment. All of it could be quickly lost should you sustain an injury, especially when caused by failure to follow established or recommended safety practices.

1

Autobody Work Defined

Naive car owners might envision autobody work as a simple dent repair or part replacement service. They may picture an easy process where technicians wield hammers at pieces of metal eventually straightening them out to smooth perfection, followed by a quick coat of paint and, voilà, repairs are done. Very small dings could have possibly been fixed that way years ago, but autobody repair work these days is different.

On today's cars, what may first appear to be just a minor dent on a fender could actually include slight hood buckles. A dent on the face of a rubber covered bumper might be deemed an easy repair until you recognize that one or two of the five or six pieces incorporated into the bumper are virtually destroyed.

Autobody work encompasses many different functions. Technicians not only flatten dings and dents, they straighten frames, weld in new rocker and quarter panels, replace doors, trunk lids and

The passenger side rear door on this 1990 Toyota 4-Runner was accidentally opened as the rig was being backed out of a garage. Impact with the garage wall forced the door to open way past its normal position. Although the vertical door dent is obvious, additional damage included uneven gap spacing around the entire door. As it turned out, the B-pillar was tweaked with resulting misalignment of the door hinges.

Autobody work is a combination of part dismantling, metal straightening and work with filler materials. Minor dings on the fender, near the door handle and along the bottom section of the door, required the removal of fender flairs, body side molding and door handle. New paint for the entire side and a complete detail will help this car look as good as new.

hoods, remove and replace broken glass, fix misaligned hatches and insert new light fixtures. About 50 percent of a technician's time can quickly be spent dismantling damaged parts and installing new ones, another 25 percent used to flatten dented metal and

The entire side of this pickup truck suffered extensive shallow metal damage in a side-swipe collision. Because repairs to the rather thin sheet metal panels would have been exhaustive, if not impossible, a new door and bed side panel were ordered and put in place. Note that some bodywork was performed on the bed just above the rear tire. Sometimes, new parts arrive with minor blemishes or suffer small dings during installation.

With all the body and paint work completed, one would never know that this truck was involved in a side-swipe accident that required installation of a new door and bed side panel. Expert body filler work on the pillar behind the door made sure that curves and contours were maintained. About half of the work included part removal and new part installation, while a quarter was spent fixing dents and another quarter devoted to sanding and shaping maneuvers. All that's left is a complete detail and this truck will look great.

the remaining 25 percent utilized for sanding and smoothing endeavors.

Along with metal straightening and shaping expertise, autobody technicians must possess a certain amount of mechanical skills. All sorts of parts may have to be removed during a repair. This must be done in an orderly fashion to guarantee that eventual replacement efforts will be synchronized to assure proper fit and part operation.

Autobody technicians are, more or less, jacks-of-all-trades. In the course of a week's work, they flatten dented metal, repair torn fiberglass, fill in punctured flexible plastic, remove and replace fenders and so on. "No two jobs are ever the same," says Mike Kane, the senior autobody technician at Dan Mycon's Newlook Autobody in Kirkland, Washington. He likes the diversity of his profession and recognizes that each job brings with it a new set of challenges and rewards.

For job scheduling and estimating purposes, Dan Mycon rates collision damage into three basic groups: light hits, medium hits and heavy hits. This determination is generally based on bottom-line cost figures. For the most part, repairs under $1,000 are light hits, between $1,000 and $2,000 medium hits and those over $3,000 are classified as heavy hits.

Light hits

Light hits include, but are not limited to, minor door dings, dented bumpers, fender creases, hood depressions and quarter panel wrinkles. Minimal damage to trim, lights, grilles, flairs and spoilers also fits into this category. Basically, a light hit is described as collision damage that, although easily seen, clearly does not involve adjacent vehicle sections or assemblies.

For example, a minor fender dent can be easily popped out and flattened with a hammer and dolly. Paint is removed from the area of repair with a 24 grit sanding disc to expose bare metal. A coat of quality plastic filler is then applied to the repair extending past actual damage by a few inches in all directions. After it is sanded smooth, a skim coat of glazing putty is put on, allowed to cure and then finish sanded. This entire process may take only thirty to forty-five minutes.

A similar dent next to a door handle will require more work, not so much for the dent repair, but for the time it takes for removing an interior door panel to gain access to the handle's fastening screws. Although this dent could still be classified as a light hit, extra labor time allotted to remove and eventually replace the door panel, any inner door mechanisms for access to the handle and the handle itself might cause repair costs to climb near medium hit levels.

Sometimes a light hit collision will cost an owner more than $1,000 just for parts. According to Mycon, a new Porsche 944 door, for example, can cost as much as $2,500 for just the shell. This does not include hardware, glass, molding, interior panel, handles, and so on.

You may not think a moderately dented door would require replacement with a new one. But when a "Nader Bar" between inner and outer door skins is damaged, you have no choice. These bars are installed in newer cars for passenger protection in case of accidents (light trucks and utility vehicles are not required to have them). They are made of high strength steel alloy in such a way that they cannot be repaired. New doors must be installed because straightening Nader Bars would require that heat be applied to them and then hammered flat. Heat and metalwork could make the metal's tight molecular structure brittle and weak.

Combine that Porsche door cost with a $1,000 price tag for Mazda RX-7 bumpers and $1,100 for the liftgate glass on a 1989–90 Ford Probe and you can understand why repair costs are so high.

You can save money on minor repairs by not only doing them yourself, but by purchasing used parts at an auto wrecking yard. Whether a door or fender is new or used, it will have to be painted to match the color of your car. As long as a used part is in excellent condition, what's the difference?

Because of this dent's close proximity to the window above, belt molding and trim around the window will have to be removed in order to allow working access to damaged metal. This kind of job requires patience and careful examination of the trim and molding so that they are not damaged during removal. Look for clips, screws or other fasteners around moldings before simply tugging or pulling on them. Few window parts just snap in place; most are secured somehow with special clips.

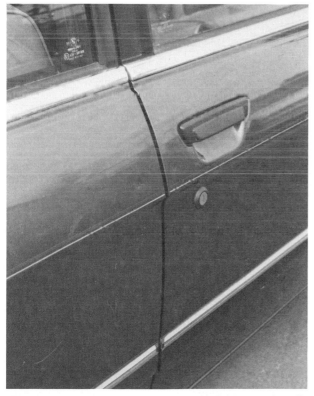

The two small dimples just to the left of this door handle are minor repair items. Extra labor will be needed to remove the front door's interior panel so access can be made for the removal of the door handle. This is an example of light hit damage where only what you see needs repairing. No other assemblies or panels are involved.

To make sure this repair turns out perfect the first time, the interior door panel was removed to gain access for door handle and window belt molding removal. This allows plenty of work room on the outside, as well as room between the inner and outer door skins for spoon and dolly work. A small section of cardboard covers the window to protect glass from grinding sparks and other work maneuvers.

Before writing off an entire grille piece as totally destroyed because of a light hit to just one side of it, be sure to look it over carefully. Many times, grille assemblies are composed of two or three pieces secured together with screws or clips. What may first appear to be a ruined grille may turn out to be damage suffered by only one section of the unit. That little section may be cheap to replace and easy to install.

Medium hits

Collision damage that includes more than one automobile section generally falls into the medium hit category. With the possible exception of a shallow crease along a door and fender, most multiple panel, door and fender accidents involve more than just dent repair. Doors or liftgates may have been sprung, pillars dented, window mechanisms bent, door handles broken, body side molding ripped off, emblems, trim or decals damaged, and so on.

In cases where fenders have been crunched, for example, you must determine how much additional damage to surrounding assemblies has occurred. Many times, inner fenders, bumpers, light fixtures, hoods and various support brackets have been directly affected by an accident. This will require more time be spent on the repair and more money allotted for parts.

A majority of medium hits can be repaired by do-it-yourself auto enthusiasts who have a general knowledge and assortment of mechanic's hand tools and required autobody repair equipment. Neither frame nor suspension assembly damage repair should be attempted, however. A novice repair person should concentrate on body panel shaping and new part installation.

Patch panels and new panel installations might be within the range of repair for enthusiasts with

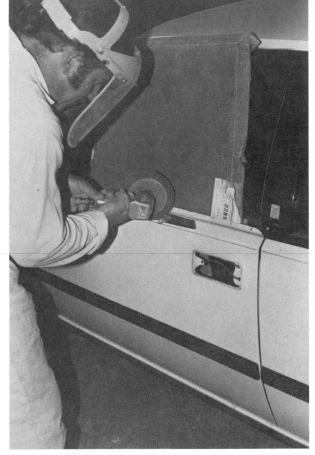

Kane uses a high-speed sander with a 24 grit disc to remove paint and any foreign debris, like rust, from the dent's area. Notice that he is wearing a full face shield and glass is protected with a piece of heavy-duty cardboard. He prefers to cut small slivers off of the outer circumferences of sanding discs to form angled points around them. These angled points work better than round edges for getting paint, rust and debris out of tiny craters or creases inside dented areas.

Kane is pointing to a Nader Bar inside Janna Jacobs' 1988 Volkswagen Jetta front door. Although most Nader Bars are wide and flat, some are round. Damage to Nader Bars cannot be repaired. Impacts strong enough to bend them call for new doors to be installed. A new door shell complete with Nader Bar can be purchased through a dealership parts department or a used one might be found at a wrecking yard.

The grille and bumper on this Corvette were removed in order to repair fiberglass damage on the driver's side front corner. Notice that a section of grille still remains behind the license plate. Not all grilles are assembled as one piece. In many cases, a number of pieces are secured together to make such an assembly. This is important to know when assessing damage and ordering new parts.

A shallow dent outlined by a crease on the front door along with a crumpled rear door edge and broken body side molding pieces might cost as much as $1,000 to have repaired at a professional body shop. Interior door panels will have to be pulled off to gain working access to the inner sides of outer door skins. The rear door hinges were tweaked causing the door to open stiffly. Notice the wide gap spacing at the front door and fender area next to lower trim. flattening the door panel dent will cause this gap to narrow within acceptable limits.

In addition to this obvious fender crunch, you have to look around the entire front right quarter area of this Nova to check for indirect body damage. This collision impact caused gaps between the fender and hood to narrow, which means that either the fender or hood, or both, was tweaked out of alignment. Also note that new headlight trim pieces are needed and the forward section of body side trim has come loose. The headlight might have been cracked or knocked out of alignment.

11

welding experience. One must recognize that welding work on newer vehicles is vastly different than for models of yesteryear. Older cars were made of heavier steel that could withstand a greater degree of hot metalwork and welding than cars of the last twenty to thirty years made with lighter materials.

Welding in a new rocker panel or patch panel on a newer automobile requires skill using low amperage welding. Too much working heat will burn away newer metal and prolonged welding exposure will cause panels to warp. Kane has found that low amperage wire feed welding works best when applied in the form of short, ¾ to 1 in. stitch welds, spaced 2 in. apart, as opposed to long, fill-in-all-the-gap, standard welding.

Doors that have been severely torn on the outside can sometimes be outfitted with new door skins. Door edges and internal mechanisms must not be damaged, just the outer door skin. Using a spot weld cutter and die grinder, you can remove outer door skins and install new ones for a fraction of the cost of an entire new door.

Trunk lids and hoods are reinforced with inner supports and assemblies. Fixing medium to heavy damage on these is almost impossible. In the first place, there is no practical way to reach a unit's top skin through underlying support metal. Second, the extra long and wide surface areas of thin metal are exceptionally prone to indirect buckles and warp-like damage by way of hammer, dolly and metal shrinking work performed on an original dent. In most cases, medium to heavily damaged hoods and trunk lids are replaced with brand new units or used pieces in excellent condition from a wrecking yard.

Medium hits cover a wide array of collision damage. In some cases, repair work may simply consist of dismantling damaged parts and replacing them with new ones. Dents and dings are pulled out to within ⅛ in. or flatter and then covered with body filler. Since newer plastic fillers have been designed for extensive autobody use, they perform admirably on thin sheet metal panels when applied according to instructions. The old school of thought that only rank amateurs use plastic filler is just that, old school. In fact, with the advent of thinner sheet metal bodies, the old style method of leading-in and brazing dent repair is fast becoming a lost art.

Mycon and Kane have watched the autobody industry change over the years from a skilled circle of talented welders and metalworking professionals to more of a part removal and replacement, body filler, fiberglass and plastic repair industry. More and more, new cars are rolling off of the assembly lines with high-strength plastic and lightweight sheet metal parts in place of what used to be standard,

The edge of a Mazda fender is featured just above a section of channel material from Mycon's 1939 Buick. It is easy to see the difference in body-metal thickness between older cars and those manufactured today. Panels consisting of thicker metal can withstand metalwork using high heat. Thinner metal panels will burn through or warp if too much heat is applied, especially if prolonged work periods are required to repair moderate to major damage.

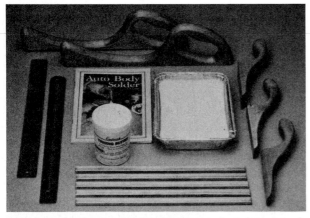

This is an assortment of soldering material and tools used to repair dents on thicker sheet metal parts familiar on older cars and trucks. The long flat bars at the bottom are solder. An area is heated and solder melted into the repair space. Tinning butter, located inside the tin pan, is put on the hard maple paddles to keep solder from sticking to them as they are used to shape molten solder. Coachbuilder's files on the left are used after solder has cooled to smooth the repair and shape it as necessary. The Eastwood Company

Dennis Laursen, jobber for Bel-Tech Auto Paints in Bellevue, Washington, points to the tip on a wire feed welder. These small welders are ideal for metalwork on thin autobody panels. Low amperage wire feed welding will not distort or burn through panels if done correctly. Only short welds can be applied at any one time and the spots have to be cooled immediately with a sopping wet towel or cool air from a compressor to eliminate warp problems. As with most other bodywork maneuvers, practice welding on a scrap door or fender before attempting work on your car.

This rear door edge damage will require extensive body hammer, dolly and spoon work with slide hammer maneuvers to repair. Note the trim piece located below. The white clip to the left came out of the trim support hole just above it. The clip for the hole on the right is missing, as its plastic support mount has been ripped off. The entire trim piece will have to be replaced, adding to the overall cost of repairs.

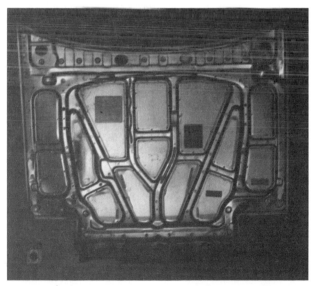

The undersides of most hoods and trunks are reinforced with inner supports. In addition, most hoods are designed to fold up when impacted so that they are not forced into passenger compartments in one piece. Repairs to severely damaged hoods on newer cars sporting these features are almost impossible. In most cases, replace damaged hoods with new ones.

Along with part dismantling and installation, autobody technicians today are well versed in plastic filler applications and sanding maneuvers. Hardeners are mixed in with filler material to help it cure within a reasonable time. Autobody paint and supply stores carry wide assortments of plastic filler. Hardeners are issued to customers from behind the counter.

13

All kinds of filler materials, glazing putty products and fiberglass repair kits are available at autobody paint and supply stores. Because of the incorporation of so many thin metal panels, plastic and fiberglass parts into newer cars, repairs to separate units or assemblies may require use of particular products. Jobbers at supply stores are well informed about the use and application of the products they sell and can help you choose the right materials for your projects.

Heavy hit damage to the front end of this Honda will require extensive work to manage satisfactory repairs. Not only will a lot of broken parts have to be replaced, sections of frame rails, fender aprons and radiator supports will have to be straightened. Damage to the front suspension and unibody frame system requires intricate repair endeavors using special equipment operated by trained technicians. Engine compartment items must also be assessed for collision damage.

heavy-duty steel units. To fix these newer items correctly, one must adhere to the modern set of body-work standards that include a great deal more body filler work and parts replacement than was experienced not too many years ago.

Heavy Hits

Although it may not take much of a collision to result in over $3,000 damage, let's categorize heavy hits as those with extensive multi-panel body damage and those with frame and/or suspension problems.

Unibody construction incorporates a series of cross members and side members with a floorboard (floor pan) to replace what used to be separate full frames and floorboards. Damage to this structure can only be repaired with special equipment operated by trained technicians. Since this single, unibody assembly is basically responsible for suspension performance and the fit of all other associated vehicle assemblies, repair and alignment to exact specifications is imperative.

Special unibody frame straightening machines support an entire car and utilize sets of measuring devices, chains and hydraulic or pneumatic units to pull damaged sections back into place. Detailed operating instructions are followed by precise measurements to guarantee that unibody assemblies are once again shaped according to manufacturer's specifications.

If a unibody frame system or full frame system was damaged in an accident, a number of other systems could be directly affected. When repairs do not meet exacting standards, vehicles could go down streets with their bodies off center in more or less of a sideways position. Doors may not open and shut as expected and gaps between hood and fender, quarter panel and trunk lid might not be uniform.

Should this kind of damage exist on your car, have a professional autobody facility do the repair work. Tow the vehicle to your selected body shop's location in an "as is" condition so that technicians may evaluate the entire extent of damage. Frame problems are unique and require critical evaluation and controlled repair by trained professionals.

Suspension damage also falls into this category; repairs should only be made by professionals. If a chunk of body filler flies off of your car at 55 mph, your safety would not be compromised, although the safety of following motorists could be. Should an integral suspension piece fail at the same speed, however, your safety and the safety of nearby drivers could be severely jeopardized. Lack of operator control at high speeds almost always results in disaster.

As with frame and chassis work, trained professionals use special equipment to measure, straighten, replace, adjust and align suspension parts. Having a qualified repair person perform this kind of work will not only save you worry about overall vehicle performance and help tires to wear normally, it will also provide you with a much smoother and more comfortable ride.

Heavy hits may include damage to more than one body panel without affecting frame or suspension members. Many times, auto enthusiasts with welding and metalworking experience can make repairs with just a limited array of autobody tools and equipment. Attaching new rocker panels or quarter panels to an existing body is tricky work but made easier when a controlled method of installation is followed. The job must be well planned and tools, like a spot weld drill, air chisel, die grinder, welder and clamps, must be available, along with the know-how to use them.

Fiberglass Repair

Fiberglass repairs include work to fix stars, cracks, tears and wear-throughs. The process is not complicated as long as prescribed preparations and methods are adhered to. The repair area must be clean and free from all contaminants. Fiberglass mat should be used along with resin when cracks are deep or part strength integrity has been compromised. Resin is mixed with a catalyst in specific doses in order for it to harden at a consistent pace.

Sanding endeavors are required to smooth and definitively shape repairs. Be alert that fiberglass dust can be irritating to skin and will cause you to itch. Wear long sleeves. A dust mask or respirator must be worn at all times while sanding.

Newer Corvettes are made with a combination of fiberglass and hi-tech Fiber Reinforced Plastic (FRP). Repairs to their bodies may require a special fiberglass material. Be sure to consult your autobody paint and supply store jobber to be certain the repair materials you purchase are compatible with your particular car.

Plastic Repair

Interiors, exteriors and engine compartments of most new cars reveal wide assortments of plastic parts, like flexible urethane spoilers, fender flairs, bumper covers, inner fender panels and a lot more.

Mycon was surprised the first time a newer Cadillac was brought into his shop for an estimate on repairs to a damaged right front fender. The fender was urethane (plastic). The driver had misjudged the distance between him and a light post in a parking lot and crunched the parking light assembly, along with tearing a small section of the fender. Repairs were easy as new light parts were installed, a urethane glue repair made to the fender tear and fresh paint applied.

Damage to urethane bumper covers can also be repaired. In fact, a company in Canada buys all of

Frame damage is corrected with special equipment, such as this featured at Wesco Autobody Supply in Kirkland, Washington. Operators have to be trained in the operation of frame straightening equipment in order to align frame rails and other associated assemblies. Specific calibrations and dimensions are measured on frame machines with the help of indicators and sight guides.

This is an assortment of chains, hooks, pulleys and bars used to move damaged body assemblies back into the proper positions. Special training in their use allows technicians to straighten heavy-duty panels, like floor pans and aprons, to within specific calibrations. Because frame, suspension and support systems are so critical to an automobile's performance, novice technicians should send work like this to qualified body shops for accurate and complete repairs.

the old urethane bumper covers from body shops across the Northwest and reconditions them to look like new. Kits are sold at auto parts stores and autobody paint and supply stores for the express purpose of repairing dings and abrasion damage to urethane bumper parts.

Broken hard plastic trim pieces should generally be replaced instead of repaired. They are attached to car bodies with an assortment of clips, pins, screws, adhesives or two-way tape. Each car manufacturer seems to have its own way of doing things and develops special clips unique to almost all others. Consult a dealership service manager before attempting to remove trim pieces whose attaching mechanisms may be unfamiliar to you.

Disassembly

A good part of any autobody technician's time is spent removing damaged parts from cars involved in collisions. Without a doubt, anyone attempting to make repairs to such vehicles must own or have access to an assortment of mechanic's hand tools. Wrenches, screwdrivers, sockets and the like are mandatory. Work on some models will require special tools, like star slotted (Torx) screwdrivers for removing star headed (Torx) screws familiar on GM grille assemblies.

The wider array of tools you have at your disposal, the easier your job will be. Kane uses large and small pneumatic ratchets to speed up nut and bolt removal. Die grinders of increasing size help him to hasten the process of removing damaged body sections. To help your work progress in an

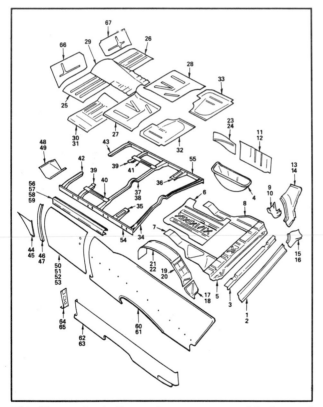

This illustration indicates the many assorted body panel sections that can be purchased for replacement purposes on cars. Although these parts are for 1955–57 Chevrolets, similar panel sections are available for almost any vehicle. Dealerships offer customers an array of panels for newer cars, and parts for older cars can be found through mail order and other specialty auto parts businesses. Check through auto related magazines and issues of Hemings Motor News *to find advertisers that specialize in new and reproduction parts for particular vintage or classic makes and models.* Drake Restoration Supplies

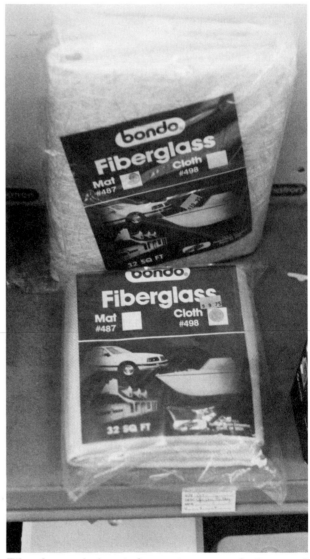

Fiberglass resin is not always strong enough alone to effect secure fiberglass repairs. In addition to resin, you should apply pieces of fiberglass mat. This material is available at autobody paint and supply stores and many hardware outlets. One large sheet is folded into a bundle for compact storage. Cut out any size or shape needed for repair work with a pair of scissors.

efficient manner, carefully examine the job in front of you to determine which tools you will need during the dismantling process. Once work starts, you should be able to work comfortably and productively with all the needed tools nearby.

During the dismantling phase of your repair operation, consider taking pictures. This will not only give you a record of your achievements, but will also provide you with a definite pattern of how parts came off and exactly how they are supposed to go back on.

Project cars are favorites among auto enthusiasts. They are generally makes or models with special meanings to owners who do not have a dire need to get them running within any specific time frame. This kind of long-term project must include a definite plan for dismantled part storage. Consideration must be given to part deterioration during storage, such as rust, corrosion, drying out and accidental damage. Bare metal parts should be sprayed with a coat of epoxy primer, and fragile parts, like glass, wrapped in a cushioned material and stored in a box or crate.

Have a number of boxes available for part storage. Be sure to label each one and keep all associated parts together in the same general location. This way, when you are ready to put your car back together, everything will be handy and easily located.

Part Replacement

Wrecking a new part while installing it makes no sense. Far too many times, novice autobody repair persons force new parts on instead of taking time to find out why the part will not go on smoothly. Sometimes, hidden body damage prevents screws or bolts from lining up or allowing fenders or panels to fit properly. Investigate the reasons for this dilemma and take corrective action before installing a new part. If parts were forced in place without breaking, you may later discover that excessive stress on them during road operation has caused cracks, tears or outright failure. Patience is a key factor during part replacement and the more you exhibit, the better your repair will turn out.

During the dismantling phase of your autobody repair operation, clips or pins from trim pieces or other assemblies may have accidentally been bro-

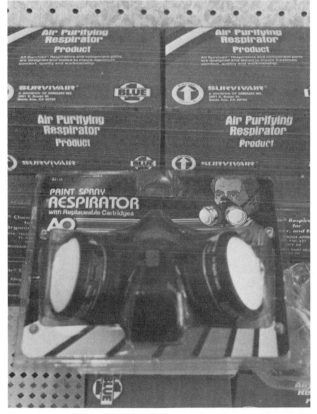

A variety of respirators and dust masks are readily available at autobody paint and supply stores and other outlets that sell safety equipment. Any kind of sanding endeavor will create dust. Respirators like this one are inexpensive, as are replacement filter cartridges. Be smart and use respirators or dust masks whenever sanding or working in dusty atmospheres.

Repairs to this Corvette fender required removal of the front bumper. An assortment of mechanic's tools is needed for any dismantling project like this. In addition, you have to carefully examine how parts are secured in place. Some assemblies are fastened with more bolts and screws than you might think necessary. Pulling or tugging on parts before all of the fasteners have been loosened or removed will cause unnecessary damage to affected parts.

ken. This is common, as even professionals occasionally misjudge the operation of particular fasteners and break them, which is why they keep storage bins full of various fasteners close by their work space. Account for these items during dismantling efforts or at least prior to beginning the replacement phase of your job.

A missing part in the middle of a job can be frustrating. Avoid this dilemma by having all of the necessary parts on hand at the beginning of your job.

Bumpers

Bent and wrinkled bumpers from older cars could be heated, hammered to shape and rechromed. Except for some pickup truck dock bumpers, this is often no longer a viable option.

Bumpers on newer cars have a number of parts. Along with a basic frame, these include support brackets, guard guide supports, a thick foam cush-

ion, end guards and a urethane cover. Parts are ordered individually.

More exotic bumpers are featured on Corvettes, Firebirds, Daytonas and the like. A sufficient amount of time must be spent learning how these items come off and go on a vehicle before attempts at dismantling or replacement are made. For instance, twenty-three separate adjustment points are common on some models and tightening one set

This is Mycon's 1939 Buick project car. Along with a complete restoration, he is lowering the top. He does not have to rely on this vehicle for everyday transportation so he can work on it at his leisure. Because this is a long-term project, parts storage must be maintained in an organized fashion.

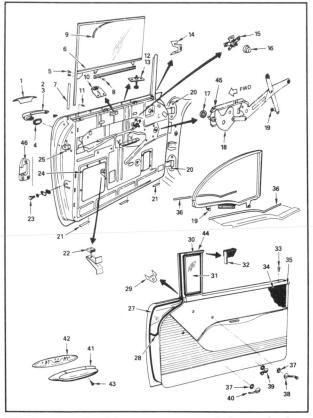

This is a sample of the many parts needed to make door latches, handles and windows operate on car doors. Although this illustration depicts parts available for 1955–57 Chevrolets through Drake Restoration Supplies, it is a clear indication of the many parts available for all makes and models. When disassembling a door, consider taking pictures or a video movie of the process to give you a firsthand guide to how parts come off and in what order they should be assembled into your new door. Drake Restoration Supplies

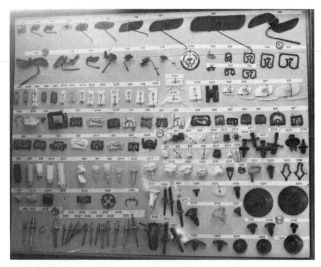

Autobody paint and supply stores carry a wide variety of clips and fasteners. Every car seems to have its own set of special fasteners for any assortment of part assembly combinations. Keep a record of those that have broken during dismantling efforts so you can purchase new ones before attempting to put new parts back on your car. To be certain that new fasteners are the same as the ones that came off, bring the old ones in to the store to compare their size and shape.

of bolts too soon will cause others to twist out of alignment.

Body shop technicians must spend time investigating how certain parts are installed before attempting to dismantle. They do not want to break any part during the process.

Bumpers on older cars come off in just minutes by loosening a few bolts. Today, a grille may have to be completely dismantled just to reach bolts that secure bumper brackets. Be prepared for labor intensive chores like these and plan extra time for removal and replacement.

Lights

Almost any front or rear end collision will result in damage to at least one light fixture. Be aware that not all light assemblies are composed of simply one part. Many include a lens, separate bulb, housing, support brackets, clips, retainer bars, screws and trim. If yours simply needs a new trim ring, purchase only that and save a few dollars by not buying unnecessary parts.

Along with obvious headlight and taillight damage, you must determine if other lights in the area are also broken. Parking lights, signal lights and side lights must all be accounted for and repaired as necessary. Don't overlook reflectors.

Lights are assembled with gaskets located between the housing and lens. Should this gasket fail, moisture will enter the space to corrode electrical connections and reflector plates. Use caution while dismantling lights so good gaskets are not damaged. During replacement, be certain gaskets are seated correctly.

Miscellaneous Add-Ons

Automobiles of the eighties and nineties sport an amazing array of decals, stickers, stripes, graphics, emblems, badges, hood ornaments and general goodies of all kinds. Be sure to include these in your estimate of repair costs. Badges, emblems and trim may be purchased at wrecking yards for less than the price of brand new pieces, but stripes, decals and vinyl graphics must be purchased new.

Glass

Some of the more expensive and totally non-reparable parts of automobiles are windows. Rear liftgate windows can cost thousands of dollars, while tinted windshields for the economical Ford Festiva may cost around $400. Door glass can commonly command prices of $200 and up, and custom-made windows might easily exceed the cost of metal repair.

Used glass may be found at wrecking yards. Especially for expensive liftgate windows, it is highly recommended you investigate the availability of such items at used part facilities.

During your initial collision damage evaluation, be sure to vacuum up all glass remnants from the in-

The driver's side of the front bumper on this BMW was involved in a minor collision. In addition to obvious damage at that point, you can see that a section of related material has popped up on the passenger side. Until the bumper is removed and thoroughly inspected, there is no way to determine how much damage was caused to inner bumper parts or supports. It is possible that the main bumper support piece has been severely bent or twisted out of shape.

This 1986 Cadillac was rear ended in a low speed accident. Along with obvious dent damage to the passenger side quarter panel, the rear bumper suffered damage. A new passenger side upright bumper piece will have to be installed, as well as a rear light lens and gasket. The total repair cost for this job will exceed $4,000. This is because the car body was tweaked to result in narrow passenger side front door and hood to fender gaps, widening of the same gaps on the driver's side and slight buckling panel damage along the roof line at the C-pillars.

terior compartment. Shards of glass can quickly tear upholstery and cause cuts on those who happen to come in contact with them.

Newer windshields are held in place with thick beads of sealer. Their perimeter edges are covered by trim. Special tools are designed for trim removal and most windshield removal procedures require two people. Many body shops rely on professional glass installers for the removal and replacement of sealed windows. Unless you are familiar with this type of operation, you might be better off hiring a professional to remove and replace the windshield and fixed glass units on your car.

Door windows are secured in place by tracks and moldings located under and around window openings. To gain access to them, disassemble doors by first removing the interior door panel. Unless a door needs major repairs or replacement, glass should be left in place.

While repairs are being made, though, always be aware of the glass location while working. Drilling holes through a door skin for body pick access may result in damage to glass if a window is not rolled all the way up. Conversely, a misplaced hammer or dolly blow near glass could shatter it.

Moldings and Weather Stripping

Thousands of different parts are integrated into the design of an automobile. Each has its own specific part to play in the overall performance of a vehicle. Moldings and weather stripping are no exceptions.

Moldings are used to hold some parts in place and to direct water runoff out of specific areas. Weather stripping is most commonly found surrounding doors and trunk lids. A tear, rip or avulsion along any stretch of these pieces will allow water, dust and dirt to infiltrate the area it protects.

Experienced autobody technicians and estimators quickly recognize damaged moldings and weather stripping and include such items on their list of new part orders. Carefully examine these items when evaluating repairs for your car. In addi-

The grille, fender and hood around this BMW headlight were damaged in a minor collision. Consideration must also be given to the headlight assembly and any other lights at the area, like the side light located to the bottom right. Cracks, deep scratches or chips will have to be repaired or their affected units replaced with new ones. Check to see that lights actually work after a collision, as bulb filaments can also break as a result of impacts.

Years	Stock #	Price	Description		Years	Stock #	Price	Description
GMC					**(HORCH, cont.)**			
'38	MP 850-A	5.75/ea.	Headlight pad.		—	MP 7971-D	5.15/ea.	Door handle pad.
'47	MP 850-B	11.80/ea.	Parklight pad.		—	MP 7971-E	9.50/ea.	Trunklight pad.
GRAHAM					**HUDSON**			
'29	MP 792-E	5.15/ea.	Headlight pad.		NOTE: Please send tracing of your metal base with all Hudson orders.			
'31	MP 791-A	5.10/ea.	Fenderlight pad.		'32-'33	MP 798-A	6.60/ea.	Tail-light pad.
	MP 791-B	4.15/ea.	Tail-light pad.			MP 798-B	4.40/ea.	Door handle pad.
	MP 791-C	5.35/ea.	Side mount pad.			MP 798-C	4.40/ea.	Spotlight pad.
	MP 797-D	4.85/ea.	Parklight pad.			MP 798-D	4.40/ea.	Parklight pad.
	MP 797-E	4.85/ea.	Headlight pad.		'34	MP 798-E	8.75/ea.	Headlight pad.
	MP 797-F	5.50/ea.	Spare bracket pad.			MP 798-F	5.25/ea.	Tail-light pad.
	MP 797-G	4.85/ea.	Tail-light pad.			MP 798-O	10.70/ea.	**Hudson Deluxe.** Tail-light pad.
'31	MP 797-H	5.15/ea.	Tail-light body pad.			MP 798-P	5.75/ea.	**Hudson Deluxe.** Fenderlight pad.
'32	MP 791	8.75/ea.	Tail-light pad.		'35	MP 798-J	7.25/ea.	Tail-light pad.
	MP 792	5.75/ea.	Headlight pad.			MP 798-Q	5.55/ea.	Headlight pad.
'35	MP 791-D	5.35/ea.	Headlight pad.		'36	MP 798-M	4.25/ea.	Tail-light pad.
'36	MP 794	8.90/ea.	Headlight pad.			MP 798-N	6.60/ea.	Headlight pad.
	MP 797-A	8.75/ea.	Headlight pad.		'37	MP 798-S	5.55/ea.	**Hudson Terraplane.** Headlight pad.
	MP 797-B	6.60/ea.	Tail-light pad.					
'37	MP 798	6.80/ea.	Tail-light pad.		'38	MP 798-L	5.15/ea.	Tail-light pad.
'39-'41	MP 795	5.90/ea.	**Graham Hollywood.** Tail-light pad.		'41-'47	MP 798-R	20.70/ea.	Parklight pad.
	MP 795-B	22.00/pr.	Tail-light pads. R & L.		'42-'47	MP 798-I	10.75/pr.	**Hudson Super Six. Fits all except Commodore.** Tail-light pads. R & L.
	MP 797-C	8.75/ea.	License light pad.					
'40-'41	MP 900	5.75/ea.	**Graham Hollywood.** Trunk handle pad.		'48-'57	MP 798-KK	4.25/ea.	Roof antenna pad.
					'49-'50	MP 798-G	6.60/ea.	Tail-light pad.
HARLEY DAVIDSON					'51	MP 798-K	5.15/ea.	Trunklight pad.
'42	MP 7972-A	5.75/ea.	Fenderlight pad.		'52	MP 798-H	11.55/ea.	Tail-light pad.
HORCH					**HUPMOBILE**			
NOTE: Please send tracing of your metal base with all Horch orders.					'31	MP 7981-A	5.90/ea.	Headlight pad.
'33-'40	MP 7971-H	4.25/ea.	**Horch, all models.** Fenderlight pad.			MP 7981-B	5.90/ea.	Headlight bar pad.
'36-'40	MP 7971-G	6.55/ea.	**Horch, Models 851, 951, 951-A.** Trunk rack bracket pad.			MP 7981-C	5.40/ea.	Tail-light pad.
						MP 7981-D	3.50/ea.	Door handle pad.
'37-'40	MP 7971-F	6.65/ea.	**Horch Straight-8.** Tail-light pad.			MP 7981-F	5.90/ea.	Headlight pad.
—	MP 7971-A	6.60/ea.	Headlight pad.			MP 7981-G	3.40/ea.	Door handle pad.
—	MP 7971-B	7.10/ea.	Luggage rack pad.			MP 7981-H	4.25/ea.	Tail-light pad.
—	MP 7971-C	5.25/ea.	Door handle (with lock) pad.			MP 7981-J	7.05/ea.	Parklight pad.

This illustration is just a small sample of myriad mounting pads used to cushion light fixtures and other parts that attach to automobile bodies. Use of these pads is important, as they prevent rigid parts from rubbing directly on painted bodies to ruin paint jobs, cause galvanic corrosion problems or simply mar surfaces. Be sure to include them, as needed, in your parts replacement list. Metro Molded Parts, Inc.

tion, determine how they are secured in place so that replacement pins or adhesive can be ordered.

Parts like these may be difficult to find for vintage automobiles. It is recommended you read through monthly periodicals like *Hemmings Motor News* and other magazines dedicated to the make and model car you are repairing. *Hemmings* is a clearinghouse of advertisements for everything from restored vintage cars to special, hard to find parts. Other auto consumer magazines also carry a wide range of advertisements for companies that specialize in rare and vintage auto part sales.

Overview

Autobody repair work is notably a profession that requires more than just a single talent. To effect acceptable results, a repair person must understand the use and purpose of mechanic's hand tools, pry bars, body filler application, sanding and auto parts installation. If such a person were to expand his or

her horizons, in-depth knowledge of welding and metalwork would be required.

With the advent of unibodied cars came the concept of utilizing a number of different parts to create what used to be one major component. In a sense, this made autobody repair easier by simply allowing for the exchange of broken or damaged parts for

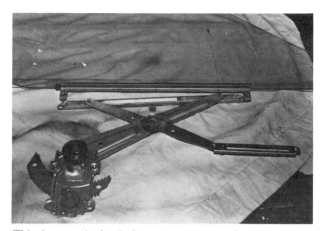

This is a typical window operating mechanism. These units are secured inside doors in a number of different ways. Most are secured with bolts and screws; others also include metal rivets. Carefully study these assemblies before randomly taking off individual parts. A flashlight will help see inside inner door spaces to accurately determine how the window parts are secured on your car. When transferring parts from an old damaged door to a new one, place both of them next to each other. As parts come off one, put them on the other or at least set them down in such a way you can easily and quickly determine which part is supposed to go where.

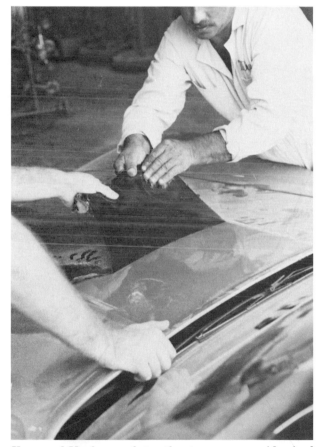

Kane and Vanhee work together to remove a wide vinyl decal from a Corvette hood. Once removed, vinyl decals or graphics cannot be used again. You will have to purchase new ones for replacement. Most vinyl stripes and decals are easily peeled off with the help of a blow dryer or heat gun. Apply enough heat to loosen the material and pull it off. Too much heat will cause vinyl to tear easily. Adhesive remover products are also available that work well.

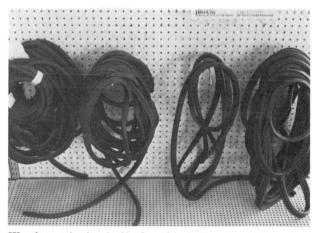

Weather stripping is displayed in bulk rolls at Wesco Autobody Supply. Customers can buy as much as they need for their repair project. It is important that damaged weather stipping be replaced with the same type and size. To be sure you purchase material identical to that on your project car, bring a small section with you to the autobody paint and supply store for comparison.

21

new ones to make complete repairs. However, it would be foolish to replace an entire fender just because a small dent mars its surface when a simple hammer and dolly effort and body filler application would make it look like new. Compromises must be met allowing some of the old school to meld with new technology.

The majority of autobody technicians practicing their craft today learned from experienced "old-timers." As new repair techniques were developed, serious technicians attended training schools and seminars sponsored by manufacturers, product suppliers and insurance companies.

One should understand the difference between a professional autobody technician and a do-it-yourself auto enthusiast. The professional makes a living by fixing collision damage. Time is money and the more time spent on repair the less money is earned. On the other hand, do-it-yourselfers are not mandated by any time frame. Mistakes can be corrected without the worry of losing money. The end result is all that is important.

Should you decide to tackle a heavy hit collision repair but lack expertise in welding, metalworking and shaping, consider attending a vocational school or community college that offers classes in autobody repair. Then save your money for the purchase of expensive autobody tools and equipment.

In the meantime, realize your limitations and concentrate on those repairs that can be easily managed with the knowledge and resources you currently have available. For the auto enthusiast, working on cars is supposed to be fun. Keep it simple by practicing repair techniques on scrap doors, fenders or hoods first. Then after you have gotten a feel for the process, tackle that repair job on your car.

Mustangs Unlimited, Metro Molded Parts, Inc., Drake Restoration Supplies, Sherman & Associates, Inc., Auto Body Specialties, Inc. and Year One, Inc., are just a few companies that specialize in after market parts and accessories for older, classic and vintage automobiles. Hemmings Motor News is packed full of advertisements sponsored by companies like these. Not all catalogs are free; some may cost a few dollars. These companies are good sources for hard-to-find parts.

This minor blemish on a new BMW fender flair is reparable. It would be foolish to spend a lot of money and time to remove this flair and replace it with a new one when repairs can be made with appropriate tools and filler material. On the other hand, if this flair were ripped, torn, mangled or avulsed, repair work would be extreme unless a new flair was purchased and installed. Be realistic with your autobody repairs. If in doubt, attempt repairs first. If they don't pan out as expected, then buy the new parts.

2

Talking to an Autobody Specialist

Collisions involving frame, suspension or heavy hit multi-panel damage will require special equipment and the expertise of a professional autobody specialist to make suitable repairs. Many newer cars include specific designs that cause particular body assemblies to collapse in a predetermined manner upon impact with another vehicle or solid object. Hoods are such items. They are manufactured with convoluted areas that, in essence, form dents in their under structure, which quickly collapse upon impact causing hood panels to fold up, as opposed to

crashing directly into a windshield and passenger compartment intact.

New cars are designed with right side frame rails somewhat weaker than left side rails so that in

The gap between hood and driver's side fender on this Volvo obviously indicates that alignments are inaccurate for the hood, fender or both. This condition might be remedied by adjusting the units at their respective attaching points at hinges or along aprons. If those corrections don't solve the problem, damage may have occurred to structural members, like frame, firewall or aprons. Those alignments will have to be done by a qualified body technician.

The front end damage suffered by this Honda reflects more than mere body panel repair needs. The front of the car has been twisted out of position as indicated by the shift of its nose toward the passenger side. A professional autobody specialist will have to remove all damaged parts and then use a frame machine to accurately reposition and straighten frame rail sections and other support structures.

the case of a head-on collision, vehicles will tend to deflect away from each other. Repairs to these assemblies must be made according to specific guidelines to be dimensionally perfect and perform as designed in order to meet governmental and manufacturer intended safety criteria.

In addition, improperly repaired or replaced parts will cause performance and handling problems. This is especially important with front wheel drive automobiles. According to Mycon, "The backyard car guy should get a full-blown, legitimate body shop to complete framework. If the framework is not right, nothing will be right." When the frame and suspension of a front wheel drive car are out of alignment just a little, parts will wear out prematurely and driver safety could be jeopardized. Where frame and suspension work starts, the novice autobody repair person should stop.

Locating a Reputable Body Shop

One of the best and most reliable ways in which to find a reputable body shop is by word of mouth. Check with friends and fellow auto enthusiasts to see which body shops have given them the best results. Talk to your mechanic and other automotive specialists to see who they recommend. Chances are, if the autobody facility used by an acquaintance provided quality workmanship, you will also enjoy the same.

In the yellow pages of almost any telephone book, you should find a number of autobody repair facilities under the heading "Automobile Body Repairing & Painting." Display ads can be impressive, but don't simply rely on them in making your decision about who will complete required repair work. Instead, talk to service managers or representatives on the telephone to get an idea of their expressed professionalism. Then visit those shops for a firsthand look at their operation.

Kane figures a minimum of fifteen years is needed for an autobody technician to gain the experience and know-how to become a qualified, independent professional. This is an important factor. A new shop supported by inexperienced technicians could cause you more problems than the ones already facing you. Along with the disappointment of unsatisfactory repair results, you could be forced into paying a lot more for additional repairs over an original repair estimate to have a real professional

Bob Thilson's 1990 Toyota 4x4 pickup truck has undergone some custom work, not only in add-ons and paint, but with a tilt bed. Chances are, he had a reputable body shop install these features and would probably be glad to recommend that shop to friends who need bodywork on their cars. Word of mouth recommendations from friends or fellow auto enthusiasts generally prove worthwhile. If you need the services of a professional autobody technician to repair major frame, suspension or other intricate assemblies on your car, ask for referrals from friends or associates.

After getting a positive response from an autobody shop representative on the telephone, plan to visit that facility for a firsthand look at its operation. Cleanliness, organization and a professional atmosphere are good indications that the shop is of high caliber. Although the shop area at Mycon's Newlook Autobody might have sanding dust on the floor and some damaged parts scattered about while technicians are working, the office and customer areas are maintained neat and tidy.

make things right. Kane says, "Improper repairs (a butcher job) is two to three times more difficult to repair because you have to undo what has already been botched."

Professional autobody technicians recommend looking for a clean and efficient appearing facility. They say the estimator should be personable and easy to converse with. Most of them prefer independent shops, explaining that large scale operations like dealerships and chain outlets may rely on volume business and quick turnaround times instead of conscientious personalized service. Of course, this is not the case with all major body shop chains, but a consideration nevertheless.

Ask an estimator plenty of questions and be sure he or she fully explains any terms you do not understand. Request permission to see some of their work firsthand. Look at any before and after photos of jobs previously completed, when available. View the shop facilities, if possible, to determine how technicians maintain their tools and equipment. Sanding dust and body repair debris on the floor are to be expected, but the entire workplace should have a sense of order about it, and it should be well illuminated.

The overall feeling about any body shop you select to fix your automobile should be one of confidence. The manner in which the estimator speaks with you, general appearance of the facility and

results found on cars already repaired are all factors that will help you with this decision.

Autobody Terms and Definitions

When asked what body shop terms are most misunderstood by customers, Kane replied, "The names of all the various parts on a car." When someone calls for information and talks about a rear fender, he takes it for granted that what they are really referring to is a quarter panel. Such is the same for a lot of different automobile assemblies.

The area on a car where taillights are located is called a rear body panel. Quarter panels are those body areas that surround rear wheels and extend back to taillights. Doors are doors, but the metal section under them that reaches to the bottom edge of the vehicle is a rocker panel. Front fenders are the only fenders on a car.

The A-pillar is located next to the windshield and runs down the forward side of front doors. The

Kane has dismantled damaged parts from this car and is now removing paint from a dented area. He figures it takes at least fifteen years for technicians to gain the experience needed to become qualified independent professionals. This may be another credential to check when looking for an autobody shop to do work for you. In a lot of shops, newer technicians complete much of the work satisfactorily. For intricate repairs, though, they are guided by seasoned veterans, like shop managers or owners who stay on top of all shop operations on a daily basis.

Many body shop owners, like Mycon, have photo albums in their customer waiting area that include before and after pictures of jobs they have completed in the past. Many have worked on special cars or trucks that have since been featured in auto magazines, which will, of course, be presented along with albums. When looking for a reputable body shop, don't hesitate to ask to see albums or magazine articles that feature work completed by the shop.

B-pillar is a post that separates the front and rear doors. C-pillars are those members that are featured behind rear side windows and span the distance between the bottom of a car and its roof.

Windows are surrounded by belt moldings, and body side moldings are those strips of metal or plastic that run from the front of a vehicle to the rear and help to protect the side of a car from accidental door edge dings in parking lots. Many other moldings are located throughout almost any automobile, including fender moldings, window moldings, door moldings and the like.

Some inner parts are called supports, others are reinforcements. Look at a parts manual or Mitchell Book for the exact reference. Fender aprons are those inner structures to which fenders are attached, and the cowling assembly includes those body parts that make up the metal piece between a windshield and hood (they hold the windshield wipers and are usually adorned with louvers) and may include the firewall.

The dashboard is now called an instrument panel and lights are referred to as lamps. The roof panel is a roof and the roof rail, or drip rail, is the thin metal piece that extends out and up from upper door edges. Its purpose is to catch and reroute rainwater so that it does not drip on you as you enter or exit your car.

A trunk lid can also be called a luggage lid and a hatchback a rear liftgate. Trucks still have tailgates. New styled, multi-part bumpers include face bars, pads, guards, deflectors, reinforcements, impact absorbers and spacers. Inner fenders are also named splash shields and the place where the nozzle is inserted to pump fuel is called the fuel housing; some are equipped with a fuel door.

A grille is still a grille but the term may only refer to one part of the entire nose of a car. Many grilles also include a valence, the part that sits below a bumper to prevent water from splashing into the inner grille area.

A dent is a dent and a ding is just a tiny dent, also sometimes referred to as a dish. Oil cans are those impressions that just never seem to settle. They may be found on newer car roofs and hoods where thin metal covers a wide area. They are characterized by the inability to pop them out when pressure is applied underneath. They simply seem to wobble like the bottom of an oil can that snaps back and forth when you depress it. Generally, oil cans are signs of pressure forced against a panel as a result of a collision to a nearby assembly.

Creases are long, thin bends caused by the impact of a relatively sharp object on a glancing blow, like from a dock bumper or cap nut on a fire hydrant. Kane says they are the most difficult to repair and that he regularly opts instead to replace panels that suffer extensive crease damage.

The term patch panel refers to an operation where a certain section of body is cut out and then replaced with a new section. This can be done to an entire quarter panel or just a small section of it. Patch panels can also be inserted into the middle of larger sections to complete a repair. Repair persons must be highly skilled welders to achieve this sort of repair.

The automotive industry has invented some unique terms for various body parts and assemblies. Modern designs utilizing a number of parts to create what used to be just one, like bumpers, have also created a need to develop new names for the parts. And autobody technicians have come up with some special terms of their own in the process. If you really want to learn the names of all car parts, study a parts book for your make and model car of interest. However, if you merely want to understand the terms used by an estimator or autobody technician, simply ask him or her to define whatever you do not understand.

Insurance Considerations

Most of us are familiar with the term "total." It refers to a vehicle so badly damaged by a collision, fire or other means that it would cost more to repair it than to replace it. Insurance adjusters are keenly aware of automobile prices and the amount of money needed for parts and the labor required to repair wrecked cars.

To keep premiums low, insurance adjusters must keep costs within reasonable limits. To do this, they must occasionally go out to body shops and in-

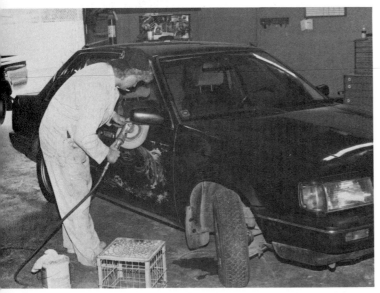

You should get a feeling of overall confidence with any body shop you select to complete work on your vehicle. Mike Link wears standard Newlook coveralls while buffing out new paint on a customer's car. Uniforms of some sort generally indicate a degree of professionalism. Along with that, an organized shop, courteous technicians and a conscientious attitude help customers to gain confidence in a repair facility.

spect additional vehicle damage that was not clearly evident at the time of an initial damage assessment and only discovered after certain parts and assemblies were removed. This keeps body shop owners honest and gives adjusters a chance to learn what can be expected with similar situations in the future.

Body shop personnel and insurance adjusters seem to haggle over the amount of time allotted for specific repair jobs. According to insurance guidelines, certain parts should be removed and replaced within specific time frames, thus allowing only a certain number of hours for repairs. Sometimes, the additional man-hours needed to remove mangled parts are overlooked. One reason a car may not be repaired as soon as expected may be because compromises have to be reached, and although frustrating, a car might have to sit while waiting for an adjuster's inspection and ultimate approval.

Many shops will work with resourceful car owners to help them save money. For example,

when a new door is called for in an adjuster's estimate, they will accept and install a used door in excellent condition found, delivered and paid for by a customer. The difference in cost between a new door and a used one can be as much as fifty percent. The difference to the shop is basically nothing, since both will have to be painted anyway. When repairing vehicles yourself, at least consider used parts in efforts to defray overall costs.

Insurance companies are only responsible for the cost of damage repair as incurred from an accident upon which a claim was submitted. Additional bodywork must be paid for by vehicle owners. In some cases, indirect body damage may be a direct result of the accident for which a claim was submit-

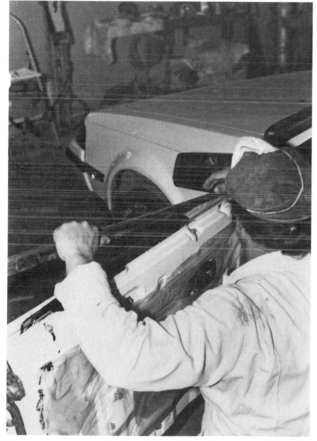

Kane removes a window belt molding in preparation for completing body work on this door. When ordering new parts, it is always helpful to refer to parts by their correct name. This helps clerks and jobbers locate them faster in catalogs or on stockroom shelves. Be very descriptive when ordering parts. Although you may not be familiar with a part's name, at least tell the clerk where the part comes from with reference to the assembly it came off of.

This is a new Toyota quarter panel section. Holes are pre-drilled for items like window trim and side lights. The old panel will be removed by drilling out spot welds and cutting any other stitch welding. Notice that new panels, like doors, arrive with nothing attached. You will have to salvage old parts like bushings, moldings and glass. New parts, such as weather stripping and light lenses, may also have to be purchased to complete a repair.

ted. In those instances, insurance adjusters must be called out to inspect the additional damage and authorize repairs.

Therefore, when you bring your car to an insurance adjuster for an estimate, be sure to closely examine the car's body for any small dings, oil cans or other imperfections that may have occurred as a result of the accident. This way, all repairs can be made at the same time to alleviate any future problems.

Getting an Estimate

Unless you prefer a particular body shop to complete your work, you should evaluate a number of repair facilities as discussed earlier. For the purpose of estimates, get at least three. Acquire estimates from the three best body shops you've located. Then, throw out the highest and lowest dollar estimates and go with the middle one.

With a clipboard, paper and pencil in hand, an autobody estimator should thoroughly examine all body damage. The obvious problems are self-explanatory, like crinkled fenders and smashed doors, but hidden damage must also be determined in order to render an accurate estimate of repair costs.

Where necessary, especially on medium and heavy hits, an estimator should go underneath the car to examine frame and suspension parts, as well as inner assembly parts and related braces and reinforcements. If front end damage has occurred, the engine compartment must be inspected for damage to mechanical parts, cooling system attributes and other associated items.

Broken trim pieces and lamp fixtures must be accounted for, and stripes, emblems, decals and badges listed as items to replace as needed. Basically, all damage repairs must be contained on the estimate sheet as closely as can be expected to arrive at a reasonable repair cost without any surprises.

If the car or truck has sustained major damage, a reputable autobody estimator will explain that re-

This is copy of an estimate sheet used by Mycon at Newlook Autobody. It includes areas for pertinent customer information, like name, address and telephone number. It allows plenty of space for detailed accounts of which parts need replacing and which ones can be repaired. A conscientious estimator will list every part that will be worked on and include current prices for their repair or replacement. A detailed analysis of repairs helps customers to understand what they are getting for their money.

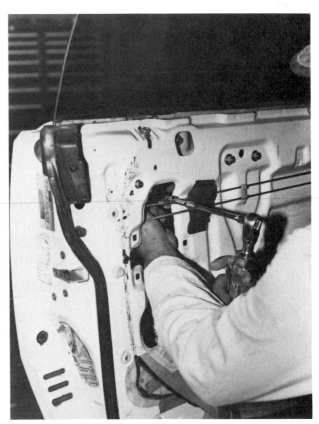

Sometimes medium to heavy hit body damage will result in hidden damage not noticed during an initial inspection. In this photo, Kane has removed an interior door panel to inspect the condition of inner mechanisms. Should new damage be located, the customer or insurance company adjuster will have to be notified. Their authorization for these new repairs has to be confirmed before work starts.

pair costs may go up if hidden damage is later discovered after some parts have been removed. This is not uncommon. As a matter of fact, most estimate sheets feature a sentence which explains that the estimate does not include additional parts or labor that may be required after work has started. In those cases, most states have enacted laws that require repair shops to notify and seek authorization for additional repairs when newfound damage will require more money for repairs than originally estimated.

The Mitchell Book

To keep autobody repairs within reasonable limits, insurance companies have gone to great lengths to standardize repair times and parts costs. In addition, insurance adjusters and autobody estimators use the Mitchell Book to determine how much time is allotted for certain part removal and replacement work. This book also displays costs for new parts on newer cars to help estimators and adjusters accurately determine the cost of repairs for almost any vehicle.

The actual title for each Mitchell Book is, "Collision Estimating Guide." After the word "Guide" is a word that signifies which type of vehicle is covered, such as Domestic, Asian, European. Separate books are published for each make and model. Each volume is updated every two months to keep subscribers on top of parts costs and the times allotted for their removal and replacement.

Starting from the front inner section of an automobile and completely going through to the rear outer sections, these guides frequently display technical drawings and blowups of various parts and assemblies to inform readers of possible additional damaged parts. Correct terms and specific ordering numbers for each part are also listed.

Use of this book by qualified professionals not only makes their job easier, but also adds uniformity to body shop estimates and insurance adjuster calculations. Estimators can make accurate estimates with detailed cost figures too.

New Part Cost and Delivery

Autobody repair shops seldom keep an inventory of new parts on hand, except for rolls of com-

Commonly referred to as "Mitchell Books," these Collision Estimating Guides help body shop estimators and insurance adjusters stay on top of current part and labor costs. Pages inside designate how much time is normally allotted for the dismantling of parts, as well as the eventual installation of new parts. Each book is specifically written for certain automobile makes and models. They are updated every two months and sent automatically to subscribers.

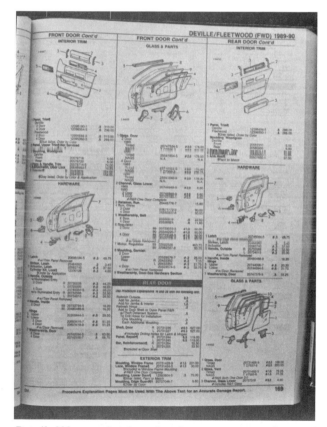

Detailed blowup sketches of various car parts are featured inside Mitchell Books to help body shop estimators and insurance adjusters understand how many individual parts may be adversely affected by collision damage to certain car or truck sections. On this page, information is displayed about parts for front and rear Cadillac DeVille and Fleetwood doors. Also included are parts numbers, prices and allotted removal and replacement times.

monly used weather stripping, nuts, bolts, clips and the like. Reasons range from lack of storage space to the inability to financially stock a parts warehouse. Therefore, body shops must rely on dealerships to supply patch panels, hoods, doors, quarter panels, rocker panels, and so on.

Many times, body shops have to call anxious customers to explain that their car will not be ready on time because parts have yet to arrive. Although the shop may have ordered them on the day a car arrived, dealerships or other parts outlets may have been temporarily out of stock.

When ordering parts, have the precise part name, part number, year, make, model, production date and serial number of the car ready at hand. Specific names and identification of parts are critically important when ordering parts for any vehicle. If a parts person misinterprets what is ordered, a wrong part will likely be received.

New parts can be expensive. According to the Mitchell Book for Fords, as of March 1990, a new door shell for a 1985–87 Ford Tempo costs $453.98.

Now remember, this is a shell. It does not include glass, window track or mechanisms, interior or exterior trim, door handles, locks, etc. You may be better off locating a used Tempo door at a wrecking yard that will cost less and also include all of the inner and outer door mechanisms and adornments. Again, if you are working with an autobody repair shop, check to see if they will accept a used door in lieu of a new shell.

Autobody shops do not make money on parts. They do not have time to scour wrecking yards hunting for used parts that will lower their cost of repairs. To them, time is money. It is much easier, faster and more efficient to order parts from a dealership and have them delivered to their door.

Parts are not generally ordered by a body shop until a car is actually taken in for repairs. This policy is more or less standard in the industry because shop owners have no guarantee that a customer will return once parts have arrived. Shop owners must pay for parts out of their business account when bills from parts outlets are due. They cannot wait until the job is done to make good on billings. For that reason they must be assured that a job is theirs before spending money on parts.

Auto parts delivery can be made in several different ways. If a complete front end, firewall to

This Mazda Sedan front fender exhibits a number of wrinkles along the flair area. This damage should be easy to repair. However, dents at the top left corner and next to the body ridge line are difficult to repair. A body shop might opt to replace the fender with a new one. It depends on how much time a technician will have to spend on repairs in relation to the cost of a new unit. The least expensive option will be exercised. Body shops do not maintain a stockroom full of various parts. A replacement fender for this car will have to be ordered from a Mazda dealership.

A brand new door shell will not include anything other than bare primered metal. Small linkages, fasteners, bushings and the like are salvaged from old doors or ordered separately from a parts facility. Installing a new door shell will entail a lot of work transferring all of the items needed to make latches, locks and windows operate. Take your time during operations like this, to be sure that all parts are assembled correctly. The two flanges on both sides of the door handle opening are where bolts are attached to secure the handle in place.

grille, is ordered from a wrecking yard, it may be delivered to your door. On the other hand, small items like simple grille pieces may have to be picked up by customers.

Dealerships will either sell parts from stock or special order them. They are picked up at the parts counter. Depending on dealerships, delivery might be arranged. Again, this depends on the size of the part and dealership policy. Mail order parts usually come by an independent delivery service such as UPS, Federal Express, or Airborne. Some companies accept COD; others require payment before shipment. This is something that has to be worked out during purchase.

Of utmost importance when ordering parts is making sure all serial numbers and part descriptions are accurate. Everything these days seems to be automated and actuated by computer numbers. If the part number is inaccurate, the part delivered will not be the one ordered.

Time Factors

Few things frustrate autobody technicians more than impatient customers who want their car repaired and delivered "yesterday." Time frames are established for all of the various tasks that must be accomplished during a repair. Time must be coordinated with a body technician and then a painter. Time must also be allotted for parts delivery and the curing of body fillers, primers, sealers and paint.

Unless a shop is exceptionally fast, you may be asked to allow your car to remain at a facility for at least five working days. It may not receive five full days worth of work, but must be fit into a series of other ongoing jobs. Most shops have two or three cars on line at the same time. While filler is curing on one, they may pound out dents and apply filler to another and then sand on a third.

Large scale operations involving frame and suspension members will require an uninterrupted segment of time for precise evaluation, equipment setup and repair procedures. If yours is a small job, it may have to wait until a larger job has been completed to a certain point. Stopping in the middle of a frame pull can interrupt a technician's train of thought and therefore cause him delays in overall job completion. However, should the big job offer an interlude where interruption would not cause problems, your small repair could easily be handled with no ill effects.

Autobody technicians, like any other service oriented professional, do not like to be hampered by strict time constraints. Most prefer to spend an adequate amount of time perfecting their repair as opposed to getting it out quickly—another factor to consider when selecting a body shop for repairs. Constant phone calls about the status of your vehicle will be irritating and do nothing to expedite the process. If you must check on your car, visit the shop in person with a six-pack of soda pop under your arm for the technicians. This small gesture of goodwill might well convince technicians of your sincerity and allow you a firsthand look and detailed explanation of the progress being made on your vehicle.

Choosing the right autobody repair facility is a definite concern. Chances are, you spent a lot of money on your car and want it to stay in like new condition. Unsightly autobody repairs are a source of irritation to concerned car owners and should not have to be accepted or tolerated. Save yourself a lot of trouble in the long run, should you have to request the help of a professional, by seeking the best shop in town and working with personnel at that facility to perform a perfect repair the first time around.

Body shop owners and managers try to schedule jobs in such a way that customers do not have to wait extended periods of time to get their repaired car back. Small jobs, like this minor dent repair, are fitted into a work schedule between bigger jobs. Although only a few hours' work may be allotted for minor repairs, time must be factored in for filler curing and paint drying times. In this illustration, Kane is using a coarse disc to remove paint from a repair area. Note he is wearing full face protection.

This striking street rod has been meticulously maintained after extensive work was done to get it right the first time. You can bet the owner didn't rely on just anybody to do the needed professional work on this vehicle. Any kind of an inferior body repair to this classic machine would stand out to ruin an otherwise perfect body. There is no doubt that whoever did the bodywork on this rig is proud of his or her achievement.

3

Tools and Materials

A professional autobody repair facility must invest thousands of dollars into hand tools, special metalworking devices and high-powered hydraulic or pneumatic equipment in order to fix the almost limitless array of collision damage that is suffered by motor vehicles every day. To stay in business in this highly competitive field, body shops must be able to satisfactorily repair everything from dings and dents to frame damage and major body crunches on just about every automotive make and model on the road. To do this, the expertise and experience of highly skilled autobody technicians must be augmented with the most useful and durable body repair tools, equipment and materials available.

Although a great deal of money could easily be spent on lots of tools and body shop materials, the do-it-yourself repair person can complete a number of autobody projects with a minimal assortment of required items. Special equipment, such as welders and Porto-Powers, can be rented from a rental yard for those jobs requiring their use.

Before you dash out to the closest autobody paint and supply store to buy every body repair tool available, shop around. You might be able to find good buys through classified ads in the newspaper from retiring body shop technicians or through mail order outlets like The Eastwood Company. For materials such as body filler, tape, sandpaper, and primer, an autobody paint and supply store is recommended.

Workplace

An ideal workshop would be one large enough to accommodate at least four cars, be brightly lit, have plenty of workbenches and electrical outlets, include a 10 hp air compressor with lots of hose connections and be supplied with the latest assortment of autobody repair tools, equipment and materials available. In lieu of that, a home garage, carport or driveway will suffice.

If at all possible, try to have at least a 6 ft clearance around that part of the car you will be working on. This will allow plenty of working space for removing parts, operating a slide hammer and maneuvering into a comfortable position for reaching specific problem areas on your vehicle. If the front of your car is what you will be repairing, park it just halfway into your garage and take advantage of extra room provided by the back half of the car sitting outside. If your vehicle's rear section needs work, back it part way into the garage.

Working with body filler and glazing putty creates a good deal of sanding dust. Protect items in your garage by draping sheets of plastic over them. Or roll plastic around pieces of lath and nail them to the ceiling. Allow the rest of the sheet to hang down and secure ends to the floor with duct tape. Use tape

A large workshop is ideal for conducting bodywork operations. In this photo, a pipe is located about halfway up the wall. It runs horizontally and slopes slightly from left to right. This is an air line that was installed at an angle on purpose. Sloping away from the air compressor, droplets of condensation can run downhill toward a dryer or moisture collector. Moisture in paint spray air lines will cause a lot of trouble with paint finishes. Moisture can also hinder operation of pneumatic tools.

to also secure side sections to walls, cabinets, and so on.

Lighting is important. If your workplace does not provide suitable illumination, use drop lights or some kind of other portable unit. Clamp-type lights equipped with bulb protecting cages can be lined with aluminum foil to offer more direct patterns toward your work. Insert foil while the unit is unplugged and be careful to place foil away from the socket, as a short could occur if it touches the base.

When needed, heavy-duty extension cords at least as big, if not bigger, than those cords attached to tools must be used. Smaller, inadequate extension cords may physically heat up and possibly short out when supplying high loads of electricity to power equipment. Be certain that cans of flammable materials, like thinner and lawn mower gasoline, are kept away from operations where sparks may occur, such as grinding, cutting or welding procedures.

Plenty of noise will be created while working with hammers and dollies, drills and other equipment during autobody repair. You might consider certain time frames for completing this work to ac-commodate sleeping babies or unsympathetic neighbors. A constant rat-a-tat with a hammer and dolly can be quite nerve racking for day sleeping neighbors who just got off a night shift or for your wife who was up with your baby most of the night.

Your workplace should be a site where you can maneuver and work with ease. Cramped quarters can only add to your frustration. Create an organized system where dismantled parts can be safely and conveniently stored and the disabled car can be handily parked for as long as necessary.

Basic Mechanic's Tools

With the exception of some very small dings, almost every autobody repair job will require use of

Small portable lights, like this one equipped with a clamp, are versatile tools when working on car sections shadowed from available ceiling light. Aluminum foil was wrapped around the cage on this unit to concentrate the light beam into a single pattern. It works great for directing solid light onto one specific item or localized area.

Laursen points to the identification label of this air compressor. Labels like this will display the rated horsepower of units, as well as their cubic feet per minute (cfm) capabilities. Most body shops use at least a 10 hp compressor. It is recommended that serious enthusiasts employ 5 hp units, while occasional users can easily get by with 2–3 hp compressors for small jobs.

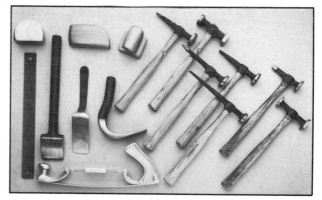

This is an assortment of body shop hand tools. Starting at the top left-hand corner in a clockwise rotation are: a heel dolly, toe dolly, general purpose dolly, cross chisel hammer, heavy-duty bumping hammer, general purpose pick hammer, cross chisel shrinking hammer, long pick hammer, cross pein finishing hammer, close shrinking hammer, adjustable file holder, flat flexible body file, spoon dolly, light dinging spoon and combo spoon. The Eastwood Company

wrenches, sockets and ratchets, screwdrivers or other mechanic's tools. Cars of today are assembled in such a way that most parts are easily removed and replaced. Certain units, like quarter panels and rocker panels, are spot welded into place. Many others, such as fenders, grilles, hoods, trunk lids, lamps, bumpers, spoilers and doors, are simply bolted, screwed or clipped on.

At the least, you should have a set of American-sized wrenches for work on American cars, metric wrenches for foreign cars, a ⅜ in. socket set with breaker bar, Phillips and slot screwdrivers, an adjustable wrench (crescent wrench), pliers, needle nose pliers, locking pliers (vise grips), ball peen hammer, plug puller and a pry bar. Without these, you

will be hard pressed to remove any intact or damaged body part from your car.

The more tools you have available, of course, the better. Removing large bumper bolts is much easier and safer with a ½ in. socket set and breaker bar. Pneumatic wrenches are great time savers, as are battery powered screwdrivers. The job you have at hand will dictate just what tools are absolutely necessary.

American car owners be advised. In many cases, you will find that nuts and bolts are actually metric! So when an American-sized wrench or socket does not fit correctly, try a metric. You will be surprised at how many parts are attached with such oddball-sized nuts and bolts as 18 mm. Do not force wrenches or sockets to fit, as this will ruin your tool or the part you are trying to remove.

Along with a basic set of mechanic's tools, you should have a can of WD-40 or Liquid Wrench handy to loosen stubborn nuts and bolts. Worst case scenarios may call for use of a hacksaw to remove those that are frozen on. An impact wrench would be ideal for extra tight screws and a small sledgehammer perfect for pounding out mangled sheet metal to gain access to mounting bolts. Before actually starting your job, assess the situation to anticipate what tools will be needed where.

Hammers, Dollies and Spoons

A wide assortment of autobody hammers, dollies and spoons is available through autobody paint

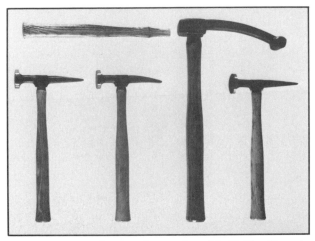

Hammers and dollies can be purchased individually or in sets. These are four body hammers with a spare replacement handle. The large one, third from the left, is called a fender bumper. It is used for bumping out dents that cannot be reached with a dolly. The other hammers are typical of blunt and fine picking models. The Eastwood Company

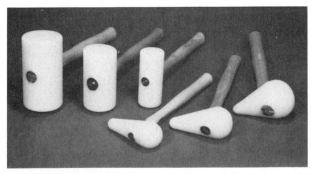

These are polyethylene mallets used to shape sheet metal parts. Metal is laid on a sandbag and then shaped with any one of a number of mallet combinations. Sandbags allow metal to move, somewhat, to effect curves. Old English panelbeaters used a similar system years ago to shape metal. The Eastwood Company

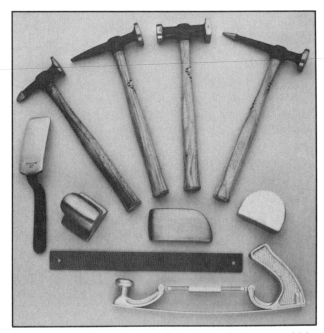

This is a small set of autobody hand tools that should be adequate for most small to moderate body repair projects. Additional tools will help more intricate jobs progress quicker. A set like this will cost between $150 and $175. The Eastwood Company

and supply stores, some auto parts stores and mail order businesses, like The Eastwood Company. It would be nice to have all of them at one's disposal but impractical from a do-it-yourselfer's perspective.

Various body hammers are designed to bump out particular metal dents in prescribed manners. Blunt hammer heads are used to pop out imperfections in relatively flat sheet metal panels. Heavier hammers are used on thick metal pieces such as braces, supports and floor panels. Picks and chisel heads work well for metalwork on creases, ridges, corners and high crown work.

Each hammer has a specific purpose, although general use hammers will also complete similar repairs with just a bit more effort. In lieu of buying a complete hammer set, you may choose to purchase just a general purpose dinging hammer and a general purpose pick hammer. Used as directed, both will accommodate most metal bumping chores handily. The Eastwood Company offers an assortment of sixteen different metal hammers as well as a wide selection of polyethylene mallets and a metal

shrinking hammer. They range in price from about $15 for a polyethylene mallet to about $60 for a twist-action shrinking hammer.

Dollies are actually miniature, hand-held anvils. Used on the opposite side of sheet metal from hammers, they can be directly pounded upon or bumped off of. A small assortment of shapes, sizes and weights is available to assist in flattening dents on large panels, rounded edges, crowns and corners.

As a semi-rigid base, dollies can be hammered upon to flatten sheet metal back to its original shape. In cases of sharply bent dent edges, you can hammer off of the edge of a dolly to reduce tension on an edge and release pressure on the inner dent so that metal can spring back to its original contour. Autobody technicians frequently pound dollies against the inside sections of sheet metal to pop out a bad spot so a hammer can be used to more carefully tap it back into shape.

Although a number of dollies are available, the do-it-yourself autobody repair person can certainly get by with just a general purpose dolly and a toe dolly. The others simply make special metalworking endeavors quicker and easier to accomplish. From The Eastwood Company, dollies cost as little as $22 for a Heel Dolly to $36 for a Heavy-Duty Dolly.

Spoons are similar to dollies in that they are generally held against a panel to support and help

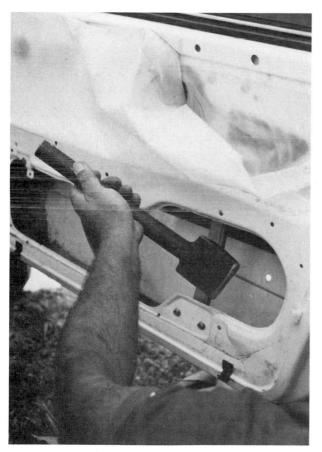

A heavy-duty spoon dolly with a long handle works great for reaching into confined spaces to offer a strong base upon which to direct hammer blows. This rugged tool can be used for a lot of chores, including some small prying maneuvers. Tool courtesy of The Eastwood Company.

With a thin rod inserted into the head of this Fitz Machine, electrical current activated by the trigger control will weld the rod to a metal surface. Kane is attaching a rod to this door section and will secure a collared slide hammer to it. When that part of the dent is pulled out, the rod will be cut off and the remaining nub ground down to be smooth with the panel surface.

shape metal from the blows of a body hammer. Their design allows insertion into tight spaces that dollies would not fit into. Like most autobody paint and supply stores, The Eastwood Company offers various body spoons.

A spoon dolly is strong and heavy with a long extension handle to reach inside door pockets, quarter panels and fenders. Fender beading spoons feature curved tips at the end of a long handle to assist in the bumping of turned-under fender edges and other such curved features. The combo spoon has a short handle but a long, slightly curved spoon face. Its length offers versatility in reaching those hard to get at spaces deep behind panels and in other inaccessible areas.

The long, curved spoon is handy for prying up dents behind curved reinforcements. It generally weighs about 1½ lb. and its face measures 2 × 7 in. A light dinging spoon could also be called an all-purpose spoon. Although heavy prying with this tool is not recommended, you can certainly hammer against it as much as necessary. The thin face allows entry into the tightest of spaces and its sturdy handle offers easy control.

For moderate to heavy bodywork, you should have a spoon dolly and a light dinging spoon available. Prices from The Eastwood Company range from about $14 for a dinging spoon to $40 for a fender beading tool, while a spoon dolly generally costs about $26.

Dent Pullers

Dent pullers range from sophisticated rod welding and special attaching slide hammer Fitz Machines, to self-tapping screws on small slide hammers, to simple drill attachments that use self-tapping screws with a collar nut reinforcement and wide bars or discs for pulling out dents. All types and brands of these handy devices are available through autobody paint and supply stores, some auto parts outlets and mail order businesses.

Some autobody technicians prefer to use a Fitz Machine. Its unique gun welds a small rod to designated areas along dents. Special rods are inserted

Kane has attached a collared slide hammer to a Fitz rod. While pulling on the hammer, he uses light taps from a body hammer to flatten a dent crown and reduce stress on the dent. He can also operate the slide to direct outward-bound pressure on rods to pop out dents. Notice that he is wearing a full face shield. He will put the shield down over his face while grinding off rod nubs.

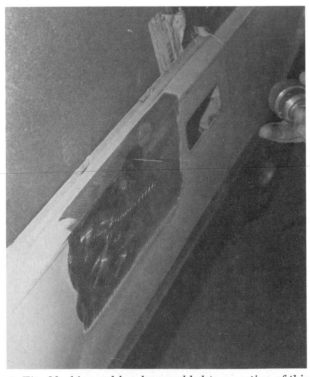

A Fitz Machine rod has been welded to a section of this door panel dent. As many as twenty rods can be used on large dents. They are placed according to how a dent impression is shaped. Dents are taken out by working on shallow impressions first. As metal stress is reduced along shallow impressions, stress is also relieved in the deeper ones. It is a methodical process that progresses in stages until all stress has been relieved and dents are flattened.

into the gun which are then pressed against a dent. Actuation of the trigger causes electricity to flow through the rod, welding it in place. Timing is critical. Too much electrical activity through rods will cause thin sheet metal to burn through, too little will not allow rods to attach firmly.

After rods have been strategically placed, use a slide hammer equipped with a special collar. The collar tightens around rods much like a drill chuck clamps down on a bit. With the unit secured, a slide is pounded against the back of the tool to pull out dents. You can also pull on the slide hammer to force out metal while lightly tapping creases and crowns with a body hammer.

After a dent section has been metalworked, rods are snipped off with cutters and then ground smooth by a grinder. Additional rods are placed as needed in and around dents to effect repairs. Depending on the repair, as many as ten to twenty individual rods

may be necessary. The rods are not reusable, so an ample supply must always be on hand. Units like this cost $200 to $300 at autobody paint and supply stores.

The Eastwood Company offers a Heavy-Duty Dent Puller that is actually a small, 3 lb. slide hammer. A ¼ in. dent pulling screw is slipped through a collar and then tightened into a hole drilled in the center of a dent. The collar screws onto the tip of the slide hammer and remains in place while the weight is pounded against the back of the tool. Other attachments, like a hook, flange type axle puller and vise grips are also available. The unit sells for about $40, with extras ranging from about $25 for an axle puller to around $9 for the vise grip attachment.

Simple to use Body Man Tools use a self-tapping screw and backing plate with a ⅜ in. drill to pop out dents. The Eastwood Company sells theirs for about $30. These units work well for pulling out small dents that are not compounded by sharp ridges or creases. Twelve and four inch bars are available, as well as a small disc.

As a screw is slowly threaded into the center of a dent, the backing plate is forced against raised dent edges. Continued tightening of the screw pulls out the center damage while the backing plate pushes down against the raised edge. The only

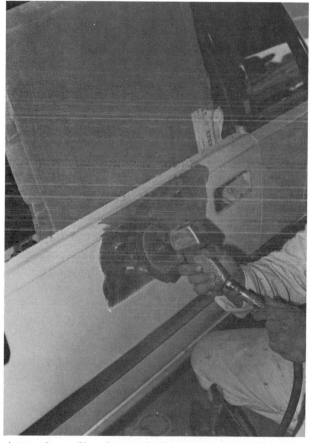

A 24 grit sanding disc is used on the end of a high-speed sander to grind off Fitz rods and paint. This tool application works quickly to remove paint, rust and other debris. Caution must be exercised while using high rpm tools like this to prevent accidental damage to adjacent panels or parts. The door handle was taken off this car to reduce worries of marring its finish with sanding and grinding operations. Note, too, that cardboard protects the window from sparks and sanding fragments.

This handy little dent puller from The Eastwood Company works quite well to pull out small dents. A self tapping screw is drilled into the center of a dent and then slowly tightened to force outward pressure on a dent's center area. The round collar maintains a solid base around the dent's perimeter so metal can be pulled out. If a variable speed drill is not available, use a wrench on the disc collar to slowly tighten the tool onto a work surface.

drawback might be that holes must be welded closed after repairs are made. This is done to prevent water from splashing through the back side of holes to dampen body filler applied over the repair.

Sandpaper

Autobody paint and supply stores sell a large variety of sandpaper for all automotive needs. Sandpaper is graded on its coarseness; the lower the number, the more coarse the paper. More than one grit is needed for bodywork, regardless of repair size.

Use a 24 grit disc on a power sander to remove paint and all signs of rust and dirt from a repair area. After dent repairs use an 80 grit disc on the sander to smooth coarse sanding marks left behind by the 24 grit disc.

After the first coat of body filler has been applied and cured, 80 grit paper is used on a dual action (DA)

sander to remove extra filler bulk and smooth the surface to a primary finish. Then use 120 grit with a hand held sanding block to complete this initial body filler job.

Next, apply glazing putty or finish body filler over the initial application of filler to give repairs an extra smooth and pinhole-free surface. Then, when cured, sand with 320 to 400 grit sandpaper and a small DA sander. Finally, sand by hand with sanding blocks and 400 grit paper.

Sandpaper grades range from very coarse 24 grit discs to extra fine 1500 wet/dry grit material used to polish certain paints. Actual autobody work will not require grits much smoother than 400. All of the softer grades of sandpaper are used during painting preparations and finish work. Because most body fillers are porous, dry sandpaper is used to smooth repairs. Wet-or-dry sandpaper is generally saved for use on painted surfaces that are moisture resistant. Water helps sandpaper to cut faster and reduce clogging from sanding residue.

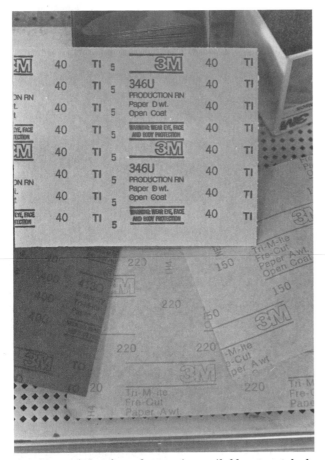

A wide variety of sandpaper is available at autobody paint and supply stores. It is graded according to its relative coarseness. The lower the number, the more coarse it is. Sandpaper comes in sheets, like this, adhesive backed discs for DA sanders and long thin adhesive backed strips for use on long boards, sanding blocks and air files. You will need an assortment of grits. The autobody supply jobber will be able to estimate how many of each grit you will need for your intended job.

This is an assortment of sanding boards, blocks and sandpaper displayed at Wesco Autobody Supply. Notice the round sandpaper discs on the right side and strips for long board use at the bottom left corner. This is an indicative array of hand sanding equipment featured at most autobody supply stores. You do not need all of the blocks and boards to complete a job. Generally, one long board and a small block are all that is required.

Sanding Blocks

As sandpaper is applied to a surface, material is removed. Coarse paper will leave deep scratches. Uneven sanding pressure can cause ripples along flat panels. To avoid these types of problems, use the correct sandpaper grit for the job and a sanding block to maintain even pressure.

Sanding blocks may be anything from thin, flat paint sticks to long, wide sanding boards. Blocks come in a variety of shapes and sizes, all designed for specific purposes. Their function is to allow users an easy way to sand flat panels with uniform pressure to make certain all parts of the sanding surface receive equal and consistent smoothing.

Large blocks are used on panels that feature wide surface areas like doors, roofs and hoods. Two hands are needed to guide them in a series of up and down and back and forth patterns. Sanding crosswise along panels ensures that all panel areas are sanded evenly without telltale grooves or ridges caused by too much sanding in one direction.

Smaller blocks are available that essentially fit into the palm of one's hand. These work great for sanding in tight places or along the surface of a small repair on a wide panel. Basically, large blocks are for large jobs, small blocks for little jobs. Autobody paint and supply stores carry an assortment of sanding blocks, both in the form of rigid wooden sanding boards and in pliable vinyl models. The Eastwood Company offers a set of wooden boards for about $24 and vinyl block sets for around $12.

To accurately sand inside body grooves and along curved edges, special sanding blocks are made with rounded bases. In place of special rounded blocks, some technicians use an old paint roller wrapped with duct tape. The firm, rounded shape of

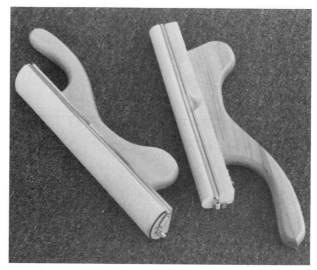

Special sanding boards equipped with rounded bases are made for sanding projects along grooved or arched panel sections. Most car bodies feature curved panels around wheel openings on fenders and quarter panels. Although sanding boards are a great aid during sanding endeavors, you can successfully sand curved panels by carefully using small blocks or hand pads.

These sanding blocks and hand pads work well for smoothing areas on panels that are confined in tight spaces. Sandpaper is inserted into slots at the front and back on some models or wrapped around hand pads. Stikit brand blocks, like the one in the middle of this photo, require the use of adhesive backed sandpaper. Be sure to sand vertically, horizontally and crossways to ensure a flat, even sanded surface.

Kane has had good luck using an old paint roller wrapped with strips of duct tape to sand curved panel sections. Here, he uses his homemade tool to smooth a rounded section along a Corvette fender. Sandpaper is wrapped around this block so that an edge can be held by the fingers on one side and thumb on the other. Instead of moving in just a straight back and forth motion, this sanding block is moved more in an up and down or crossways direction.

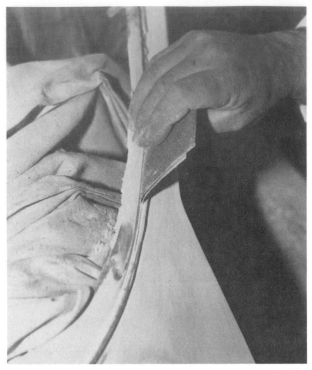

A fold on a sheet of sandpaper is used to smooth body filler caught in the groove of this Volkswagen Beetle engine compartment opening edge. You have to occasionally be creative with your efforts.

an old paint roller works well for sanding around flared fender panels and inside grooves along the sides of many body styles.

To reach inside thin grooves, use thin wooden paint sticks wrapped with sandpaper. They are inexpensive and maneuverable. During tight sanding operations in gaps between panels or along grille pieces, a sandpaper's folded edge can be used. Although it is best to always use a sanding block of some type, concessions have to be made and ingenuity allowed to take over in those special situations where normal tools will not work.

Power Sanders

To make their jobs easier and to complete projects faster, professional autobody technicians rely on power sanders of all types. Most of their tools are pneumatic, powered by compressed air. Some that operate on electricity can be found at various tool stores.

A basic high speed disc sander is simply a tool that looks like a power drill but operates at higher speed, up to 20,000 rpm. The Eastwood Company's High Speed Sander costs about $70 and uses both 3 and 5 in. backing pads. Sanding discs with adhesive backs are applied to pads for smoothing metal and also grinding off paint, rust and other metal contaminants.

For sanding wide, flat panels, use an air file. Its size and shape are similar to a long sanding board.

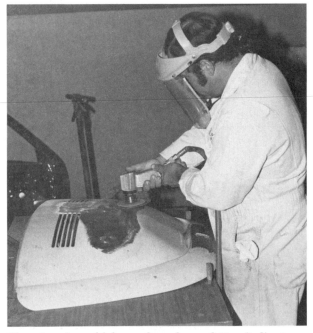

Kane is using a high-speed sander and 24 grit disc to remove paint from this Volkswagen Beetle engine compartment lid. Sanders like this commonly operate at 20,000 rpm. Paint and rust are no match for this type of intense sanding. Note that Kane is wearing a full face shield for protection against sanding sparks and flying debris. Gloves would offer even more personal protection.

Air files work fast to remove bulk body filler from wide flat panels. Kane has plenty of experience with this equipment and can, therefore, effectively use an air file on a curved VW bug engine cover. Power sanders should never be left in one position; rather, they should be constantly moved along panels. When left in one spot too long or operated in one direction only, they sand so quickly that grooves or ripples can easily be created.

Pneumatic power causes the unit to vibrate, reducing the amount of pressure a user has to apply. Since air files are long and flat, wide panels are easily sanded to smooth perfection as long as the unit is operated in all directions. Sanding in only one direction will cause grooves in panels and make the final finish uneven. The Eastwood Company's Dual Piston Filer/Sander sells for around $190. Along with strips of 14 in. sandpaper, you could attach a body file to their machine for smoothing steel panels or body solder repairs.

Although they can cut one's work in half, power sanders and air files are not required tools for the occasional do-it-yourself autobody repair person. However, if you were planning to spend money on a power sander, purchase a dual action model. DA sanders are available in both large and small sizes with the small size more appropriate for both body and painting work.

On DA sanders, the sandpaper attaches to a round disc. Unlike a high-speed sander's, the DA's disc does not spin. Instead, it is powered by an off-center mechanism that forces its disc to move in an orbital movement to quickly knock down rough surfaces. Novice autobody technicians should practice a lot with DA sanders before actually applying them to finish work. Since discs may not appear to be moving on a work surface, it may seem that no sanding is being accomplished. But the unit is definitely sanding. An inexperienced user could easily sand too much, which would then require additional coats of body filler to be applied to repair gouges or uneven strokes.

Body Fillers and Fiberglass

Bondo is the brand name for a plastic body filler product that has been around for years. Many auto enthusiasts believe that Bondo is actually the proper name for body filler. However, like Kleenex is a brand name for tissues, Bondo is simply a brand name for an assortment of various body fillers and glazing compounds. Autobody paint and supply stores generally stock a number of name brand body fillers. Talk with a jobber to find out just which brand will work best for the type of repair you are contemplating and the kind of paint that will be applied afterward.

Amost all plastic body fillers require a catalyst (hardener) be mixed in to help the material cure and harden. Without a catalyst, filler material will simply sit for hours and hours, possibly lumping down to cause an uneven finish. Too much catalyst will cause mixtures to set up too fast making them impossible to apply. Read directions carefully whenever mixing a catalyst with any plastic filler or other material.

Initial coats of plastic filler are designed for strength and adhesion to bare metal. They are not intended to be applied as a final coat. Glazing putty

Dual action sanders do not spin like high-speed units. An off-center mechanism causes the head to move in an orbital motion. Caution must be exercised in their use, as they too can sand a lot more material than expected. Never let them sand on one spot alone; keep machines moving at all times. Tool courtesy of The Eastwood Company.

Body fillers are manufactured by a number of different companies. This is just a small sample. Some brands profess to work better with certain paint systems and others are advertised as the strongest. Unless you have used a certain brand before, or have a friend that highly recommends one brand over others, let an autobody supply jobber assist you in your choice of a filler that is suited to the type of job you are doing and chemically compatible with the paint system you will employ.

41

Mycon has used Dynatron's Dyna-Hair body filler with good results on a number of occasions. He feels that extra strands of fiberglass help to strengthen repairs and add support to assemblies. In the autobody field, this product is commonly referred to as "Kitty Hair." Once again, if you are not familiar with this type of product, let an autobody supply jobber assist you.

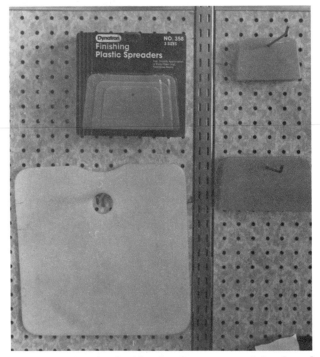

Body filler is mixed with a hardener on a mixing board like the one featured here. Essentially, a board is an autobody technician's working easel. Filler is scooped up with a plastic spreader (squeegee) and then applied to a panel surface. Spreaders come in sets with generally three sizes: small, medium and large. They can also be purchased individually, as shown in this photo.

is a similar product that is used for the final coat. Its base material is much smoother and finer than plastic filler. After its application, sanding will smooth glazing putty to a fine finish ready for sealer, primer and paint.

Fiberglass resin and mat may be needed to repair rips, tears and dents on fiberglass bodies. Resin must be mixed with a catalyst in order to set up and harden. Too much catalyst will cause resin to harden very quickly and will even cause it to become physically hot. Read and follow mixing instructions carefully.

Fiberglass mat is used along with resin to strengthen fiberglass repairs. It comes in packages as single folded sheets. Pieces are cut off in sizes and shapes to fit a repair area. After a coat of resin is applied with a brush, mat is laid down and then covered with another coat of resin. From one to four layers of mat may be needed for deep repairs. Resin, catalyst and fiberglass mat are available at autobody paint and supply stores and some auto parts outlets.

Metal Cutting Tools

Except for removal of mangled metal, cutting tools are usually saved for panel patches and other, more involved body repair procedures. Equipment used for cutting metal range from tin snips to die grinders and nibblers to air chisels.

Tin snips look like garden pruning shears. Their blades are heavy duty and cut sheet metal easily. About the only problem with their use is that they tend to distort metal edges by causing them to curl. The Eastwood Company's Mini Nibbler is a tool used in much the same way as tin snips. This hand held tool cuts up to 15 gauge aluminum, brass or cop-

Dynatron's Putty-Cote is a polyester glazing and spot putty product. Use this after applications of filler have been sanded smooth. A skim coat of glazing putty will seal filler material to offer a smooth, pinhole free surface, ideal for eventual coats of paint sealer and primer-surfacer. Technicians have had good results with other brands too. Be sure to follow label directions when mixing in hardeners and applying to panel surfaces.

per and up to 18 gauge mild steel. A great feature about this $29 tool is that it does not curl or distort metal on either side of cuts. A groove in the center of the Mini Nibbler allows waste metal to curl up away from your work.

Power nibblers are available from The Eastwood Company in both a pneumatic unit and as an attachment for power drills. Both make quick work of cutting up to 18 gauge mild steel. The power drill nibbler is simple to operate and even allows for cutting curves. The air powered nibbler operates at 90 psi and only uses 4 cfm of air. It sells for about $50. The drill attaching nibbler costs around $30.

Die grinders and utility cut-off tools operate at 20,000 to 22,000 rpm. Special abrasive wheels attached to their shafts grind away a thin line of metal to effect cuts. Use caution while operating these tools to prevent sparks from igniting combustible or flammable materials and wear gloves and eye protection for personal safety.

Air chisels are power tools that look like heavy-duty ½ in. drills, but instead of spinning, they incorporate a reciprocating impact system that forces a special chisel through metal. They can be used to cut sheet metal and heavier gauge steel components, like brackets, supports and reinforcements.

Newer cars are loaded with spot welds that secure everything from quarter panels to door skins. To remove assemblies attached with spot welds, it is best to use a spot weld drill bit on the end of a ⅜ in. or larger drill. The special design of these bits allows top metal to be cut around spot welds, yet stops short of drilling through base metal. The Eastwood Company offers these bit units for around $15. They are also available at autobody paint and supply stores and tool houses.

Welder's torches can be used to cut metal but their high heat will tend to warp thin sheet metal panels. Along with that, torches leave behind ragged edges and are more difficult to use to cut perfectly straight lines. Nibblers and die grinders cut a cleaner line and do not heat the metal enough to warp it.

Welders

Kane believes nobody can call themselves a professional autobody technician unless they know how to weld. Amateur autobody repair persons can

This is a drill nibbler tool. It attaches to the end of a power drill and works fast to cut sheet metal. As seen here, it can even cut around corners with no problem. If your project requires that sheet metal be cut, seriously consider using a nibbler like this. They are inexpensive and work very well with little noise or edge curling. Tool courtesy of The Eastwood Company.

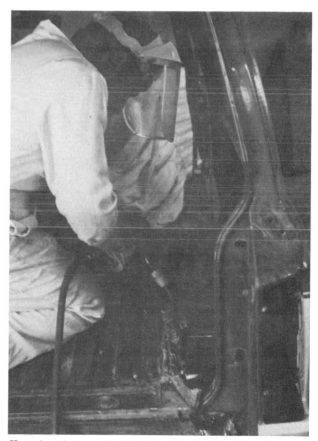

Kane is using an air chisel to cut out welds along the quarter panel and floor pan seam. He wears a full face shield and heavy leather gloves while cutting metal. Air chisels work fast to cut metal. They do leave ragged edges that have to be flattened before patch panels can be welded to them. Air chisels require a substantial amount of air pressure to operate on a continuous basis.

practice welding on pieces of scrap material to learn how to effect secure welds with few problems. Solid welds with less than desirable finishes are ground smooth with a grinder and coarse disc.

If you are contemplating a major autobody repair with inevitable welding needs and have little or no experience welding, consider taking a welding class at a local community college or vocational school. Weak shallow welds will not only result in visual blemishes, but could easily become major safety hazards should they break during operation of a repaired vehicle.

Most thin sheet metal is welded with low amperage wire feed welders. Too much amperage causes base metal to burn away, leaving behind large holes. In addition to attending a welding class, novice welders need practice to become proficient. Be sure to have a fire extinguisher or garden hose handy during all welding operations and to wear quality welding gloves and a hood with the recommended view lens.

Most autobody technicians use wire feed welders for plugging holes and stitch welding sheet metal panels. Stick welders produce too much heat for thin sheet metal and their use is not recommended. A variety of welders are available from a number of outlets, including tool houses, autobody paint and supply stores and mail order facilities like The Eastwood Company. Prices range from $200 for a small unit to more than $700 for wire feed machines.

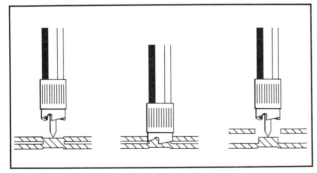

This spot weld cutter can be adjusted to set the depth of cut in order to prevent weakening lower metal panels. The unit cuts around spot welds on the top layer of metal only. Residual nubs are ground smooth with a grinder. Spot weld cutters are a must for those projects where sheet metal panels have to be taken off. Dip cutters into cutting oil after each cut to preserve the bit. The Eastwood Company

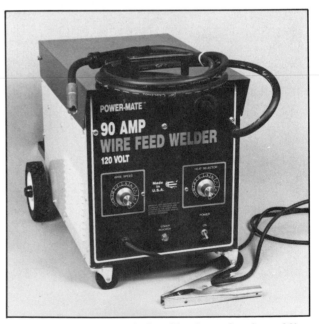

A small, 90 amp wire feed welder is perfect for welding thin sheet metal panels. This unit requires no special electrical supply wiring. It can weld up to ¼ in. material as long as the metal is beveled and multiple passes are used. Should you need to do some welding on your car, consider buying or renting a unit similar to this.

Frame and Suspension Straighteners

Hydraulic and pneumatic jacks, Porto-Powers, mechanical body pullers and large-scale frame straightening machines are part of a professional autobody technician's arsenal of equipment used to align frame members, pillars, floorboards and other heavy-duty assemblies. Your need for such expensive equipment is debatable.

A regular hydraulic jack can be used to force small parts back into position. Blocks of wood may have to be used to shore up work and also protect metal from gouges caused by small jack tips. Mechanical jacks and screw jacks will also work as long as room is provided for their operating handles.

A Porto-Power combines a hydraulic unit with various attachments by way of a high strength hose. Pipe fittings of different lengths are assembled together with a power ram to apply outward pressure between two items spaced as much as 6 ft. apart. Other attachments, like chains, hooks and bases, make this a versatile body shop tool. When set up correctly, a Porto-Power can force out metal pieces and even pull sections together.

A Mechanical Body Puller costs about $90 from The Eastwood Company. This type of tool has been around body shops for a long time. It employs a

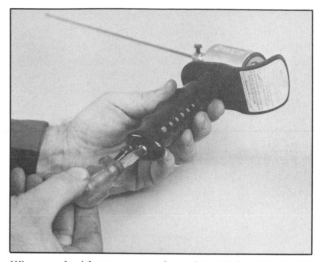

When used with 80 amps or less, this stitch weld attachment works great for welding on thin sheet metal panels. Rods are slightly maneuvered by the machine in quick, almost unnoticeable up and down spurts to help novice welders maintain good beads. Adjustments to any piece of power equipment must be done according to manufacturer's recommendations and directions. Improper adjustment of this stitch welding attachment can cause problems with welds and also equipment. The Eastwood Company

This Eastwood Company welder is supplied with stitch and spot welding attachments. The hand-held attachments have a simple pin located at the end of the power cord that is placed between the welding rod handle jaws. Grounding is effected by the grounding clamp and welding is done as needed. This little unit is perfect for occasional do-it-yourself auto restorers.

This heavy-duty Yellow Jacket pneumatic machine makes quick work of pulling out smashed metal from this Bronco II quarter panel and floor pan. Expensive equipment like this is mandatory for professional technicians. Should you need major collision work done on your car, seriously consider having a professional complete the work for you. Inexperienced use with powerful machines like this can cause more trouble than satisfaction.

mechanical jack mechanism along with a 5 ft. steel pole and a multi-purpose head to enable users to push or pull misaligned body parts back into position. Used with chains or straps, this tool can be manipulated into a multitude of configurations.

Heavy-duty frame straightening and aligning machines must be operated only by qualified personnel. These machines must be used in a prescribed manner if unibody frames and other chassis and suspension systems are to be repaired correctly. Repairs of this nature should be undertaken only by a legitimate body shop. Although the machines are available at most autobody paint and supply stores, training in their use must be done through a qualified community college, vocational school or private facility.

Miscellaneous Equipment

Whenever a vehicle must be raised to gain access to undercarriage areas, extreme caution must be exercised to assure it will remain securely in that position. Use heavy-duty jacks and jack stands for any procedure of this type.

Bumper jacks may certainly be able to lift cars, but they are in no way capable of keeping them steady, especially while you are pulling and tugging on various body parts. It is mandatory that you place jack stands under your car and then lower its body onto sturdy stands. The only recommended use for bumper jacks is lifting cars for the immediate placement of jack stands.

By far, the best piece of equipment to use for raising automobiles is a hydraulic floor jack. But once again, do not rely solely upon it to keep a vehicle secure. Use jack stands whenever working under any part of a car body. Always lower vehicles onto jack stands and make sure they are steadfastly in place before crawling under any car.

Should half of a car be raised onto jack stands, the wheels still in contact with the floor must be

Porto-Power is a name brand for tools like this. Units incorporate a hydraulic ram and high pressure hose along with various attachments to push and pull metal sections back into position or out of the way. Just about every body shop has at least one of these tools. You can rent them at rental yards for nominal fees. Practice with the attachments will render a multitude of different ways to move mangled sheet metal or reposition tweaked supports.

Mechanical body pullers have been around body shops for years. Here, two of them support the roof structure of a Bronco II whose demolished passenger side quarter panel has been removed. Many different uses for these tools are available to inventive technicians. The main structure is a 5 ft. steel bar, complemented by a hook at one end and a mechanical jack assembly that can be adjusted anywhere along the bar. Another multi-use part complete with an assortment of hooks can also be slid anywhere on the bar when needed. Tool courtesy of The Eastwood Company.

46

blocked. Use chunks of wood, concrete blocks or any sturdy item that will prevent the wheels from rolling.

All sorts of optional body shop equipment are available from autobody paint and supply stores, tool houses and mail order businesses. You could easily spend thousands of dollars on nifty items like trim removing tools, profile gauges, clamps, punches, metal fabricating machines, bead rollers, rivet guns, and sandblasters. But you may not need nearly that much to complete the job you have at hand.

Look at the basics and purchase only those tools and pieces of equipment really needed for your job. As you progress through projects, you will surely find new repairs to tackle and will be able to clearly justify purchases of more tools and equipment. Be sure to buy only quality tools so that you can depend on them to last a long time. And always make certain that you use each tool as it was intended to be used. Improper tool or equipment use will not only increase chances of failure, it may cause damage to otherwise undamaged parts or, more seriously, a personal injury.

Heavy-duty hydraulic jacks are mainstays at body shops. This one is used to raise a Corvette front end while jack stands are placed under frame sections. Jacks work fine to raise cars, but they should never be allowed to support a car while you are working under it. Place jack stands to support its weight.

Before crawling under any raised vehicle, be certain sturdy jack stands have been strategically placed and the vehicle's weight clearly rested upon them. No other means of vehicle weight support is as dependable as jack stands. Here, a Corvette is supported by two heavy-duty jack stands placed under frame sections. Almost all jack stands are adjustable to fit whatever height needed.

Bel-Tech Auto Paint is just one example of an autobody paint and supply store. Jobbers, like Laursen, stay up to date on the latest autobody repair materials and painting products by reading information sent out by manufacturers. In addition, they carry a lot of body shop tools and equipment. For all intents and purposes, you can purchase just about any tool or product needed through autobody paint and supply stores.

Safety Equipment

Foremost, especially when working around metal, you must wear eye and/or face protection. Whenever using a grinder or power cutting tool, always wear a full face shield. This protects face and eyes from flying metal sparks and debris. Also wear a face shield, or goggles, when working under vehicles. Undercarriages collect a multitude of dirt, grease and debris. No matter what project you are working on in that position, something always seems to fall off the underbody, generally close to or into your eyes.

Heavy leather gloves are also important for safety. Especially when removing mangled sheet metal, be aware of sharp edges that can cause deep cuts in hands and fingers. The operator should wear gloves for grinder and cutting equipment operations. Hot sparks can burn skin and a simple slip with a power tool could cause grave tissue injury.

When sanding plastic fillers, wear a dust mask or respirator. Once this type of operation begins, you will be amazed at how much sanding dust is created. Masks and respirators can be purchased at autobody paint and supply stores.

Overall safety with any job begins with a solid plan of what you will be doing and how you will be doing it. If hot sparks are anticipated from cutting equipment, be sure all combustibles and flammables are safely located away from the operation. Use only those extension cords that are as big or bigger than the cord attached to the tool in use. Make certain the vehicle you are working on is safely and securely held in place, whether raised on jack stands or simply parked. Autobody work can be fun and give personal satisfaction upon completion of a project. Do your part to guarantee this reward by performing projects safely.

Angled cuts around the circumference of this sanding disc allow for the removal of paint, rust and debris from deep inside dented sheet metal. Kane has used this technique successfully for years. Alongside the high-speed sander is a full face shield from The Eastwood Company. You should never attempt grinding maneuvers without the use of eye or face protection.

Respirators with replaceable cartridges are excellent pieces of safety equipment that should be worn whenever you are confined in a dusty or contaminated atmosphere. These units are inexpensive and readily found at autobody paint and supply stores. Cartridges are easy to replace and do an excellent job of preventing foreign material from entering your respiratory system.

Rubber gloves should be worn anytime your hands might be subjected to harsh chemicals, like lacquer thinner or enamel reducers. Painters' rubber gloves are designed to hold up to such chemical use. More and more, notes Laursen, body shops are using respirators and rubber gloves. You should too.

Special hand cleaners, like this, are designed to remove paint and other body shop materials from hands and skin. Harsh cleaners designed for tool cleaning are not safe for cleaning skin. Products made just for the purpose of removing paint products from hands are. You will be better off in the long run to use hand cleaners like this instead of washing hands with lacquer thinner or other harsh chemicals.

4

Assessing Damage

Perhaps one of the most critical parts of autobody work falls into the realm of damage assessment. What might initially appear to be a minor dent could actually turn out to entail a major repair operation. A fender problem, for example, might also include damage to side lights, inner fender apron, a mechanical part attached to an inner fender, A-pillar buckles, and so forth.

It would be nice if primary damage inspections could reveal all damage initially and allow for im-

The most obvious sign of damage on this vehicle was a dent on the passenger side rear door. However, closer examination revealed that the gap between the front and rear door was more narrowed than the same gap on the driver's side. Eventual repairs included work to straighten a tweaked B-pillar and rear door hinges.

The front fender on this Toyota 4x4 was severely crunched. A more detailed assessment showed that the wheel hubcap was scraped and chipped, and will have to be replaced. Note that the splash shield (inner fender) was also wrinkled in the collision. All damaged parts and assemblies have to be accounted for in detailed damage assessments.

mediate and complete ordering of new parts to be on hand at the beginning of repair operations. But in many cases, damaged assemblies need to be removed before a thorough inspection can be made to all areas surrounding obvious damage to assess just what parts will be needed.

Professional autobody shops insist customers plan on leaving their moderately damaged cars at their shop for at least five working days. This generally allows plenty of time to order and receive required new parts and also a bit more time to order replacement parts for those damaged items that were not recognized during an estimate inspection.

The Obvious

It is pretty hard to overlook a bumper, fender or hood that has been crunched in a collision. However, it might be easy to pass over a cracked lamp lens, creased trim piece or torn inner splash shield made of high strength plastic (urethane). Although dam-

age to a minor, rather insignificant part of a larger assembly may seem to be of little consequence, missing it during an initial damage assessment will only mean that attention to it will have to be given later, possibly at a time when you thought the project had been completed.

While assessing obvious damage, look deeper than just the outward, most significant problem. A front end crunch, for example, might reveal some major part damage, like fender, bumper and grille. But smaller items are also obviously damaged and must be accounted for.

Obvious, in this context, means that damaged parts are clearly in plain view but may be overshadowed by the larger parts mangled around them. If a lower quarter panel came in contact with an immovable object, for example, a dent would be outwardly obvious and its recognition immediately identified. But what about other items located close to the dent? Could a small bracket or support be bent on the inner side of the panel? Is a side lamp

The grille assembly on this 1990 Toyota 4x4 pickup truck has a number of separate parts combined together to make one grille and front end section. If a collision occurs to this area, each individual broken piece will have to be located to determine which parts are needed to put the assembly back together correctly. There is no sense in ordering a whole new grille for the truck if only a few pieces are actually broken.

A minor dent at the front of this fender also included a slight buckle at the rear side section of the hood near its hinges. Follow the path of force that impacted your car to accurately determine whether indirect damage has occurred. Especially with lighter metal unibody cars, dents and buckles are commonly found a few feet away from where actual impact was made.

lens cracked? How about body side molding clips? Are they all intact, or could one or two have suffered broken housings?

Newer cars are assembled with a multitude of small pieces connected together to make one large assembly. In the case of some grille sections, two or three pieces may be joined by clips to form an entire grid-like pattern on the front of the vehicle. If only one part of that assembly is damaged, you need to buy only that part, not an entire grille section. The same for lamps. If just a lens is cracked, why spend extra money for a new housing, trim ring and gasket?

Collisions can also produce indirect damage such as buckles or dents located away from the initial point of contact. A small dent might be quite obvious at the front of a fender where it smacked a post, but a smaller dimple located closer to the door might have resulted because the entire fender assembly absorbed the impact. That dimple will also have to be repaired along with the fender dent.

Where cars of thirty and forty years ago were built with heavy materials and could easily withstand the force of a minor impact with minimal damage, lighter cars of today may display collision damage in a number of different spots. A quarter panel that sustained a rather minor impact toward the rear might show wobbles all the way in front of the rear wheel. Until tension and stress created by the initial dent are relieved, those wobbles will not go away.

Indirect damage can occur almost anywhere. Look at roof panels for signs of buckling or dimples. Unibody cars utilize all structural parts together to form a solid, single unit. When one part of the structure receives force from an impact, additional pieces may also absorb some. The degree of absorbed force may be insignificant and the car may show no signs of damage because parts sprang back into position. Since metal does have a memory, this is common. However, if the force is great enough, a piece may fail and a dent, dimple or bulge appear.

Obvious body damage should be anything that can be seen or felt. A wobble in a door skin of a white car may not be noticed when viewed straight on. But

Almost all of this passenger side door panel is marred with lots of tiny dings and dimples. Waves in the reflections of the door show where imperfections exist. You can easily feel these blemishes, especially if you place a soft cloth between your outstretched hand and the car body. Look at damaged areas from different angles to determine the extent of damage. Light reflects in different ways and you need to take advantage of the best reflection to get a detailed look at damage.

The door panel was repaired by working on metal damage with hammer and dolly maneuvers. Then, instead of just filling in and sanding each individual ding and dimple, the entire door panel was covered with a coat of filler material. After sanding to a smooth, flat and even condition, a skim coat of glazing putty was applied and sanded accordingly. The results, as you can see, are excellent.

looking at it from the front or rear with light reflecting off the side may reveal additional wrinkle damage above, below, in front of or behind an obvious dent. This condition can also be felt when the door is lightly massaged by one's hand.

Because of design characteristics, you should look under front and rear ends, fenders and quarter panels when those areas have sustained body damage. Any number of associated pieces could be dented, broken or marred by a collision. Spoilers and splash guards are commonly overlooked items. Since newer bumpers are comprised of a number of parts, what may outwardly appear as a minor problem could actually be major damage to supports or braces located behind the unit.

Glass is another obvious thing that could go unnoticed. Minor nicks or cracks in corners or along sides will get bigger once a vehicle resumes road operation and subjects them to bumps and jolts. Leaks are another problem with glass involvement, especially when trim has been damaged or a seal broken.

A host of incidental problems could result from just one minor collision accident. You can do little about assessing hidden damage until parts are removed to allow for visual inspection. But to ensure that the job starts out and then progresses smoothly, you should get an accurate assessment of

obvious problems before you begin. Not only will you be able to have needed replacement parts and repair materials handy from the outset, you will also be able to devise a systematic plan of repairs for the completion of your project in an efficient manner. Anything less will add to confusion and frustration, as parts fail to fit properly and minimal dent repairs fix only small segments of larger problems.

Trim and Moldings

Trim and moldings are attached to vehicles in more than one fashion. Older cars relied on holes in body panels into which protruding support pins from trim pieces were inserted and then secured by nuts or clips. Newer cars utilize the same basic principle for some trim, emblem and badge pieces but may also feature sections secured by adhesive, two-way tape or small screws hidden, somehow, by weather stripping or interior trim sections.

Decorative, vent-like trim parts located on C-pillars behind the rear windows of some import cars are secured by screws hidden behind interior trim in the passenger compartment. Prying on them is inappropriate; they will break. Carefully investigate

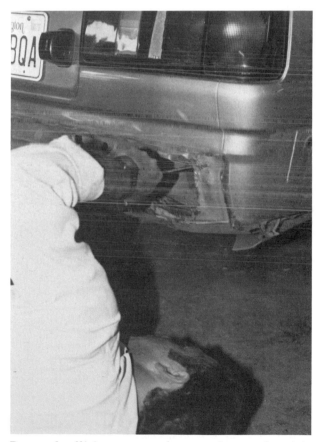

Rear end collisions commonly cause damage deep into rear body panel areas. Look for broken wires, seals, bumper brackets and quarter panel problems. Check exhaust pipes and other assemblies under the vehicle for signs of damage or breaks.

The center of this photo shows cracked fiberglass at the base of a Corvette driver's side rear doorjamb. This was caused by stress applied to the area after a side-swipe collision. Because the sides of the car were severely damaged, it would have been easy to miss this spot of indirect damage.

how pieces like these are attached to your car's body. Do this by scanning their entire perimeter and gently lifting an edge to see if tape or mount supports are present. Go slow. If need be, remove an adjacent piece of molding or weather stripping to determine if it is fastened by screws or clips.

A section of body side molding may have popped off in one piece after a collision. At first, it may appear to be in perfect condition. For plastic parts especially, look at each individual clip supporting mount to determine if it has been cracked or damaged in any way. Just because the face may look great does not mean inner supports are intact. If damage has occurred to any of the mounts, repairs may be impossible and the trim pieces will have to be replaced by a new one.

Trim and moldings cover a wide range of autobody attributes. Replacements are easy to locate at dealerships for newer cars and a surprising number of mail order outlets offer a vast assortment of trim packages for older, classic, vintage and general use

vehicles. One of the best ways to locate the suppliers of special auto accessories is through *Hemmings Motor News*. This auto enthusiasts' telephone book-sized monthly magazine of classified and display advertisements is absolutely packed with information about the acquisition of parts and service for every kind of auto related assembly, project endeavor and business you could imagine for just about every make and model car or truck ever manufactured.

As with other auto parts, trim packages also have specific names, like ground effects for those trim and molding parts adorning rocker panels and lower door sections of cars and trucks. When ordering replacements, be sure to clearly identify the exact piece you want.

Trim and molding are not limited to just metal and plastic pieces that dress up the side, front or rear parts of vehicles. Many times, these terms include vinyl stripes, decals, graphics and the like. When assessing damage, be sure to include the cost of these items when estimating overall cost factors.

Fenders

Experienced autobody restorers with expertise in welding techniques can repair almost any older,

This Corvette fender was scraped against a yellow metal post filled with concrete. Luckily, all that happened was a couple of abrasions and a small crack. In addition to the fiberglass work, vinyl pinstripes will have to be replaced. Rolls of striping material in all sorts of patterns are available at auto parts stores and autobody supply houses.

The fender, hood and splash shield on this truck will have to be replaced with new units. There is really no easy way to repair them. In addition, grille pieces, bumper, signal lights and the lower front panel will have to be closely assessed to see whether they can be repaired or will have to be replaced.

thick metal fender or body part. They can cut out bad metal and weld in new patch panels, solder or braze the edges and then file the repair to perfection. Newer cars with thin sheet metal panels will not allow that kind of heavy, heat reliant metalwork as they will burn through or warp.

Crinkled fenders suffering deep creases or multiple, accordion-like folded dents are almost impossible to repair on newer automobiles. The amount of time, energy and technician expertise needed for this type of metalwork is not worth the effort when replacement fenders are so easy and inexpensive to acquire. A new Mustang fender, for example, costs just over $100; trim, lamps and other add-ons will cost more, of course, unless they could be salvaged from the old fender.

This is not to say that you shouldn't attempt repairs on your own to save the cost of a new fender. It may sound contradictory, but you are doing this project to save money and learn how autobody repairs are completed. You may never know what the limits of your abilities are until you try.

Quarter panels

Collision damage to quarter panels may also include metal buckles to floor pans, inner fenderwell splash shields, trunk sides and/or floors, gas tank filler housings, and so on. A careful assessment of damage to these areas is imperative.

When assessing damage, try to determine the mechanism of impact. In other words, picture the inertia at the point of impact and estimate what kind of effects radiated out from that point. Does the roof show signs of buckling? Any oil cans along pillars? What does the floor and wheel housing look like under carpeting? Do you see signs of paint peeling or cracking along the rear doorjamb? These are all things to look for when digging into the depth of damage created by an impact to quarter panels.

In cases of extreme damage, entire quarter panels must be removed and replaced with new ones. A complete quarter panel for a Ford Bronco II includes both inner and outer panels, B-pillar and assorted brackets and costs around $740. Plenty of autobody expertise is required for this type of project as damage will first have to be pulled out to square away the floor pan, wheel housing and roof, if damaged. Spot welds must be cut out and all dimensions of the area set up uniformly to accept a new panel.

Pickup truck beds can be likened to quarter panels in that they cover basically the same part on a truck as a quarter panel covers on a car. Most newer beds are double walled. This means two pieces of sheet metal are used to make a truck bed. An inner piece will absorb shocks from cargo and keep those impacts from affecting an outer skin.

When pickup beds are crunched in a collision, assess not only the damage to the outer skin but the inner section as well. In some cases, repairs may call for a new bed. Used ones from a wrecking yard are much less expensive. Another alternative, if you are familiar with welding operations, is to remove that side of the truck bed that has been damaged and replace it with a new panel. Prices vary according to which company purchases are made from. The Mitchell Book shows 1987–90 Ford pickup truck side panels, both inner and outer, costing about $325.

Brackets, reinforcements and supports may also be located behind truck bed side panels. They must be accounted for during damage assessment. In what condition are fenderwell trim pieces? Gas tank filler door? Mud guards? Stripes, graphics and reflectors? These are all items that must be repaired or replaced if you want the entire job to turn out looking like that part of your truck was never involved in a collision.

Rocker Panels

Rocker panels are located directly below doors and constitute that part of a car or truck that runs

A rear end collision caused definite damage to this Cadillac quarter panel. In addition, buckles were found on the roof between the side windows and rear glass, gaps were narrowed on the passenger side between the door and fender and gaps were widened on the driver's side door. Some frame and structural member alignment will have to be undertaken to straighten out this car.

along the bottom side, from the lowest part of the body to the bottoms of the doors, and from the front of quarter panels to fenders. They are frequently damaged when a driver scrapes against a tall curb while cornering or from accidents involving vehicles with bumpers located at the same height as rockers.

Like most other body assemblies, rocker panels can be removed and replaced. This will require drilling out spot welds and maybe some metal cutting. Be certain that the floor pan and affected pillars are put back into their proper positions before inserting a new rocker panel; that may necessitate some special hydraulic or pneumatic body pulling equipment. Once a new panel is placed, spot and stitch welding will secure it.

Along with obvious damage to rocker panels, investigate whether doors were sprung, pillars twisted or front fenders knocked out of alignment. Unusual buckles along body sections and peeling or cracking paint are indications that these areas were damaged.

Most rocker panel dents are popped out with dent pullers or picks, while severely damaged sec-

tions may have to be cut out and replaced with patch panels. This operation requires knowledge and experience with welding techniques on thin sheet metal, as rockers are made out of the same basic material as other body panels.

Doors

Sometimes assessing door damage is easy. A dent incurred somewhere on a door is obvious. As long as the door opens and closes smoothly, and handles, locking mechanisms and glass operate correctly, there is little need to look further for damage. However, if any of the above do not function properly, remove the interior door panel and assess what damage has also occurred inside the door.

Nader Bars are strong steel beam-like structures located horizontally inside passenger cars. Their function is to add a greater degree of protection for passengers in case of collision with another vehicle or solid object. As mentioned earlier, once

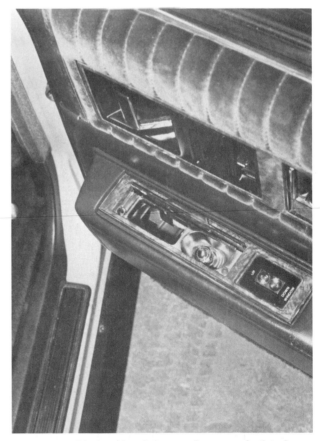

To remove this interior door panel, screws had to be removed by way of the ashtray slot. If there is no reason to remove interior panels, don't remove them. However, when repair efforts will be made easier by the removal of door handles or other items, take your time to remove parts in a controlled manner. This way, unnecessary damage will not occur to unaffected parts during dismantling endeavors.

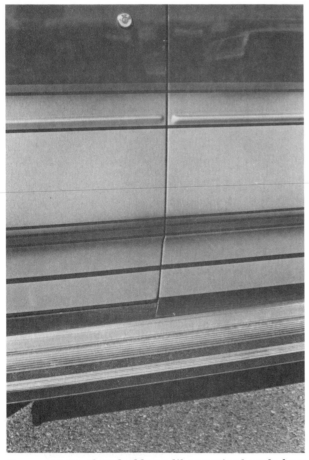

Fancy paint work and add-ons, like running boards, have to be accounted for in any damage assessment. This vehicle sports a trendy paint design that might be a bit difficult to match and will definitely add to any cost estimate.

they have been bent, the door must be replaced. Nader Bars cannot be repaired.

Broken door latch, lock and window mechanisms can easily be replaced. Depending on the make and model, a series of linkage rods connects handles to actual locking and latching mechanisms. If you notice that the dented metal has put pressure on a rod, pulling out the dent might be a simple solution to the problem. But if the rod itself has been broken or badly bent, replace it with a new one.

Window crank assemblies use a set of gears to operate a bar attached to the bottom of a window assembly. While the bar moves in an up or down direction, the glass slides along a set of channels accordingly. Bends or creases in the slide channels will prevent glass from moving smoothly. Damage to the gear unit will render an assembly useless. These items are replaced individually. Carefully study layouts of such equipment as their removal and replacement are hampered by a lack of access. The outer door skin blocks all visibility to the area and inner panels only allow access through a set of specific inspection openings.

If the door you are working on has suffered so much damage to the outer skin that it will be impossible to repair, consider cutting out a large area of outer skin to allow for full inspection of all the inner door assemblies. This will also permit easy removal of all internal working parts and installation of those parts into a new door.

Along with investigating the possibility of damage to inner door mechanisms, check if hinges, weather stripping, pillars or interior door panel parts have been adversely affected. Look for cracks, unusual bulges, tears or rips on materials located close by.

Glass is an important concern. Small shards will quickly cut your hand or arm as you prod an inner door assembly for damage. Before anything else, in cases of broken glass, use a strong vacuum cleaner to remove all traces of glass. Then, as you feel inside

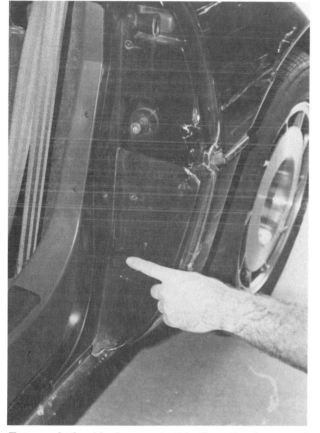

Extreme body side damage to this Corvette also caused damage around the driver's side doorjamb. Mycon is pointing to a hairline crack in the corner of the jamb. Along with that is damage just to the right of the door latch pin and at the bottom of the jamb. Damage assessments have to be very detailed in order to determine all of the damage suffered by a vehicle so repairs can be made.

The passenger side rear fixed glass on this Bronco II is under a tremendous amount of stress. It is surprising that it did not shatter upon the collision impact. Note the wobble reflections at the top of the glass. This shows that surrounding sheet metal is buckling glass. Before attempting to remove glass in this condition yourself, seriously consider having a professional glass installer do the work. Just one wrong move with this unit and it will shatter.

a door panel, be especially aware that broken glass could easily be laying on top of window and latching mechanisms and could cut your hand. Shake doors with broken glass to try and make pieces fall to the bottom of doors. Use the crevice attachment to your vacuum cleaner for reaching inside to remove glass particles.

As with all other body sections, trim and molding also figure into a final new part inventory. Order enough clip assemblies to complete the job and be sure to use the correct adhesive when installing new weather stripping. Door handles and window cranks are ordered through dealerships for newer cars and through catalog sales outlets for older, vintage and classic cars.

Hoods, Deck Lids and Hatches

Because hoods are designed with an inner panel full of convoluted characteristics, repairs to moderately and heavily damaged units are almost impossi-

Brand new door shells will arrive with absolutely no attributes. You will have to completely outfit these units with all of the inner mechanisms, weather stripping, trim, latches, glass, etc. In your damage assessment, include new clips, screws, bolts and fasteners of any kind. Emblems and decals will also have to be replaced so include them on your parts list as well.

ble. In most cases, professional autobody technicians simply replace smashed hoods with new ones.

In cases of heavy damage, pounding out dents and crowns in hoods is exceptionally difficult because there are two closely connected panels with which to work. It is extremely hard to work on an outer skin when the inner skin is in the way. Dual panels make strong units as welds used to connect them prevent one panel from reshaping while the other remains rigid, then vice versa.

The best thing to do when your car has suffered a mangled hood is to locate a used hood in excellent condition at a wrecking yard. Barring that, new hoods can be ordered from dealerships and some mail order companies.

Older hoods do not present autobody technicians with the dual panel problems of newer cars. Basically, they are single sheets of heavy metal formed to prescribed shape specifications. Normal metalwork should be sufficient for dent, crease and buckling repairs.

The mechanism of impact must be considered when assessing damage to hoods. Was the car hit from the front or did something fall on top of it? Front end collisions will almost always involve grille work, lights and bumper. Are they damaged? What about the hood's hinges and metal surrounding them? Are buckles, chipped or cracking paint visible? If so, where are they lcoated and what kind of impact would have caused their condition? Should you look even further to assess damage to cowling and/or firewall?

Dents caused by falling objects should not necessarily affect other supporting hood features unless, of course, the damage source was a very heavy object, like a tree trunk. In such cases, check fenders, aprons, engine parts and all assemblies located around the hood.

Deck lids fall into the same category as hoods. Newer cars feature a series of inner structural members that help to give lids strength and support them during opening and closing. Crunched deck lids, like hoods, are generally scrapped in lieu of new ones.

Along with assessing the deck lid's damage, look at the hinges, locking mechanism, rear body panel, quarter panel sections and that part of the body that extends from the base of rear glass to the deck lid.

Rear hatches, or liftgates, usually contain a large piece of glass. Because of their weight, most hatchbacks are outfitted with a set of piston-activated supports that hold the assembly in place while raised. Should a hatch become damaged, make sure these supports are intact and functioning properly. Determine this easily by simply raising the hatch to see if it will stay in place.

Depending on how a unit was damaged, check hinges, locking mechanism, rear body panel and roof for damage. Should you think that a part of the roof has buckled, lay your hand on top of a soft cloth and gently feel the area for imperfections. A cloth will increase your hand's sensitivity to quickly and easily feel any disfigurement along the roof panel.

All associated assemblies close to the damaged hatch must also be included in your damage assessment. Check lamps, emblems, badges, moldings, weather stripping, glass, trim and quarter panels. The entire rear section of your car must be evaluated for any direct or indirect collision damage. Be sure to include clips, screws, nuts and bolts with your parts replacement order.

Engine and Drive Train

Seldom does midside impact significantly damage engine or drive train units. If it does, impact inertia had to be strong enough to cause major body damage. Generally, front and rear end collisions result in damage to engines, transmissions or rear differentials.

As with most assessments, envision what kind of force was absorbed by your automobile. Immediate results could be a crunched grille and front end, but additional energy may have been expended on the radiator and its supports, battery, inner fender panels and anything else in line with the front part of your car.

At first, look around the engine compartment for obvious signs of damage. A leaking radiator, hoses or water pump are good indicators. Are fan blades bent? Do they scrape against the radiator? If so, that assembly will have to be replaced or repaired. What has the force of that impact done to the crankshaft?

Engine blocks are very sturdy. It takes a tremendous collision to break them. But a number of associated engine parts may have sustained damage. Physical defects are first indicators. A more definitive check of the engine and its associated parts will offer clues as to their disposition. These inspections could include pressure checks of the cooling and fuel system, a check for crimped brake lines and damage to the heater assembly.

The transmission could be damaged if an engine was forced back in a collision. Leaks, of course, would be a definite problem indicator, as well as the inability of the transmission to go into gear.

Rear differentials have few indicators of damage. Bolts attaching leaf springs could be severed or marks designating their previous location could be exposed, signifying that they have moved. Pinion seals on differentials could be cracked, which would allow fluid to leak from housings.

Cars on the road that are seen going in a crosswise direction, as opposed to straight in line, have experienced rear end problems. One wheel has smacked a curb very hard to dislodge that side of the axle from its point on leaf springs. In essence, one rear wheel is ahead of the other by a few inches. This condition must be corrected to ensure safety and normal tire wear.

Suspension

A car's suspension must be positioned correctly or it will not ride as designed. Bumps will be unusually hard and steering could be compromised. All front end collision damage assessments must include thorough inspections of all front end suspension assemblies.

Broken suspension pieces could easily lead to dangerous driving encounters. A part could be slightly bent at one point and then suddenly snap while in operation, leading to a serious accident. Other misalignments will simply cause related parts to wear out prematurely.

For all intents and purposes, suspension problems should be corrected by a competent professional. Special equipment and expertise are needed to align everything under the car that needs to be in an exact position for performance dependability.

Frame

Collision damage to frame members also falls into the same category as suspension damage. All repairs should be done by a qualified professional.

The engine and drive train for front wheel drive cars are all located in the engine compartment. Severe front end collisions like this could cause a lot of damage to mechanical assemblies or parts. Should body panels be smashed against engine parts, a certified mechanic should check out all of the drive train assemblies before putting the car back on the road.

Clues as to frame damage include obvious buckles and/or cracks to frame members. Since that part of the car's underbody receives so much dirt and grit debris, it is easy to notice where a certain pattern of dirt build-up has been disrupted. This is a good sign that an impact has been absorbed.

Side collisions often damage frame members. Crawl underneath your car to visually inspect damaged areas. Anything that appears unusual is cause for attention. Frames are nothing to take lightly, as their function is to hold an entire vehicle together.

Grille and Lights

Newer automotive designs have incorporated so many different multi-part assemblies, it is hard to distinguish a solid part from one that is composed of a number of different items. Grilles and headlights are just those sorts of assemblies.

Older cars had a grille. It was one unit designed into the front of a car which allowed air to pass through to the radiator. Headlights were sealed units. If a light went out, you simply bought a new bulb complete with element and heavy glass lens.

Today, it is common to find grilles made up of a number of different parts. The actual grid work can easily be a composite of three or more different individual parts. The mechanisms that hold all of those parts together might be simple clips or could be high-tech plastic, reusable rivets. The only way to determine this is by close and careful inspection.

Headlights are far superior in illumination ability today than ever before. Halogen lights are capable of putting out more candle power than previously imagined. But their bulb elements, since they are so expensive, are now integrated into the headlight unit as a separate part. So if you need to replace a headlight, be sure to order a glass lens and a separate bulb.

Damage assessment for grille assemblies might appear easy at the beginning. A certain part is broken and you need to order a replacement. Don't be too quick to write off a grille, headlight or other trim piece. You may save money by slowly dismantling the grille section to positively identify just exactly which piece is broken and needs replacing. Instead of spending a lot of money on an entire grille, you

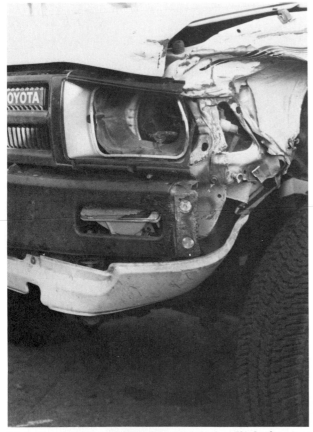

Note that the plastic trim piece over the headlight features a line between it and the rest of the grille. This shows that it is a separate piece combined with other parts to assemble a grille unit. Also look closely at the mangled metal section. You can see that another light fixture was located next to the headlight and some small brackets are broken just below that. All of these little items have got to be accounted for if repairs are to be complete.

Due to the force of collision, the driver's side door mirror was forced into the dashboard to dent the vinyl material. This small spot of damage could have been overlooked had it not been for Mycon's keen eye for detail.

may save by just ordering a small section that was really the only piece damaged anyway.

Interior Compartment

In your zeal to detect all of the damage suffered by your car on the outside, don't overlook the inside to determine just what damage has occurred there.

Interior door panels often split, crack or bend from the force of a collision. Trim around windows is blemished as well as seats, dashboards and headliners. Consideration must be given to stereo speakers, seatbelt connections, sunroofs and many other items located within a damaged area. All of these parts must be calculated into an overall part replacement estimate.

It might be surprising that a side mirror could be forced into a dash panel to cause a blemish. It may also be odd to consider that a collision could damage the alignment of seats, glove compartment and console components.

Once again, you have to extend your damage assessment investigation into all areas surrounding the immediate impact area. Look at it, if you will, as a pebble thrown into a pond. Although the pebble makes an immediate splash, ripples continue to move on to greater circumferences. The same principle holds true for autobody damage assessment. Look at the most obvious damage, but hunt further into the vehicle for those things that may have also absorbed shock from the impact to present misaligned or actual damage characteristics.

Wheels

Unless they are obviously bent or broken, wheels are a common automotive component that go unrecognized as a possible victim of a collision. Many times, damage is not determined until a repaired vehicle is taken out on the highway. It is then that drivers notice a shimmy, shake or an inability to adequately control their automobile.

Even a light hit can result in balancing weights being thrown off wheels. This can cause tires to shake violently at speeds as low as 30 mph. Look at the outer parts of wheels for extra clean spots. This is generally an indication that a weight has been lost. You will have to take your car to a front end alignment business to have the assembly properly balanced.

The general consensus among car people is that damaged wheels should be replaced by new ones. In the case of expensive spoked wheels, you may find that a professional spoke wheel specialist, although hard to find, can true spokes to perfection. It may take a bit of work on your part to find such a specialist, but could save you money in the long run when compared to the purchase price of a new wheel.

Along those lines, look at tires. Deep cuts or gouges in tread or sidewalls are definite signs of damage. Do not take chances with damaged tires.

Instead replace them with new ones to guarantee as safe a ride as possible.

Overview

Auto collision damage assessment is a combination of determining which new parts are needed and which areas of a vehicle can be repaired with standard body shop dent mending procedures. Much of this process depends on your knowledge of body shop operations and your limitations with regard to bodywork experience and equipment availability.

With the exception of minor dings and dents, newer cars are designed in such a way that damaged parts are easily interchanged with new ones. It may appear that repairs will be expensive with the purchase of new parts, but a lot of grief and frustration can be saved over attempts to repair panels made of thin sheet metal or reinforced with sections of convoluted bracing supports.

Overall, make a concerted attempt to assess all damage from the onset of a project. This will allow you the peace of mind that all replacement parts and their proper securing mechanisms are readily at hand and set for timely installation. Projects flow faster and much smoother when preparations have been properly planned.

It would be pretty tough to miss the damage on this wheel. Some companies advertise that they can fix and true damaged wheels. Not all car enthusiasts agree.

5

Part Replacement versus Repair

The choice between repairing damaged body parts or replacing them with new ones relies upon the degree to which parts are damaged, your ability to effect needed repairs and your budget. It might be easiest to simply remove a dented fender and put on a new one, but is that really necessary in every case? Why spend a lot of money on a new fender when minor repairs could make the damaged one look new again?

In some cases, there is no choice. Parts are so badly damaged that no amount of repair work could

A small dent on the forward section of this Toyota fender has been repaired with metal and body filler work. The fender flair was destroyed, so it will be replaced. The side light was removed to facilitate overall repair efforts. A new fender could have been installed but that would have been a waste of money, since this one was easily repaired. You have to decide when to fix parts and when to replace them. When in doubt, attempt repairs. If your work fails to produce satisfactory results, resort to new parts.

This is the bottom side of a Corvette hood assembly; notice the headlight at the bottom right corner. The driver's side of this car was severely damaged in a side-swipe accident. The hood assembly will be replaced because deep fiberglass damage has extended into structurally significant areas.

62

make them ever look new again. For those, replacements are inevitable. You could save some money by purchasing used parts from a wrecking yard.

Locating replacement parts for older cars may not be as easy as a simple visit to a dealership. You may have to search wrecking yards or contact a number of mail order specialty parts outlets before finding exactly what you need. In extreme cases, special parts for vintage cars may have to be fabricated by a professional metal shop.

Overall, the bottom line with any autobody repair operation is to make a damaged vehicle look undamaged. This is accomplished in only one of two ways, by repairing blemished items or replacing them.

Cost Effectiveness

The key factor with any autobody repair project is cost effectiveness. It would be foolish to spend more money on repairs than it would cost to buy another, like-new vehicle of the same year, make and model. Exceptions are classic, vintage, special and irreplaceable automobiles.

Body shops frequently choose to install new replacement parts instead of spending extra man-hours repairing panels, fenders and doors. To them, time is money. A do-it-yourself autobody technician doesn't have to worry about time and can easily afford to spend however many hours necessary to repair damaged items. By doing this, do-it-yourselfers save the cost of new fenders, for example, where a body shop saves labor time by simply removing bad fenders and putting on new ones. The price of a new fender will about equal the labor cost for repairing an old fender, so customers pay about the same. But since the replacement operation takes less time, body shops are able to complete more projects to make more money.

A low speed, light hit to the driver's side front corner of this Jeep resulted in quite a bit of damage. The urethane fender flair is buckled, fender wrinkled, bumper guard and bracket bent, bumper twisted and signal light trim cracked. In addition, a small dimple is located on the corner of the hood. Body shops would not always choose to repair fenders in this condition because of labor time and cost effectiveness. However, a serious do-it-yourselfer could make satisfactory repairs on this kind of moderately damaged item.

Dismantling efforts can sometimes involve more than removing the damaged parts. In this case, the entire Jeep grille had to be removed in order to reach bolts that secured the bumper. Notice, too, that the lower splash shield was bent in the low speed collision. This item and its supporting bracket can be straightened with a little hammer and dolly work. Be sure to check for damage behind items like these that encompass an entire involved area.

63

Attempts should be made to fix damaged parts whenever possible. This is cost effective. But when parts are too badly damaged or designed in such a way that repairs would be nearly impossible, you will have to purchase new ones. Shop around to find the best deal. Be aware that some inexpensive after market parts from companies other than original equipment manufacturers (OEM) may not fit exactly as they should; sometimes bolt holes are misaligned and other dimensions are slightly off center. OEM parts might cost a little more, but their overall quality and dimensional characteristics are worth it.

New Part Identification and Ordering

Each individual auto part has its own separate identification number. This number catalogs parts in books and on stockroom shelves. Without a number, it is difficult and in some cases impossible to order new parts. When you go to a dealership to order something, one of the first things the parts person will do is look up that part in a book. From that, he or she will retrieve a part's identification number and then locate it according to a numbering system designed on the stockroom shelves.

To help a counterperson correctly locate the exact part you want, make sure you have the vehicle's year, make, model, production date and serial number on hand. Production dates and serial numbers are found on stickers located on either a driver's doorjamb, firewall, radiator support, glove box or other position as determined by the manufacturer. Serial numbers are also normally located on dashboards at the base of windshields in front of the steering wheel. Information from this number can tell an experienced counterperson a lot about a vehicle, including at which manufacturing site it was assembled and what body series it is.

When ordering antique parts such as special brackets, lamp pieces, lenses or small body parts, it

Paint has been removed from the area surrounding a small dimple. It is difficult to see dings and imperfections with paint removed. This is why Kane does as much metal flattening as possible with paint in place. Body filler will easily repair this minor imperfection. Tape has been placed on top of pinstripes behind the ding to protect them against accidental damage from grinding operations. Body filler will be applied to an area much wider and longer than the ding spot. This is done to make sure that the whole area is smoothed out perfectly flat and even.

This brand new Jeep fender arrived with a slight ding. Repairs are indicated by a body filler application just above the wheel and tire. New trim and wood grain vinyl will have to be put on this fender after paint work has been accomplished. In this case, it was more cost effective for the body shop to install a new fender than to repair the old one, even when a slight imperfection had to be fixed on the new unit.

may be a good idea to bring the damaged item into the parts department with you. This way, once a counterperson has found a replacement part, you can compare the two to make sure the new one is correct. Many times, new parts might initially look like old ones but are slightly different. Even though they may be identical parts that serve the same purpose, their use may be intended for different car models. Bolt holes or other minor features could be positioned differently, which would make its installation on your car impossible.

Locating Used Parts

A lot of money can be saved by purchasing used parts, such as fenders, doors, bumpers, emblems, and interior panels, from a wrecking yard. Not all wrecking yards or auto salvage businesses operate the same. At some, you will have to bring your own tools to remove parts yourself from wrecked vehicles in the yard. Other yards prefer their employees

remove parts and then sell them to you over the counter. Call wrecking yards first to determine if the parts you need are available and who would be responsible for removing them.

Large items, like hoods, deck lids and doors, are heavy and someone should help you carry them out to your pickup truck or trailer. If you plan to purchase more than one large item, wrecking yards may be able to deliver units for you. When body shops purchase entire front end assemblies, for instance, wrecking yard personnel generally deliver them to the shop.

If you are lucky, the body part you find at a wrecking yard will be in excellent condition. However, in many cases you will have to repair a minor ding or dent and then paint the unit to match the color of your own car. Be alert to trim pieces. If a part on your car that is being replaced has no trim,

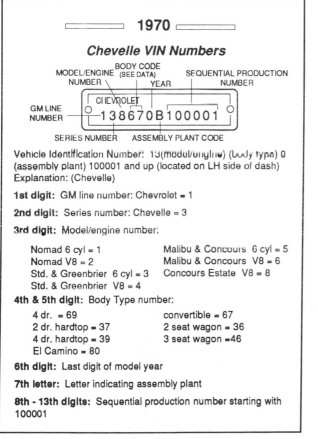

1970

Chevelle VIN Numbers

MODEL/ENGINE NUMBER · BODY CODE (SEE DATA) · YEAR · SEQUENTIAL PRODUCTION NUMBER

GM LINE NUMBER — CHEVROLET — 1 3 8 6 7 0 B 1 0 0 0 0 1

SERIES NUMBER · ASSEMBLY PLANT CODE

Vehicle Identification Number: 13(model/engine) (body type) 0 (assembly plant) 100001 and up (located on LH side of dash) Explanation: (Chevelle)

1st digit: GM line number: Chevrolet = 1

2nd digit: Series number: Chevelle = 3

3rd digit: Model/engine number:

Nomad 6 cyl = 1	Malibu & Concours 6 cyl = 5
Nomad V8 = 2	Malibu & Concours V8 = 6
Std. & Greenbrier 6 cyl = 3	Concours Estate V8 = 8
Std. & Greenbrier V8 = 4	

4th & 5th digit: Body Type number:

4 dr. = 69	convertible = 67
2 dr. hardtop = 37	2 seat wagon = 36
4 dr. hardtop = 39	3 seat wagon =46
El Camino = 80	

6th digit: Last digit of model year

7th letter: Letter indicating assembly plant

8th - 13th digits: Sequential production number starting with 100001

In the front pages of a Chevelle parts catalog from Year One, Inc., are displays of serial number meanings for various model years, like this one for 1970 Chevelles. VIN stands for Vehicle Identification Number. As you can tell, it represents a lot of information about the vehicle. Newer cars even show what paint color was used originally. Numbers like this can help parts people locate new parts quicker and more accurately.

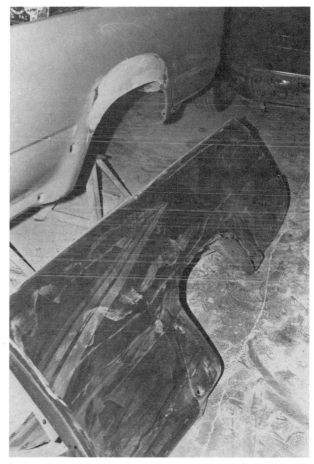

The side of this Toyota pickup truck bed was badly damaged in a collision. Too much work would be needed to repair it and there are no guarantees that repairs would turn out to be acceptable. In this case, a new bed side was purchased from a Toyota dealership and installed. Spot welds were carefully drilled out and sufficient time given to the repair project. When ordering large parts like this, be certain to indicate left or right side and whether special trim packages should be included.

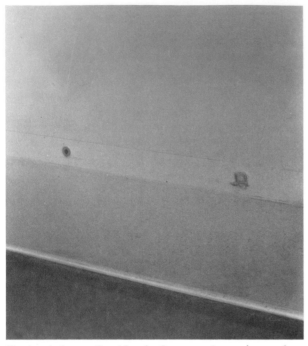

The two holes on the side of a door panel are places where trim pins will be inserted. The hole on the left has a receiving bushing in place. The one on the right has a pin in place, evidence that a support mount was broken off that trim section. The presence of trim holes is an important consideration when buying new or used body parts. Be sure to specify what is needed when ordering parts or while searching for them at a wrecking yard.

Terry Skiple points to a rusty spot on the fender of his 1957 Thunderbird project car. Already, paint has been taken off with chemical stripper. This fender can be repaired with no problems. But had it been rusted completely through, he might have had to locate a new unit. A vintage salvage yard is one place to look for old car parts. Another means to locate hard-to-find items is through specialty auto parts catalogs and monthly periodicals, like Hemmings Motor News.

you must be sure that an identical part from a wrecking yard does not have trim access holes drilled in it. Should trim be in place, look at it carefully to make sure it is not secured by clips, but rather with tape or glue. This way, trim can be removed to match your car and you will not have holes to weld up.

Another way to locate used parts is through newspapers and periodicals with classified ads for automobiles. Many times, you will find ads for parts cars. These are generally older cars that no longer run and whose owners simply want to get a little money out of them by selling off parts a few at a time. Should you come across a make and model similar to yours with body parts in good condition, you might be able to purchase the entire car for a fraction of what new parts would cost.

In other cases, a vehicle like yours might have sustained collision damage to an area opposite of what your car did; that is, it has front end damage and yours has rear end damage. You might be able to buy this wrecked car for next to nothing and then salvage all of its good parts to repair your car. When the project is complete, sell what is left of the parts car to a metal scrap yard.

With the interest in automobiles at an all-time high, a number of auto swap meets are held regularly. You might be able to locate items you need at one of these gatherings or even find a fellow auto enthusiast who has access to them. Check newspapers and auto-related magazines to find out when the next auto swap meet will be held in your area.

Hard-To-find Vintage Items

More and more, auto enthusiasts are restoring older, classic and vintage automobiles. Locating parts is one of the biggest problems that face restorers. Because of this, a lot of companies have been started that deal specifically in new and used parts for specific automobiles. Some of them have even gone so far as to develop machine shops to manufacture certain hard-to-find parts like fenders, floor pans, quarter panels and other items. In addition, periodicals like *Hemmings Motor News* have sprung up to offer enthusiasts greater means to locate parts through nationwide advertising.

Salvage yards that specialize in vintage auto parts are becoming more popular around the country. These kinds of facilities offer enthusiasts thousands upon thousands of used parts from older cars that have been dug up from barns, pastures, abandoned garages and elsewhere. Vintage auto salvage yards are generally quite neat and tidy when compared to generic wrecking yards. Most of these businesses will not allow customers to remove parts from their stock of cars, preferring instead to have qualified employees dismantle items so that adjacent parts are not damaged in the process. find listings for these outlets in the yellow pages of your telephone book under the heading "Automobile Parts—Antique and Classic."

Car clubs are made up of true auto enthusiasts. Most organizations support certain auto makes, like Ford, Chevy or Dodge, and some even get more specific as members must own a particular model, like Corvette or Mustang. These folks can offer new members a wealth of informtion when it comes to finding replacement parts. If you are having difficulty locating parts for your special car or truck, talk with car club members. Clubs may be listed in auto-related magazines and publications or you might find them in the yellow pages under the heading of "Clubs and Organizations."

Locating hard-to-find clips, trim and other accessories may not be easy. However, sooner or later, parts can be found if you persist. Browse through automobile sections in telephone books to find the various auto-related services where you can inquire and gain insight as to who to contact next. If all else fails, you may have to have special parts custom-made.

Custom Fabrications

Almost any kind of metal part can be fabricated at a professional metalworking or sheet metal shop. Again, the yellow pages list both types of business under the headings of "Metal Fabricators" and "Sheet Metalwork," respectively.

To get a better idea of who specializes in automotive metalwork, check with local autobody shops, parts stores, automobile machine shops or professional auto restoration services. Their experience in the auto field may have given them the opportunity to see what type of metal fabrication work has been completed by particular companies and they can therefore recommend their services.

A metalworking person cannot simply pull a design out of thin air, but needs a guide plan or model. If at all possible, bring along the old parts you want duplicated so the metalworker can get an idea of size and shape dimensions. If a part has been totally destroyed, make a detailed drawing complete with accurate measurements.

A cardboard template could be made, in some cases, which characterizes the size and shape of the piece you expect to be made. Make a template yourself by using thin cardboard about the thickness of a shoe box. Bend or curve it in exactly the same design you expect a new part to resemble. Use sturdy tape to hold it together and mark any significant spots, such as bolt holes, braces, and supports, with a felt pen.

Make sure you talk to your metalworking specialist about templates or drawings before authorizing any work so that both of you will be in complete agreement as to just exactly what the fabricated piece will be used for and what it will look like when completed. Communication is critical in this area. Not only does the part have to fit and be secured correctly, it must be made of the right gauge metal

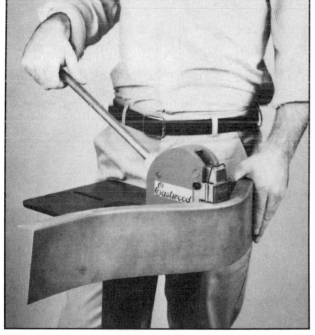

Especially for vintage automobiles, you may not be able to find replacement parts and might have to have them custom-made. Tools like this Shrinker and Stretcher set allow do-it-yourself technicians to make inside or outside curves on pieces of stock that have been properly prepared. Some knowledge of metalworking procedures is needed before actual fabrication work can be accomplished. The Eastwood Company

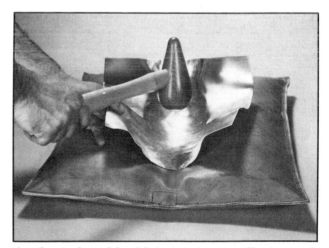

Another tool used by fabricators is a panelbeater sandbag. Specially designed mallets are used to shape metal panels while they rest on the sandbag. Because a sandbag can "give" under mallet blows, shapes are easily accomplished. Like any other metalworking tool or piece of equipment, practice with scrap material is mandatory before atempting repairs or actual fabrications. The Eastwood Company

Metal that is too thin may fail during use and metal too thick may cause undue wear or stress on adjacent parts.

Fasteners

During many autobody repair jobs something breaks, most commonly hidden fasteners or clips. Each car manufacturer seems to have developed different ways of securing trim, interior door panels, grilles, lights and so on. No two makes or models are exactly the same. While a Volkswagen Jetta's interior door panel will be attached to the door with screws, another car will feature simple pop-on and pop-off clips. Pulling and tugging in an inappropriate fashion will surely break clips, requiring new ones for replacement.

Hundreds of clips, snaps, plastic rivets, clasps, hooks and fasteners are available at most autobody paint and supply stores. Always bring broken clips or fasteners to the autobody supply store when shopping for replacements. It is imperative you retrieve exactly the same size and shape as broken ones. If not, you will have a difficult time making items function properly, if at all.

Few fasteners are reparable. In newer cars, many of these items are made of plastic. Once they crack, they are ruined. In some situations, glue repairs have been successful. These are generally plastic trim pieces that support little weight and are also lightly wedged into position and held there by adjacent parts. Reliance on glue to repair cracked or separated plastic fasteners is not recommended. You will be better off to replace damaged plastic pieces with new ones.

Metal fasteners may be a different story. Using the correct hand tools, you might be able to bend or force them back into their original shape. As long as tensile strength has not been unduly compromised

This is an assortment of small screws, nuts, clips and other fasteners found at an autobody paint and supply store. In a lot of situations, tiny parts like these are accidentally broken while dismantling. Many times, items like these get frozen in place and break when attempts are made to loosen them. Be sure to keep a list of broken parts so that replacements can be ordered before efforts to put a vehicle back together are started.

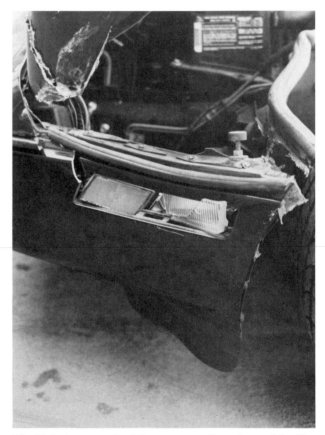

The light lens on the left appears to be salvageable. The one on the right is not. Some plastic parts can be repaired with special glues or products designed for that express purpose. In many cases, though, plastic parts cannot be fixed and must be discarded in lieu of new replacements. Look at the top part of this lower Corvette fender skirt. Notice that a thin plastic bar next to the adjustable hood bumper that extends horizontally is broken into three parts. Items like this will have to be ordered individually when replacing major body parts like fenders and hoods.

and cracks are not present, these items could be metalworked back into a usable condition. Should any metal fasteners appear weak or more than moderately damaged, replace them with new ones.

Along with certain clips and fasteners, spring-type clips are featured on various car parts. One of the most common are the C-shaped spring clips that hold window cranks on shafts of door and window operating mechanisms. Nothing other than these specific clips will work to hold those handles in place. Should a clip become lost or broken, it will have to be replaced with a new one of identical size and shape.

Repairs to Used or Damaged Pieces

The degree to which you repair damaged parts depends on your metalworking skill, tool availability, time and patience. You also have to be realistic about the repairability of some parts. For example, if a door skin had been repaired once before with extensive metalworking and plastic filler applications, chances are that a repeat repair to a set of new dents would not work. Thin sheet metal can only be worked so much. Once a second collision has caused

The original door on this Toyota pickup truck was dented and creased in a collision to a point where Mycon and Kane decided to replace it with a new shell. This was done strictly from a cost effectiveness standpoint for the shop. Although damage to the door is extensive, conscientious metalworking and filler maneuvers might be able to result in acceptable repairs. You will never know if repairs will turn out satisfactorily until they are attempted. Should they not, you can always purchase a new part.

This door was hit from the rear and pushed forward, as indicated by the distinctive V-pattern displayed by wrinkles on the lower door panel. Slide hammer, dent puller, hammer and dolly work can make this door look good again. In extreme cases, new outer door skins are installed using spot welds and special crimping tools to fold new skin edges over door edges. Should this skin be repaired, another collision of this sort will stretch metal to a point where a second set of repairs would not be feasible. Thin sheet metal panels can generally only accept one moderate repair. Collision damage suffered after that will require, in most cases, a new panel.

Instead of purchasing a new hood just because a small dimple marred this one's finish, repairs and new paint made this corner look like nothing had ever happened to it. By far, repairs of this nature are much less expensive than total part replacement. Deciding which items can be fixed and which ones have to be replaced is all part of thorough assessments.

medium hit damage, you should seriously consider replacing the door, or at the least the door skin.

Using the above example, let's say that you found a replacement door at a wrecking yard for a reasonable price. Minor dings or dents should be repaired before the unit is installed. Although this will require extra time, you will save money compared to the price of a new door and save time and effort by not having to transfer window and door latch mechanisms from the damaged unit to a new one.

Fenders, grilles, lamp assemblies, trim, bumpers and other separate assemblies may also be reparable, depending on their condition. If you are not sure whether a piece can be fixed or not, make attempts at repairs before spending extra money on new parts. Should your efforts produce less than satisfactory results, buy a replacement from a wrecking yard or a new part.

Overview

Decisions pertaining to the replacement or repair of damaged parts are based on a number of factors. When items have been totally mangled, shredded or ripped off their base, repairs are just about impossible. The decision to replace them is obvious. The only choice that has to be made is whether to purchase a brand new replacement or try a used one from a wrecking yard.

When parts are just slightly marred, though, you have to decide whether repairs will give you the results expected or if new parts are the only satisfactory option. For regular drivers, one would have to surmise that quality repairs could indeed make a vehicle visually and operationally acceptable.

Show cars, vintage, classic and special custom automobiles fit into a slightly different category. Repairs to parts on these vehicles may not quite fit within the realm of expected display qualifications.

Vinyl stripe tape is available in a variety of colors, sizes and patterns. You should be able to find replacements at almost any autobody paint and supply store. New body panels will, of course, need new stripes. In the case of dent repair, paint removal, filler and sanding operations might destroy existing tape located close to damaged areas. If the vinyl tape designs on your car are unique, you may have to order replacement packages from a dealership.

How an automobile is used by its owner will sometimes determine where repairs should be attempted or new parts ordered right away. Show cars and those entered into concours d'elegance competitions cannot be haphazardly repaired and then expected to win shows. This Corvette, for example, has suffered a good deal of body damage. Extensive fiberglass work could probably make most of the body look good again, but will repairs equal the high standards of new part installation? In this photo, note that the windshield is cracked and its vertical trim piece damaged.

Plastic filler, for example, may discredit a vehicle from championship status in a concours d'elegance competition. A minor trim repair flaw, although hardly noticeable to an enthusiast's eye, could stand out like a sore thumb to a concours judge.

Likewise, as far as concours judging is concerned, replacement parts must be authentic in order for automobiles to pass inspection and amass enough point credits to win competitions. In situations where acceptable part replacement is not feasible or possible, professional repairs have to be attempted that make a damaged original piece look and feel like new.

When all factors have been taken into consideration, final determination usually rests on cost. If making repairs to an item that can be fixed is least expensive, do that. If not, check with a wrecking yard to see if a replacement part can be located in satisfactory condition and at a cost substantially less than a new one. Failing that, buy a new part from a dealership parts department or through a specialized auto parts mail order company.

The round engine compartment part resting on top of the battery is a cruise control mechanism. It had been torn off of its mounting support in the collision. Items like this are put back in place after mounts have been repaired or replaced. If mounting brackets on the mechanism itself were broken off, you will have to find a new housing, possibly requiring a complete new part purchase. When mechanical parts like this are jarred loose or broken off their mounts, you must also question the unit's ability to operate correctly.

The lower Corvette fender panel has been ripped off of the car body and broken in half. A replacement panel will be used to fix the area. In situations like this, look around the entire area to determine what other pieces or parts were destroyed or damaged. The mounting clips for this piece are still in place, but are they in good condition? Can they be used again with a new panel? If not, new ones have to be ordered before parts can be put back on.

Major fiberglass repairs to this Corvette area would be noticed by show car judges and would not be acceptable. However, daily drivers are another subject. Conscientious fiberglass work followed by intricate sanding and smoothing techniques could make repairs acceptable and sturdy. The amount of time needed to effect quality repairs versus the amount of money required to purchase new parts are the main considerations. The choice in most cases is up to you.

6

Minor Ding and Dent Repair

When metal is forced beyond its original shape, it is stretched. Older cars with thicker sheet metal bodies can have dings and dents treated with heat and blows from hammers and dollies to shrink them back into shape. This process is called metal shrinking. Newer cars are not manufactured with heavy enough metal to easily accept metal shrinking endeavors. Panels will warp and holes are quickly burned through sections to make old style metal-working operations extremely difficult.

Therefore, ding and dent repairs on these newer automobiles are done without heat. Metal is worked with hammers and dollies and then covered with thin coats of plastic filler to effect a wrinkle, warp and dent free surface. A final skim coat of glazing putty fills small pinholes and sand scratches to effect a very smooth, paint ready finish.

Every square inch of an automobile's body is susceptible to some form of minor ding or dent. Sides are highly susceptible to parking lot door dings by inconsiderate people who fling open their

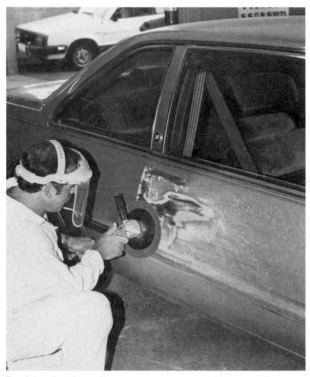

Parking lot door dings are common problems suffered by the sides of most daily driven cars. The entire door panel on this vehicle is riddled with dings. Since all of the blemishes are very shallow, Kane has elected to simply cover the entire panel with a coat of filler material and then sand it flat. Deep dings or dents will have been flattened first with hammer, dolly and spoon work. Here, a large sanding disc is used to remove paint. To make this job easier, the door handle and key lock could have been removed.

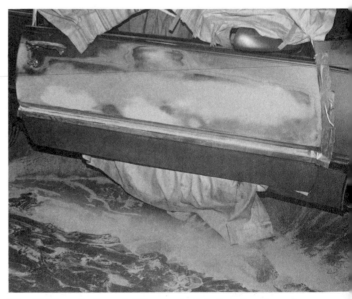

The lighter shades of filler material denote where low spots have been filled, while darker shaded areas show only a very light skim coat of material. Heavy-duty duct tape was used to protect the fender edge and trim from scuffs by sanding discs. Eventual coats of primer-surfacer will fill in feathered edges and controlled sanding with a small dual action sander and 400 grit paper will smooth it all to an even finish.

car doors without regard to where or how hard they smack into your car. On occasion, we may even miscalculate the force of our own door opening power to accidentally have it thrust into a post, wall or other solid object. The end results of these dilemmas are dings or dents.

Hoods, fenders, quarter panels, rear body panels and deck lids are just as likely to receive minor collision mishaps through accidental bumps. Once damage has occurred, work must be done to repair these visual flaws so that our vehicles can once again look new, fresh and undamaged.

Access Considerations

In a few cases, access to minor dings and dents is no problem. Holes are drilled through sheet metal skins to provide a hold for dent pullers or picks. Outward pressure is applied directly to the center of dings or dents while body hammers are gently tapped along a dent's crown to reduce stress and free metal to spring back into its original shape. If operations are successful, these repairs are quickly completed with no need to remove parts that block perimeter or interior access.

Dents next to, or very near, door handles require handle removal. To gain access to almost all exterior door handles, you have to first remove interior door panels. This can take from ten to thirty minutes depending on the type of vehicle you are working on and your level of experience. Once metal and paint work have been accomplished, you will have to replace the handle and panel.

Dings and dents along front fenders near bumper assemblies or grille sections may require those adjacent parts be removed to allow suitable access for dolly and hammer work and provide enough clearance so that paint removal, plastic filler applications and sanding can be achieved without marring their finish.

Dents to rear body panels almost always require rear bumpers be removed so that body hammers can

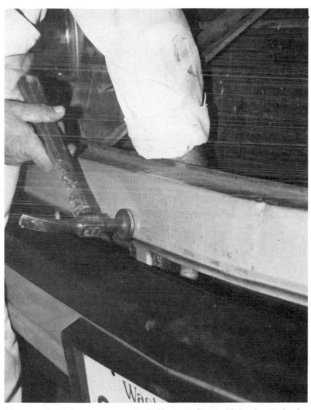

To conduct hammer and dolly work on this front body panel, grille pieces had to be removed. Adequate access to work areas is always a primary concern. It is still a tight squeeze between the panel and radiator but enough room is maintained for work efforts. A dolly is located below the hammer head just behind the panel bracket extension. Light hammer hits off the dolly help to straighten a minor bend at the junction between the panel and its bracket extension.

Careful examination of this dent will indicate a V-pattern with the point of the V at the top. This is evidence that the dent was started at the bottom of the panel and moved upward. Autobody technicians start dent flattening procedures at their most shallow part, the open end of V-patterns. Metalwork will start on the lower part of this panel to begin reducing metal stress over the entire dent. As work makes its way up to the deeper part of the dent, a lot of the stress will have been relieved and, therefore, dent depth decreased.

be swung freely without accidental nicks to parts of them, adding to the list of needed repairs. Quarter panel dent bumping (another term for hammer and dolly work) will necessitate the removal of trunk or hatchback compartment interior panels to allow access for dollies and spoons.

All in all, you should remove any body assembly that blocks total accessibility to the area in which you need to reach for repair maneuvers. Trim pieces, weather stripping, glass, emblems, badges and wheels all fall into this category. Make the job easiest by allowing yourself plenty of work room. Repairs are difficult enough by sheer autobody design that you do not need to add to this confinement by trying to work around some part that could be easily removed by loosening a few nuts, bolts or other fasteners.

Hammer and Dolly

A novice autobody technician cannot possibly expect to hammer out perfect repairs the first time out. He or she must practice. Acquire an old door, fender or other piece of sheet metal body from a wrecking yard, body shop or scrap yard. Use this piece to practice hammer and dolly techniques. If need be, smack a hammer or crow bar against the piece to make a dent. Then place a dolly under the dent and lightly tap a hammer along the top crown surface above the dolly to flatten metal. In essence, use the dolly as a blacksmith would use an anvil.

A variety of autobody hammers and dollies are available for all sorts of metal shape designs, like flat panels, ridges and curves. Additionally, you can use a combination of hammer heads and dolly shapes to pound out dents in tight spaces, as well as those of precarious characteristics. For example, pointed dings with tightly arched peaks caused by impacts from sharp objects, such as rocks or door corners, might be best bumped out with the pick end of a body hammer while a dolly puts pressure on the

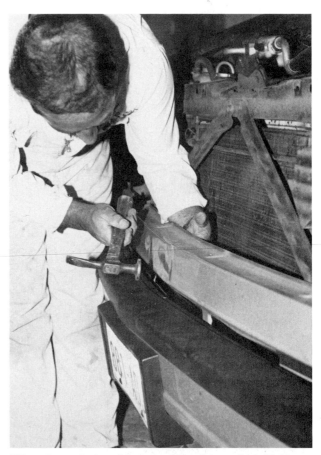

When the majority of dent depth has been reduced by hammer off the dolly work, hammer directly on dolly operations are used to flatten small high spots and generally even out the area. Again, light hammer taps are used instead of heavy hits. Heavy concussions will only cause metal to stretch and create more defined wrinkles. Along a sharp corner, use the edge of a dolly like an anvil to shape metal around it. You have to strongly support dollies in their positions to allow them to be a solid base for hammer taps.

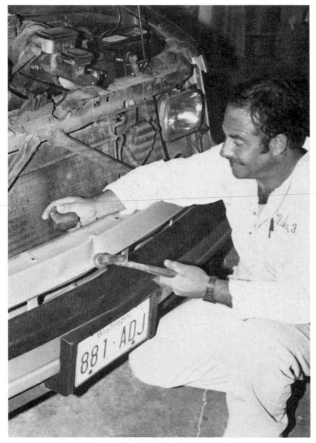

Kane uses a hammer and dolly to flatten the dent on this front body panel. Hammering off the dolly techniques will be used. As the dolly is placed in the center of the dented area, light hammer taps will be concentrated on the outer dent crowns. This action will help reduce metal stress overall without causing new wrinkles.

dent from below. Crowned creases are best flattened by the blade of a hammer's chisel head.

Hammer and dolly techniques include direct hammer on dolly blows, hammer off the end of dolly bumping and use of dollies to pound out metal from inner dent side locations. Practice will help you perfect these techniques. Practice, practice, practice.

Body hammers are seldom pounded on metal with great force. Most often, they are simply tapped against sheet metal to slowly and gently reduce stress and enable metal to spring back into its original shape. Instead of one harsh smack, autobody technicians rely on a series of maybe twenty to thirty very light taps in rapid succession to bump a dent into shape.

Dents usually display signs that indicate where damage started and finally stopped. Like the wake of a boat, as an object is forced against sheet metal, a pattern with a point is formed. The point shows in which direction the force was aimed. Behind it is where the force started. Autobody technicians attempt to reverse the direction of impact as they apply metal bumping operations, starting with the last occurring damage first and ending up where the force first came in contact with the sheet metal panel. Because newer sheet metal is so thin, you will have to walk out dent repairs; a 3 in. dent will eventually encompass a 1 ft. repair area.

Hammering off the end of a dolly is usually most effective when trying to reduce the size of a crown. While a dolly is positioned slightly toward the center of a dent away from a crown, a hammer's blows are directed at the top of the crown. Pressure pushing outward by the dolly allows pressure from tapping

hammer blows to reduce stress on the crown to let it fall back into position along with the adjacent sheet metal. Once a crown has been reduced, hammer blows on top of the crown with a dolly directly behind it will allow for final metal flattening.

Bump off the dolly around the entire perimeter of the dent's crown. As you work, you'll notice how dent depth shrinks. Work slowly; a large number of light blows is more effective than a few solid hits. Harsh slams with a hammer will not decrease a crown's stress; rather, it will simply cause little dents to form around the crown. Use as much pressure as possible on the dolly during these operations. Outward pressure from a dolly combined with inward force from hammer taps will reduce metal stress and help the overall dent to flatten.

Sharp but shallow peaks, crowns and creases are best reduced by direct hammer-on-dolly concus-

This Eastwood Company small dent puller attachment at the end of a variable speed power drill has a self tapping screw that will go through sheet metal and apply an outward force against dents. The round collar maintains a firm base against the dents' outer crown ridges so that dented metal can be pulled out to the surrounding flat level. For more precise control and when variable speed drills are not available, a nut on the collar allows for slow wrench turning. Operating a tool like this too fast will cause the screw to strip out before metal can be pulled into its proper position.

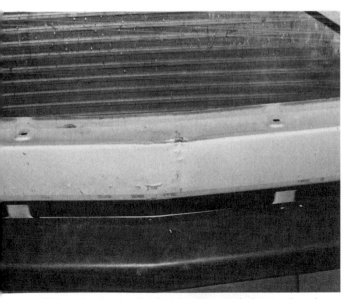

Chipped paint on the front body panel shows where hammer and dolly work was conducted. Because of its thin metal design, this panel dent will have to be covered with body filler to finish off the smoothing process.

sions. A dolly will serve as a solid base while light hammer blows force metal to flatten. Dollies of different shapes are used to effect specific curves, ridges and corners. As a dolly is forced into the shape, light hammer blows force metal to conform around the dolly corner to flatten out metal in the pattern intended. Additional light tapping with a hammer on top of a dolly's edge along a design line will eventually flatten metal so that it conforms to the intended shape.

Hammer and dolly work is improved with only one thing, practice. Attempting to repair dents on your car without first trying hammer and dolly techniques on a piece of scrap sheet metal is foolish. Do not use your car's body as a testing ground. find a piece of scrap sheet metal to practice on first.

Dent Pullers

The Eastwood Company, along with autobody paint and supply stores and other automotive tool outlets, makes special tools available that are designed to pull out dents from car bodies.

These tools operate on the premise that an outward force pulling directly on the center of a dent, while an outer stabilizer bar or disc holds perimeter metal in place, will pull impacted metal out to its original shape. For the most part, these tools work well.

Small, wrinkle free dents are easily fixed with a dent puller. Complex problems involving wrinkles, deep creases or multiple hits may pose some problems; reposition the tool a number of times for these.

Although dents will pull out, several holes may be left to fill in with low amperage welds. In cases where one or two applications of a dent puller are needed, supplement the tool's operation with hammer and dolly work.

While using Eastwood's dent puller, Kane noticed that very slow revolutions of the power drill worked best. Spinning the self-tapping screw too fast caused it to drill through sheet metal with far too little pulling force. Optimum results were accomplished when Kane allowed the tool to pull out a small part of the dent and was then stopped. While maintaining a pulling force on the unit, he lightly tapped the outer dent crown with a flat faced body hammer. A few more revolutions of the drill pulled out more dented metal and additional light hammer taps helped reduce metal stress and dent depth.

The process of slow and controlled drill revolutions with six or seven intermittent stops for light hammer tapping of the dent's crown perimeter was successful on light to medium hit dents. When the dent had been pulled out as far as the tool could progress, additional hammer and dolly work flattened

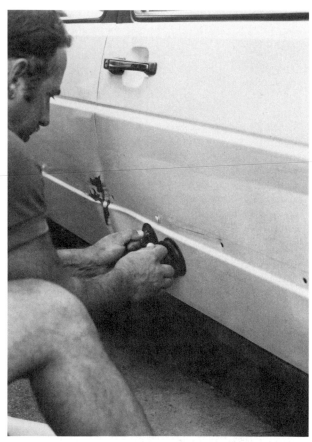

The strength of two suction cups together is sometimes needed to pop out deeper dents. Here Kane uses two different-sized suction cups in an attempt to pop out a shallow dent on the door panel. Be sure to brace yourself in the event a suction cup loses its grip.

Dent pullers create holes in body panels that have to be welded shut before body filler is applied. In some cases, shallow dents can be popped out with suction cups. Heavy-duty suction cups must first be moistened with water before being attached to car bodies. This helps them to create a much stronger suction grip. You can spray their surface with a squirt bottle or dip them in a bucket of water. Tool courtesy of The Eastwood Company.

metal to a satisfactory smoothness. Low amperage welding (50 amps) with an Eastwood welder quickly sealed the screw's holes.

Another way to apply dent pulling tools is to first start the self-tapping screw with a power drill and then progress using a wrench on the screw's collar, instead of using the power drill. This technique allows greater control. You can keep a drill motor attached to the tool's bit and use it as a means to put additional pulling force on dents. Slow rotation of the screw's collar forces out more of the dent with each turn and light hammer taps flatten crowns to reduce overall dent metal stress.

Suction Cups

Use suction cup pullers to repair light impressions where a dent perimeter's crown is very slight, like those on hoods or roofs caused by leaning on them too heavily with an elbow. first moisten suction cup bases with water to help create a tight seal. Then, gently apply enough pressure to flatten the cup against the center of an impression. Steady outward pressure will pull metal with it causing impressions to pop out.

Additional pressure may be firmly applied to the outer perimeter of an impression to keep that part of the sheet metal from giving with the section that is being pulled on. Do this by having a helper spread his or her hands around the impression and applying firm pressure. Be sure that hands which touch the car are free of rings, watches and any other adornments that could possibly scratch paint. You might even be wise to place a soft towel down first and then have them put their hands on the towel instead of bare paint.

Suction cups may also be used on tighter dents. In lieu of drilling holes for picks or dent pullers, try using a suction cup to apply outward pressure while tapping a dent's perimeter with a body hammer. In many cases, the amount of pulling force accomplished with suction cups is sufficient to pull out dented metal and also permit light hammer blows at the same time to flatten dent crowns.

Along with making dent pulling jobs less complex, successful suction cup endeavors also alleviate

Suction cups are used in conjunction with light hammer taps to flatten out a dent. This system works very well on shallow dents and those that cover a wide area without sharp creases or wrinkles.

To reduce most dents, outward pressure is applied to the center area while light hammer taps are directed to outer crown ridges. Along with dent pullers and suction cups, picks are used to apply needed outward force. Small holes are drilled along the center of dents as pressure is needed to force out metal. The pick end is simply inserted into a hole and outward force applied through pulling on the handle. While one hand pulls on a pick, the other maneuvers light hammer taps around the dent's crown.

77

the need to drill holes in sheet metal for the insertion of picks or dent pullers. This in itself is a good reason to at least attempt repairs using suction cups. If

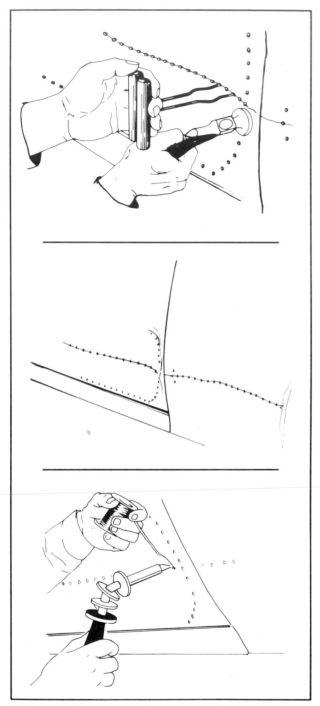

This is an illustration of how pick and hammer work is accomplished. As you can see, a lot of holes are necessary. Experienced autobody technicians scribe lines along the patterns of deepest impression and drill holes on them to maintain a uniform pattern of repair. Holes have to be filled with solder or low amperage welds. Be sure that the paint system you plan to use is compatible with the flux and solder products used. The Eastwood Company

their pulling strength is not enough to repair the dent, a dent puller or hammer and pick will have to be used.

Pick and Hammer

For many years, autobody technicians relied on picks and hammers to repair sheet metal. Today, use of machines like the Fitz Tool make pick work unnecessary. The Fitz Tool welds a thin rod to body panels to which a collared slide hammer is then attached. A securely welded rod will not break loose from metal, which allows a slide hammer to apply as much force as necessary to pull out dents or apply enough outward pressure so hammer blows reduce dent crowns. When the dent has been flattened, rods are cut and then ground off to leave the metal surface smooth.

To repair a large dent, ten to twenty rods might be needed in order to apply outward pressure in various locations around it. The same technique is used for picks. But wherever a pick is needed, a hole has to be drilled for its insertion. When a repair is complete, all holes must be welded up, adding to the work load.

The essence of pick work is no different than dent puller or suction cup endeavors. Basically, outward pressure is applied to a pick while light hammer blows are concentrated along a dent's crown. As a pick is pulled out, metal is obligated to follow as much as it can with regard to the amount of stress put on it by surrounding crowned or wrinkled metal. Hammer blows reverse that stress, to a degree, and allow dented metal to spring back closer to its original shape.

Before arbitrarily drilling pick access holes, first try to determine exactly how a dent was made and from what direction damage began. Generally, as metal is pushed forward, it forms a V-shape. The point of the V is where impact stopped.

Repair operations should start where the most shallow damage is found, generally farthest away from a dent crown's V-point. As dents are reduced and shallow dented areas are flattened, stress is relieved at deeper points. Attempts to pull out the deepest dents first will cause metal to stretch all around it and complicate repairs. Conversely, when shallow areas are straightened first, some stress on deeper dents is reduced so that when it comes time to pull them out, less metal is stretched and metal springs back easier.

Once a pick is inserted, apply a series of rapid yet light hammer blows along all crown edges surrounding the pick. Additional holes may have to be drilled in line with the first to follow a dent's path. As stress is relieved, start the same procedure a little further into the middle of the dent to reduce metal stress there.

Continue to work from the dent's most shallow point back toward the deeper end as indicated by the V-pattern, accomplishing just a little flattening with each series. Then go back to the starting point and do it again. Do not expect to pop out dents with just one series of pick pulling and hammering. You might have to repeat the process a number of times, reducing dent depth slightly each time until the entire dent is pulled out evenly.

Remember, dents are caused when metal is forced beyond its normal shape. Irregularities in that shape put stress on surrounding areas, which keeps metal in a dented condition. To remove dents, stress must be relieved so metal can once again spring back to its normal shape. One or two blows, in most cases, is not enough to relieve that stress. Repeated light blows are needed to slowly and uniformly redirect metal stress until it no longer forces irregular patterns but keeps sheet metal flat, like the way it was initially manufactured. Professional autobody specialists have been known to strike up to 120 light blows per minute when pounding out dents.

Many autobody technicians prefer to leave paint on cars while removing dings and dents because painted finishes help them to see body damage more clearly by highlighting surface imperfections. Once paint has been removed, shiny metal reflects light in such a way that slight indentations are hidden from view, making feel by hand the only accurate way to determine progress.

Removing Paint

After dings and dents have been flattened, paint is removed in preparation for body filler application. This is very important, as filler is intended to be applied to bare metal and will not adhere nearly as well to painted, primed or other covered surfaces. Make sure paint is removed at least 6 in. from repairs in all directions. This is so that filler can be feather sanded away from repairs to blend in with surrounding undamaged sheet metal. Additional bodywork with different hammer heads can also be employed after paint removal to further smooth noticeable metal peaks, creases or irregularities.

Use a 24 grit disc on a high-speed power sander to remove paint, rust and any other residue deposits left on a damaged piece of sheet metal. Get the surface as clean as possible without grinding away material from an already thin sheet metal panel. Cut off parts on the outer edge of 24 grit discs so that the rounded circumference is changed into a series of points. These points allow you to reach deep inside tiny crevices to remove rust, dirt, paint and primer.

When sanding has been completed, the sheet metal surface will be rough to the touch. Sanding scratches left behind by coarse 24 grit discs make an excellent base for filler adhesion. Smooth the perimeter of sanded sections with 80 grit paper to feather an edge between bare metal, primer, sealer and paint. The area between filler and paint, which exposes a feathered edge of bare metal, primer and underlying paint, will be filled with sealer and then

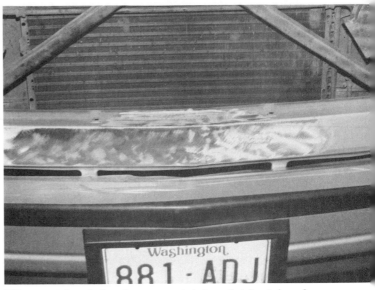

When metalwork has been completed, paint is stripped from the area of repair in preparation for filler application. Body filler is not designed to adhere to paint, as it will eventually crack and chip off. Bare metal bases scuffed with a coarse 24 grit sanding disc will give filler an excellent surface to attach to. Because of the way bare shiny metal reflects light, it is difficult to ascertain minor imperfections without feeling the surface. As you can see from this photo, the metal appears perfectly flat. In reality, very small imperfections and tiny low spots still exist to be leveled with body filler.

Paint is removed from car bodies in a number of ways. It can be sanded off with coarse sanding discs or strippers like this one from 3M. Although their thin edges cannot remove material as fast as flat sanding discs, these strippers work quite well to remove paint and other foreign debris from dented areas. They are available at autobody paint and supply stores.

79

primer-surfacer to eventually build up so that paint will have a flat surface to be sprayed onto.

Paint can also be removed in other ways. Sandblasters, when used according to instructions and with the correct media and pressure, will quickly remove all traces of paint, primer, rust, dirt and so forth. Sandblasters are required to be used after any brazing work to remove all flux impurities left behind; grinding efforts are not sufficient. Should brazing efforts not be cleaned completely, body filler will not adhere well to it and will eventually break loose.

Caution must be exercised when sandblasting car bodies, especially on newer cars with thin sheet metal panels. Too much pressure, coarser than called for media (abrasive) or prolonged blasting in one spot can cause panels to warp. It is important to

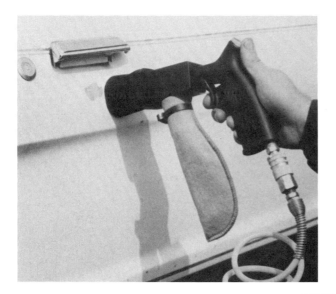

check with an autobody paint and supply store jobber or sandblasting equipment facility to see which media and pressure combination will be safest to use for your project. And be absolutely certain you follow all operational and safety recommendations provided with the equipment you employ. A sandblasting hood and heavy-duty gloves must be worn at all times during the procedure and you should wear long pants and a long sleeved shirt or jacket.

Chemical paint removers are safe and work well as long as all directions for their use are closely followed, including safety precautions like wearing heavy-duty rubber gloves and, with some products, a respirator.

Taking paint off panels with chemical strippers is messy work. After stripper is put on, a putty knife is used to scrape off wrinkled paint. More than one application will probably be necessary, especially for cars that have been repainted. A few layers of newspaper can be used under car sections to catch falling paint peels. For large jobs, consider driving your car on top of a wide sheet of plastic. Cut out sections around wheels so when stripping has been completed, plastic can be pulled from under the car, rolled up and then thrown away according to any hazardous waste disposal rules in your geographic area. For information on hazardous waste disposal regulations, sites and facilities, look under the heading "Waste Disposal-Hazardous" in the yellow pages of your telephone book for companies that specialize in the disposal of hazardous waste. Use those facilities to dispose of old paint residue, thinner and the like.

Determining Smoothness

Autobody professionals only trust their eye for detail to a certain extent. Instead, they mainly rely

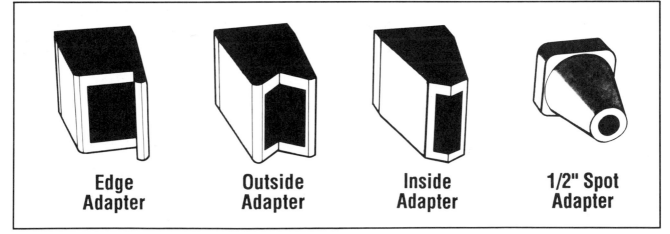

A good way to strip just spots of paint from very small nicks, chips and rusty dings is with a spot blaster. This handy unit comes with five nozzle adapters, which will easily fit over just about any kind of a ridge or corner. The tool's design is such that sandblast media is not sprayed out all over. Rather, almost all of it is confined within the unit and reused more than once. It operates at 90 psi and one bag of media is generally good for fifty blasts. Each spot blast covers an area about the size of an American quarter. The Eastwood Company

on the feel of a panel before deciding that a repair is complete. With fingers outstretched and grouped closely together, they move their hand in a forward direction with fingers leading the way. Massaging the metal back and forth allows them to feel ripples, wobbles, peaks, creases and any other irregular conditions.

This sense of feel is enhanced when a clean soft cloth is placed between your hand and the metal. Maneuver your hand across a damaged panel a number of times until you are certain that all damage has been corrected to within ⅛ in. or less. Although plastic fillers have been successfully used to thicknesses of ¼ in. and more, it is best you keep it at ⅛ in. or thinner.

As tiny peaks or creases are found, use a pick or chisel body hammer head to force them down. Leave a finger on a spot that needs flattening so that you don't lose its location while retrieving a hammer with the other hand.

Feel damaged sheet metal frequently throughout repair endeavors to determine progress and also pick up spots where minor bumps persist. If needed, use hammer and dolly to flatten metal or apply light blows with a suitable hammer head to reduce imperfections.

Initial Filler Application

Like car wax and polish, it is tough to get two bodymen to agree on which filler is best. Unless you or a friend have a preference, follow the recommendations of an autobody supply store jobber.

Plastic body fillers must be mixed with a hardener. Generally, hardeners are creamy substances that come in small tubes. You are given one from behind the counter when you bring up a con-

Body filler is scooped out of its gallon-size container with a putty knife. The star shaped material is hardener. Because Kane has mixed literally thousands of body filler batches, he does not measure out specific amounts of filler or hardener. He goes by sight. You should follow mixing instructions on the filler label. The putty knife is used to mix filler and hardener. Just before application, Kane likes to flatten and smooth the material with a squeegee to force out any trapped air bubbles. The mixing board will be taken to the job and filler will be scooped off of it with a squeegee.

Body filler is applied to this front body panel with a medium-size squeegee. As he starts out, Kane holds a squeegee in more or less a perpendicular position with a panel. As he moves the material along a panel, the squeegee is laid down until it is almost flat with the panel surface at the end of a pass. This ensures that enough material is being fed off of the squeegee to cover low spots and imperfections. You can go over spots more than once to perfect passes. Remember, too much squeegee work is not good. Slight blemishes on filler surfaces are easily sanded off once the material has cured.

The application of filler to this front body panel extended past the area of damage to include seemingly unaffected parts. This was done on purpose. Just because a panel may look perfectly flat does not mean it really is. Extend filler coverage out from damaged areas 6–8 in. in all directions when possible. This will guarantee that all of the repair will be flattened out and feathered into adjacent areas.

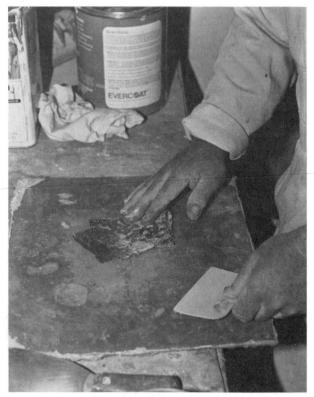

Body filler material will harden quickly on your mixing board, squeegee and putty knife. After every application, clean the board and all tools with wash thinner and a Scotch-Brite scouring pad. Kane's mixing board has been used thousands of times and although it looks used, the main surface area is smooth and clean. For maximum personal safety, painter's rubber gloves should be worn whenever using harsh chemicals like lacquer thinner.

tainer of filler (mud) for purchase. Read the directions carefully to determine how much hardener to use with specific amounts of filler. Too much hardener will cause mixtures to set up too fast making smooth applications to metal surfaces impossible. Too little hardener allows mixes to sit idle without setting up for extended periods of time. This can cause filler material to sag, possibly forming horizontal lumps or ridges across the middle or lower sections of a repair.

Use a putty knife to scoop out enough filler material to complete a job. Place it on a small piece of plexiglass that measures about 1 ft. square. This flat mixing board is the easel. Add hardener according to directions and thoroughly mix both materials with a putty knife. Since hardeners are usually a different color than fillers, continue mixing until one solid color has been achieved. After that, use a squeegee to work filler into a flat, smooth consistency. This flattening process helps to remove air bubbles trapped in the material, which could otherwise show up on a car surface as pinholes or other flaws.

Apply filler with a plastic squeegee. Small, medium and large size squeegees are sold at autobody paint and supply stores. Use a medium size for most applications. Occasionally, a small one is required for tight spaces or for very small repairs.

Mixed correctly, plastic body filler will have a consistency similar to creamy peanut butter. It spreads evenly when a squeegee is smoothly flowed over a surface. Start out with the squeegee in a position almost perpendicular to the surface. As you move horizontally, gradually lay the squeegee down so that more filler material is applied to the surface. This procedure takes practice, so don't think you will be able to complete it perfectly the first time. Luckily, mistakes can be sanded off.

As much as possible, apply filler in such a way that strokes provide even coverage. You should attempt to maintain a similar depth with each pass. Ridges between each pass are normal and can be smoothed out during the sanding process. Your main concern during this procedure is to apply a consistent layer of plastic filler onto a panel in an effort to cover all imperfections with an equal amount of material. It sounds easy but it does take a little practice.

Extend filler coverage to at least 6 in. past all repairs in all directions when possible. This will guarantee that filler has covered the repair and also flat, undamaged metal surrounding it to offer a broad, wide, flat surface. Imagine that repairs have sunk very slightly. If you were to apply filler to only the dish, there may be a very slight ridge surrounding the dish that will eventually stick up around the repair. Once painted, this will stick out like a sore thumb.

If you extend filler coverage to include those areas surrounding the dish, sanding maneuvers will just about guarantee a completely flat repair encompassing all direct and indirect damage areas and feathering into the undamaged areas.

Tools and mixing board must be cleaned after every filler application. Use regular lacquer thinner and a Scotch Brite Pad to scrape off excess filler from the board, putty knife and squeegee. Wear rubber gloves to protect your hands. Wipe off remaining residue with a clean rag. Unless tools are cleaned immediately, filler material will harden on them and be almost impossible to remove without damaging the tool. Squeegees can be sanded, if necessary, to smooth out rough gouges on the application surface edge.

Sanding

Without a doubt, the most laborious task involved with autobody repair is sanding. About 90 percent of all plastic filler you apply will be eventually sanded off. This may sound like a ridiculous waste of time and filler material but in reality it guarantees complete filling and the opportunity to sand repairs down to a perfectly flat, smooth and even finish. For your own health, always follow recommended safety procedures. When sanding, wear a respirator.

Following directions on the filler label, wait the prescribed time to allow material to set before sanding. Initial sanding of ridges and other blobs of hardened filler are knocked down by hand with a sanding block and 40 grit sandpaper. Maintain equal pressure along long boards or any other sanding block used. Uneven pressure will cause very slight waves that might not be noticed until that part is painted.

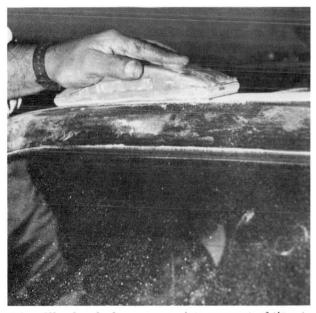

After filler has had an appropriate amount of time to cure, as indicated on the label directions or when it is hard to the touch and exhibits a light dry color, it has to be sanded smooth. Initial knock down of extra bulk filler is done with a piece of 40 grit sandpaper and a sanding block. Cautious use of an air file on wide panels or a dual action sander is fine, as long as you have practiced with the tools before. Feel the panel with your bare hand frequently to determine how sanding maneuvers are progressing. You can also place a clean cloth between your hand and the panel to accentuate your hand's sensitivity.

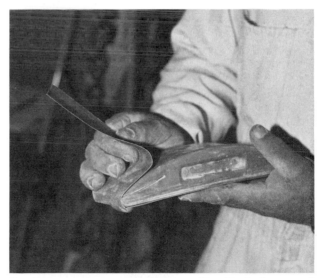

Sandpaper strips are fitted into sanding blocks by way of slotted openings equipped with teeth. Here the other end of the sandpaper strip has already been fed into and secured by the opposite slot. On this end, the extra length of a strip is folded over and torn so its end will fit into the slot and keep base material stretched tight.

Use your hand to feel the entire area to determine progress. Should you notice a ridge or hump, knock it down by sanding back and forth, up and down and side to side. Always sand in more than one direction to ensure that all surface areas are touched and that a pattern of grooves, humps or ridges is not established. This goes for hand sanding as well as machine sanding.

Basically, there is really only one way to determine when sanding has been completed—by feel. Again, as you did while repairing dents, extend your fingers and group them next to each other. Run your hand back and forth in the direction your fingers are pointing. Let the full length and width of your hand feel every square inch of the repair to make sure that the surface is flat, even and smooth.

Another tip is to look at filler material edges. They should exhibit a lot of bare metal, even though you applied filler to an area 6 in. wider and longer than the repair. If metalwork was done correctly,

there should be about 1–3 in. of bare metal showing as filler is knocked down. This is because mud has filled voids lower than undamaged sheet metal and sanding has now leveled them out.

You should also notice some spots inside the repair area that exhibit signs of bare metal. This shows that sanding has made the surface level because these minimal high spots have been blended into the entire repair. Feel the surface again to be sure all segments of the repair are flat. If you find low spots or blemishes, apply a second, lighter coat of filler. If, on the other hand, high spots are, in fact, sticking up through the surface, you will have to knock them down with an appropriate hammer head (pick, chisel, small flat head).

Sanding with power tools requires practice. Even a small DA sander can remove filler material much faster than expected. Practice filler application and sanding techniques, especially with power sanders, on an old hood, door or trunk lid.

To knock down an initial filler application, use 40 grit paper on a large DA sander. Never let the sander sit still, not even for a second. Constantly move the machine in all directions.

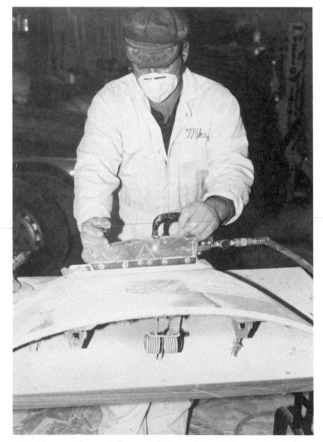

Air files make quick work of sanding filler material on panels. Kane uses one in this photo to smooth filler on a VW Bug engine cover panel. Since the panel is rounded, careful attention to air file maneuvers is critical. Operating the tool incorrectly will cause unnecessary gouges or ripples on the panel. Unless you have plenty of experience with this type of equipment, you might be best off using sanding blocks on rounded panels like this.

When body filler maneuvers have achieved a smooth, flat and even surface, it is time for a skim coat of glazing putty. This material is a finishing filler used to fill any tiny pinholes or slight sanding scratches. It is specifically designed as a finishing material as compared to body fillers that are designed for strength and versatility. You will quickly notice this material's smooth texture while mixing and applying it to panels.

When the majority of excess filler has been removed, start sanding with a long sanding block or air file equipped with 80 grit paper. Hand sanding is the only way to smooth a surface down to perfect dimensions. All the while you are hand sanding, feel the surface with your free hand. Hand sand until the surface meets your satisfaction.

It would be nice if one or two specific directions could tell you exactly how a certain procedure was accomplished from beginning to end. Unfortunately, this is not one of them. You have to practice filler applications and especially sanding techniques in order to get a feel for the tools you use and the texture and smoothness you desire. For those of you who plan to use power sanders, practice is mandatory.

Finishing Glaze

Just like filler material, no two autobody professionals seem to agree as to which finish glazing putty is best. Be open with a jobber at the autobody paint and supply store as to the job you are doing. He or she will be able to recommend a combination of plastic filler and finish glazing putty that will be compatible with each other and also with the type of sealer, primer-surfacer and paint that you will apply to your car after repairs.

The function of finish glazing putty is to seal off minor imperfections like pinholes and sand scratches in plastic filler. A skim coat is generally all that is needed. This material differs from plastic filler in that it goes on much smoother and sands to a finer finish. The basic role of plastic filler is to give strength to a repair. Glazing putty is designed to go on thin, be sanded to a thinner mass and seal off imperfections in the stronger filler coat.

Before applying glazing putty, be sure to remove any sanding dust from your work. You can blow it off with an air hose or carefully wipe it off with a clean, soft cloth. Mix and apply glazing putty just like regular plastic filler. Add a hardener to speed curing time. Use a putty knife to dig material out of its container, add hardener and mix with a putty knife, smooth and then apply with a squeegee. This application should be as perfect as you can make it. Spend an adequate amount of time smearing putty on in smooth, even and equal proportions. A skim coat should be all that is needed. In no time at all, you will notice how much smoother this material goes on compared to regular filler.

Final Sanding

Use 80 grit paper to initially knock down finish glazing putty. After obvious ridges and blobs are

Before filler material or glazing putty is applied, be sure the surface area is clean and free from all previous sanding dust. Kane is putting on a skim coat of glazing putty over a fiberglass repair. Notice that the deck area is quite clean. Dust or debris on a repair area will prevent spots of filler or putty from properly attaching to the body surface.

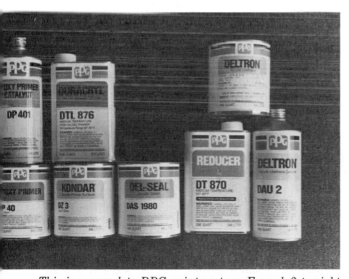

This is a complete PPG paint system. From left to right are epoxy primer, surfacer-primer with lacquer thinner, sealer, and paint with its reducer and catalyst. Not all paint systems are equally compatible with other materials. Some may fare better with certain body fillers than others. To be confident all the filler and paint products you use are totally compatible with each other and any existing paint on your car, be sure to openly discuss your project with an autobody paint and supply store jobber for product recommendations.

smoothed, 100 to 120 grit paper is applied to a small DA sander or long board to continue the smoothing process. An air file with 120 grit can be used on flat panels but you have to be careful not to sand through all of the glazing putty down to the filler material.

Final sanding is accomplished by hand, with either a long board or short sanding block. As with all other work, use your free hand to continually feel how your efforts are progressing while sanding in all directions. Never use sandpaper with your bare hand to smooth panels. Hands are not flat and it is almost impossible to get a flat sanding attitude without using a flat sanding board or block.

"Feel" is the key. Your sanding efforts will be complete when the area you are working on feels flat, even and smooth. Fill any pinholes that remain by applying another very thin skim coat of finish glazing putty. Let it set up and then sand to perfec-

First 80 grit sandpaper is used, followed by sanding with 100 to 120 grit sandpaper for smoothing glazing putty on a panel surface. Strips of sandpaper are fed into sanding blocks as described earlier. In addition, autobody supply stores sell strips of adhesive backed sandpaper like this one. Just peel off the backing paper and strips will tightly adhere to most sanding boards and blocks. Adhesive backed sanding discs are also available for dual action sanders.

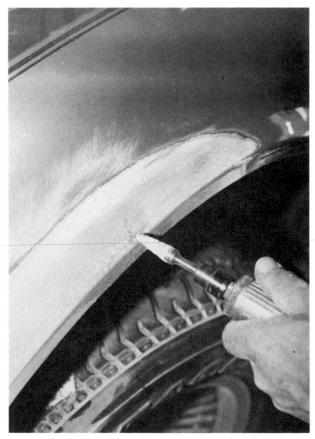

The crack on this Corvette fender was initially channeled out with a small die grinder and tapered rasp. Cracks have to be cleaned out and opened up so layers of resin and fiberglass mat can be placed inside for strength. If fiberglass repair materials were simply placed over the top, they would certainly be sanded off when the repair was smoothed in preparation for paint. If you do not have access to a die grinder and rasp, use a triangular file. Make the channel span to a forty-five degree angle all the way to the bottom of the damaged area.

Repairs to the front body panel on this Chevrolet Astro Van turned out quite nice. Had you not seen pictures of it before, you might not believe it was the same rig. With autobody metalwork, you have to trust your hand's sense of feel just as much if not more than your eyesight. Light reflections can cast unusual shadows on panels to make repairs look complete. But your hand will be able to feel slight imperfections readily.

86

tion. Minor accumulations of putty on the edges of doors or seams are easily removed by sanding with a piece of folded sandpaper.

Fiberglass Repair

Corvettes are not the only cars on the road featuring fiberglass body parts. You would be surprised at how many fenders, fender flairs and other parts are now made of fiberglass or fiberglass derivatives.

Body repairs to fiberglass parts are not difficult. In many ways, they are similar to plastic body filler work. You will need some fiberglass resin, catalyst (hardener), fiberglass mat and a small paintbrush.

Rips or tears on fiberglass need to be grooved into a V-shape so that mat and resin can fill the void to join both sides of a rip or tear into one strong section, sort of like a weld. A small die grinder with a

little tapered cylindrical rasp at its end works great for shaping Vs into fiberglass cracks and tears.

Barring that, you will have to use a triangular file. Be aware that fiberglass sanding dust can be very irritating to skin and respiratory systems. Wear gloves, long sleeves, goggles and a dust mask or respirator.

After a forty-five degree channel has been burred into a fiberglass crack, rip or tear, clean it out with air pressure or a stiff paintbrush. Cleaning is very important during this operation so that all resin and fiberglass mat strictly adhere to each side of the channel. Debris caught in the channel will prevent perfect adhesion.

Cut pieces of fiberglass mat to fit over the V-channel. They can be as long as the channel but not much wider. Have at least three pieces ready.

Use a small parts cleaning brush or a 1 in. wide paintbrush for applying fiberglass resin. After mixing resin and fiberglass in their proper proportions and in a quantity that should provide adequate

Damaged fiberglass at the driver's side front corner on this Corvette is being ground down with a high-speed sander and coarse disc. Notice that Kane is wearing a full face shield for protection against flying debris. Torn fiberglass chunks are smoothed down or cut out so new resin and fiberglass mat can fill voids and once again give the area strength and stability. Only those damaged sections of fiberglass are sanded that are loose or in the way of prescribed repairs.

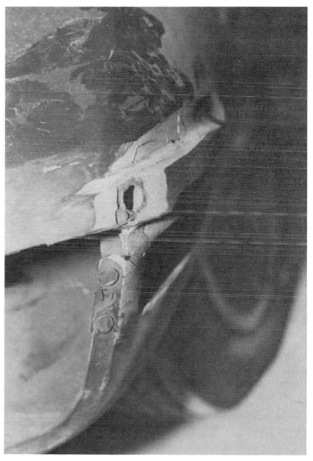

This is what the damaged fiberglass looked like after all of the loose material was sanded off. It is a clean repair area. Now fiberglass resin and mat can be used to build this area back up to where it is supposed to be. Sanding endeavors will shape the section to match the identical area on the other side of the car.

87

Pieces of fiberglass mat are cut out to fit repairs. Scissors work fine for this chore. Strips are cut to fit whatever sized channel has been developed for the crack or tear. Each piece should be wide enough to completely cover the channel after it has been pressed inside the void. Excess material will be sanded later, after resin has cured.

coverage, dab resin onto all parts of the exposed channel with your brush. Then place one piece of mat onto the channel. Dab it with resin until it is completely saturated.

Depending on how deep the channel is, determined by the depth of initial damage, as many as three or four pieces of fiberglass mat must be applied. After the first one has been covered with resin, lay down the second and saturate it with resin. If the new resin and mat do not fill the channel void to a point where it sticks above adjacent areas, apply a third piece of mat and cover it with resin.

Unless the fiberglass is extra thick, three pieces of mat with resin should be enough to build the repair up to surrounding panel height. If not, apply a fourth and/or fifth piece. For those jobs that require more than three pieces of mat, make sure that all mat sections extend over the tops of channels for added support. You might even consider putting wider mat sections underneath to add extra support to that part's structure.

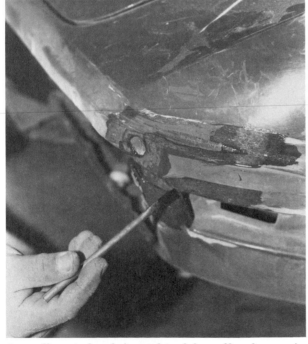

A small parts brush is used to dab on fiberglass resin. Resin is mixed with a catalyst to help it set at a reasonable rate. Read label directions for appropriate mixing formulas. Do not try to build up areas with resin, let the fiberglass mat do that. Apply enough resin to cover the entire repair area. Newspapers or rags can be placed on the floor below repairs to catch drips.

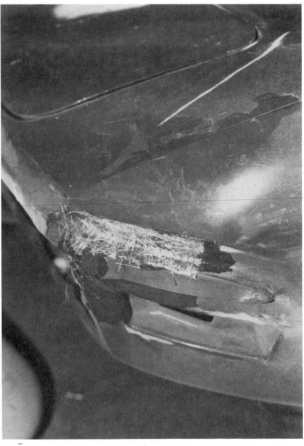

Fiberglass mat has been placed over a resin base. Note that the mat covers the entire width of this particular repair area. In addition to building up a damaged area, mat offers strength to repairs insofar as it is a type of material that will harden along with resin and because it is made up of continuous, interlocking fibers that set up to form a solid layer.

Allow the repair to cure as per directions on the resin container label. If the repaired area's height matches or is greater than surrounding fiberglass, great. Sanding will smooth out repairs so it will match the rest of the assembly's surface. However, should the channel repair not fill the void, you will have to build it up with more resin and mat.

Sanding procedures for fiberglass are not much different than those for glazing putty. Use 120 grit paper for initial knock down and finish up with 240 grit. Should 120 not seem to do the job, you can lightly try 80 grit. If you do not have a DA sander, be sure to use a sanding board or block.

For a really smooth final finish, apply one skim coat of finish glazing putty to fiberglass repairs. This ensures that no pinholes mar the surface and also adds a good base for primer materials. You must confirm this procedure with the autobody paint and supply jobber at the time you purchase repair materials to be certain that all materials are compat-

The basic fiberglass repair has been completed and sanded smooth. Use 120 grit sandpaper to start out. Then, as shapes and contours begin to fall in line, graduate to 240 grit. If a lot of excess resin and mat has to be sanded off, you might start with 80 grit and then move to less coarse paper. Use small sanding blocks or sandpaper wrapped around thin sticks as needed to effectively control sanding maneuvers. Compare your progress with the same dimensions on the other side of your car to be sure that the shape and contour are the same.

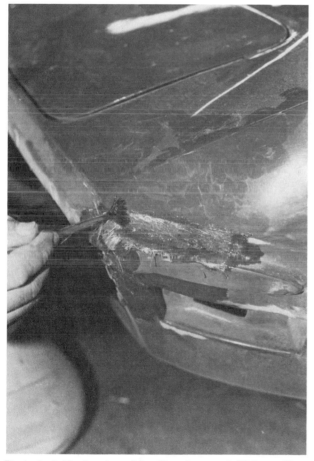

Resin is dabbed on top of dry fiberglass mat. This application makes mat material pliable so that it can conform to the shape of a repair. As more resin is applied, you will notice that the mat can be moved if needed into a more strategic location. Too much resin is not good. If voids still exist, apply more mat material with a top coat of resin.

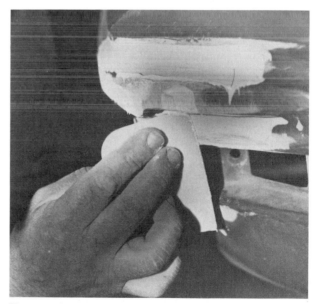

Kane prefers to coat all fiberglass repairs with a skim layer of glazing putty. He believes this helps to fill any lingering fiberglass pinholes and give paint products a better surface base. Application is the same as for any application over body filler. Use a small squeegee for small jobs, employing your fingers as needed to better shape the material into tight contoured areas.

89

ible with your car's body and intended painting products.

Newer Corvettes are designed with a special fiberglass-type material called Fiber Reinforced Plastic (FRP) that can be repaired with only a specific compatible material. Be clear with the jobber at your autobody material supply store as to what year Corvette you are repairing in order to purchase the correct repair materials.

Deep cracks or long tears may require extra support on the underside of their structures. This is accomplished by cleaning the underside completely and then applying a coat of resin and subsequent fiberglass mat sheets in a size that extends past both sides of a crack by at least 6–10 in. The size of mat pieces depends on the amount of strength and support needed by the damaged piece. The more support needed, the larger mat sections should be. In unusual cases, consult an autobody specialist with experience in fiberglass repair.

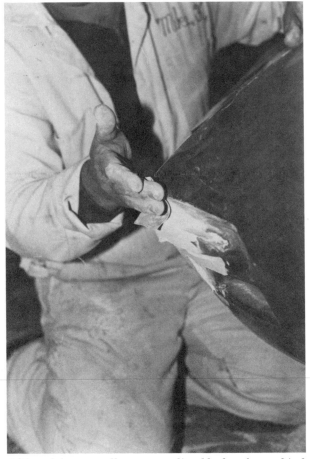

Although he normally uses sanding blocks of some kind, Kane uses the contour of his fingers as sanding blocks while sanding this rather tightly curved Corvette front end section. Like sculptors, autobody technicians must use their creativity to sand shapes out of layers of body filler or fiberglass. In this case, a small rounded sanding block might be better than fingers.

The completed fiberglass repair on this Corvette front end piece looks great. Conscientious sanding efforts proved worthwhile, as this section matches the passenger side section perfectly. Consideration was given throughout the repair for grille mounts and the side light opening. Fiberglass was shaped around these objects so that neither was blemished in any way.

7

Moderate Damage Repair

If another car backed out of its parking stall into your car's door while you idly sat waiting for a different parking space to open up, the slow collision would probably just cause a small dent in your door, fender or quarter panel. Providing this was a simple hit, with the other bumper merely punching a small dent on your car's body, repairs should be easy to complete as described in the previous chapter.

However, should this collision involve a vehicle backing out of an end parking space while you are driving around the corner, speed would be increased

Rear end collisions can cause more than just body damage. You should check deck lid hinges for signs that they have been knocked out of alignment. Cracked or peeling paint that goes unchecked could result in formations of rust because bare metal was allowed to be exposed to moisture and airborne rust inducing agents, like saltwater atmospheres.

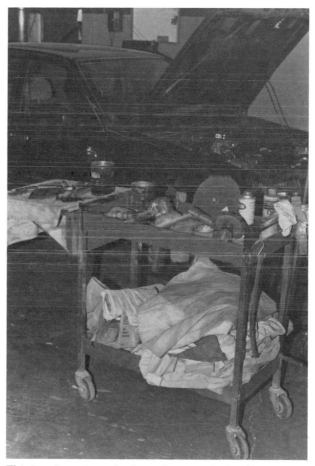

This handy cart on wheels works great for hauling needed tools to a job site. Rather than have to go back and forth to a workbench to retrieve tools, carts like this can stow sanders, hand tools and other items. Whenever working on an automobile to dismantle parts or install new ones, mechanic's tools will be needed. Be sure to use correctly sized wrenches and sockets on nuts and bolts.

and the other car's bumper and quarter panel corner could cause damage to your front fender, headlight assembly, grille work and bumper. In this case, damage repairs would be more extensive. Not only could they include dent repair for the fender, but also part replacement endeavors for headlight, grille and bumper assemblies.

Moderate damage repairs can basically be described as those autobody projects that entail more than one operation—most generally, a combination of dent repairs and part replacements. This generic category includes those collision damage problems that present repair persons with more than simple ding or dent repair work, but much less than technical operations involving frame, suspension, panel replacement and the like.

Determining the Extent of Damage

Aside from damage directly incurred from a collision, look beyond to determine what kind of indirect problems have surfaced. In front end mishaps, has the radiator support been buckled, a hole in the radiator perhaps? How about those sheet metal panels located on each side of the radiator?

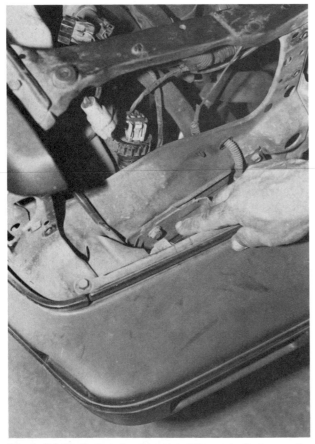

The bolt being pointed out is one of the main fasteners for the front bumper on this vehicle. To reach it, the entire grille had to be taken off. This kind of problem is common on newer cars.

Has the hood suffered small buckles back toward the cowling where it attaches to hinges? Have front doorjamb gaps narrowed?

These kinds of in-depth questions should be asked and pursued with regard to any collision problem. On the sides of cars, inspect rocker panels, pillars, door hinges, and so on. At the rear, look for indirect damage to deck lids above their hinge points, trunk floor buckles, quarter panel dents and problems associated with assemblies located below the rear bumper, like exhaust tailpipes and trailer hitches.

Oftentimes, damage cannot be accurately assessed until some mangled parts have been removed. Such is the case with crunched front fenders. Sheet metal fenders can be folded over in such a way that you are unable to accurately inspect light assemblies, inner splash shields, radiator supports or other objects located nearby.

Spend an adequate amount of time assessing damage. This will not only help in determining which new parts are needed, it will provide a systematic approach to repairs. Be sure that any parts removed are placed in a box and labeled. These will have to be accounted for later when you begin putting the car back together or for reference when ordering replacement parts.

Disassembly

Photos of collision damage before and during dismantling efforts may prove quite valuable when the time comes to reassemble what has been dismantled. Home video units offer do-it-yourself autobody technicians a means whereby voice instructions complement photo illustrations. Small segments of indirect damage can be highlighted to remind repair persons they need attention. Reviewing a tape after a day's work might be an excellent source of reference to help plan the next day's repair schedule.

Sharp edges are often along sections of mangled sheet metal. While removing those pieces, wear

New styled plastic clips, like this one from an import car, operate like Molly Bolts that secure to standard walls. When the center pin is pushed in, legs below are forced out to fill a void and secure a lightweight part. More and more, ingenious little clips like this are used to secure all kinds of interior and exterior accessories. Use a good plug puller to gently lift center pins when taking these clips off.

heavy leather gloves for protection against cuts. Quite commonly, technicians suffer cuts to the backs of their hands while breaking loose nuts and bolts. Always be alert to where your hand will go once a nut or bolt breaks loose. We have all had occasions where a lot of force had to be applied to a wrench or ratchet to loosen a stubborn nut or bolt. When it finally broke loose, our hand went crashing into something else to scrape and bruise knuckles. With sheet metal, be extra careful to avoid slamming hands into or along sharp metal edges.

An assortment of mechanic's hand tools is necessary when removing parts from cars. At the least, you need a socket and ratchet set, open end wrenches, slot and Phillips screwdrivers, locking pliers (vise grips) and any special tools designed specifically for star-like Torx screw heads or Allen heads. In addition, you may need a pry bar to move mangled metal away from nuts, bolts, screws and other fasteners.

Older cars are easy to take apart. Nuts and bolts seem to always be in plain view; intricate plastic clips and fasteners had not been invented. Today, all kinds of automotive pieces are connected together by seemingly invisible clips and fasteners of all shapes, sizes and ingenious designs. In many areas, especially front bumpers and grille assemblies, more time can be spent trying to figure out how to reach and operate a certain fastener than it will take to loosen it. Sometimes, plastic clips break, even when professionals attempt to unhook them. Be prepared by having new ones ready when reassembly operations get under way.

Trim pieces are easily bent during removal. Take your time and work at a slow pace. Special trim removal tools work better than screwdrivers or putty knives. Be careful when prying with these tools to avoid creating minor dings or dents at the fulcrum point. Lay a thin piece of wood or heavy cardboard under the tool before prying up on it to dislodge trim pins. This buffer material will spread the tool's prying force over a wider area to help pre-

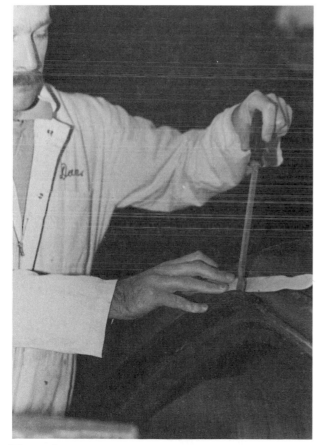

Mycon demonstrates a safe way to pull a section of drip rail cap trim. Using a wide puller, he places a paint stir stick behind the fulcrum part of the tool to protect paint against scratches from the metal tool. In lieu of stir sticks, you could use stout cardboard, rubber or anything else that will offer support and not damage paint.

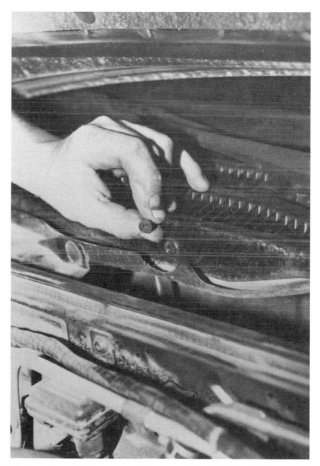

This unique little screw fills a void with its width as opposed to cinching up tight like normal screws. To get it out, apply as little pushing pressure as possible and gently twist the handle of your Phillips screwdriver. Link has complained more than once that unusual fasteners like this can be very frustrating to loosen. Be aware for items of this nature when working around cowling areas.

93

vent accidental damage to paint or sheet metal. Try prying upward at first to prevent fulcrum point blemishes.

Although many newer cars feature trim attached with adhesive or two-way tape, some are still connected to car bodies with pins and clips. Some trim piece ends are secured with screws. Emblems, badges and other similar items have pins that insert through manufactured holes in bodies secured with flat metal clips. Clips are most easily removed by reaching behind them with a long-bladed trim tool or plug puller instead of tugging on them from the outside. Those pieces held on by adhesive or tape can be loosened by spraying adhesive remover along their tops, which will then flow to the adhesive area behind. Be sure to follow instructions provided on the label of any adhesive removal product.

Except for light fixtures located around grille work, most lenses are removed by taking out screws from the front. Clips or other screws may hold housings in place from the rear. Some are removed from the outside, others from inside a trunk or quarter panel space. Since no two auto makes seem to incorporate the same designs, you will have to inspect every assembly to determine just exactly how each unit is dismantled.

Lights in and around grille sections are another story. Although some parking and signal lights appear to be combined into one unit, they may actually be separate pieces connected by sturdy clips. Access is not always easy and you may have to remove additional grille sections just to inspect them. Patience is the key. Use a flashlight, when necessary, to get a better backside view of light assemblies. This can help tremendously when trying to figure out how parts are dismantled.

Some bumper units include more than just bumpers. Directly attached to them could be splash pans, spoilers and an almost entire grille assembly. Body shop folks refer to them as noses. You will find them on Camaros, firebirds and other sporty cars with flexible front end pieces. Disassembly of these units is time consuming. There may be as many as twenty-three individual screws or bolts, all of which play a role in overall nose alignment.

Front end body assemblies should be supported by jack stands as bolts are loosened. As soon as you think all fasteners have been removed, you will probably find that a few more are hidden somewhere in the structure. Rather than try to hold the piece up with one hand while searching for nuts and bolts with the other, allow a loosened unit to rest on jack stands. This is also a safety factor, as the unit's entire weight could be supported by the last few bolts and when they are removed, the whole thing could quickly fall down on you.

If doors must be removed, be aware that they are a lot heavier than you may think. Just because they swing in and out easily does not mean they are lightweight. Have a helper support the outer edge while you remove hinge pins or bolts. Remove lower hinge fasteners first and then place a crate or five gallon plastic bucket under the door for support. You might have to shim supports with pieces of wood. With that done, have your helper support the door while you dismantle the top hinge.

Hoods and deck lids are also heavy and cumbersome. In nearly all cases, two people are needed to remove these items. Place folded towels at both corners of the base near hinges to protect paint and sheet metal located below the bottom edge. As hinge bolts are loosened, hoods and deck lids tend to fall slightly. Towels will absorb that light impact and prevent damage to an underlying surface.

As you progress in your dismantling efforts, be aware of what you are doing. Don't take off more than is necessary, and yet, take off enough parts so that you will have adequate room to work. Be certain that all dismantled parts are put into containers. Screws, nuts and bolts might be replaced into their assemblies so that they do not get lost and also so that you know which one goes with what unit.

The cowling on this vehicle is secured by screws hidden under plastic caps. Unless you knew they were there, you might become quite puzzled as to how that cowling was held in place. Gentle use of a plug puller will pop caps off easily. To guarantee that the metal part of a plug puller does not scratch or chip paint, you may want to lay down a piece of tape at the base of the cap upon which the plug puller can rest. A thin piece of cardboard could be used as a cushion also.

This is important, as some assemblies may feature both long and short bolts or screws situated around the perimeter.

When wires have to be disconnected during dismantling, mark them with a piece of masking tape. Write on the tape while still on the roll. Then take off the written sections and place them on the wires. Label them according to whatever method works for you.

Keep in mind that you will have to put your car back together after repairs have been completed. If an assembly is intricate, take pictures during various stages of dismantling so that you will have a photo schematic later to serve as a guide for reassembly. Once again, a video camera is great for this kind of how-to-put-it-back-together-again endeavor.

Metal Straightening

Just because a sheet metal part has been bent, dented or otherwise damaged does not always mean it has to be replaced. Many times, these parts can be satisfactorily repaired.

The tweaked rear door and pillar on this Toyota 4-Runner is being straightened with the use of a Porto-Power tool. A hydraulic ram forces pressure through a high pressure hose to activate a piston driven ram on the assembly you see spanning the front door area. This spreading power is, many times, strong enough to correct misaligned parts. To avoid scratching paint, consider placing small pieces of wood between actual car parts and the ram heads.

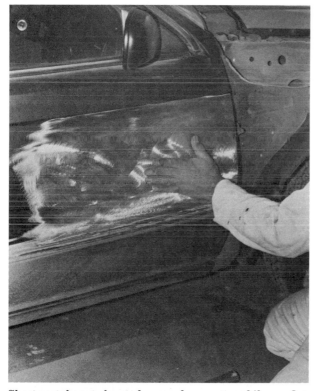

Sheet metal parts located around an automobile are flattened and smoothed much the same way as door skins, fenders and quarter panels. Hammer and dolly work flattens the big stuff and filler applications blend it altogether. Here Kane uses his hand with fingers outstretched to feel for any minor imperfections left behind after initial dent removal operations. As low spots or crowns are perceived, he flattens them out with a hammer and dolly or spoon as necessary. This panel is just about ready for a coat of body filler.

Not all interior door panels come off in the same fashion. Some are screwed on, others feature pop-on clips and others slide in place on channels. Carefully inspect these items before randomly pulling and tugging on them. Most armrests are removed by loosening two large Phillips head screws, as is being accomplished here. Door handles and window cranks on older cars are held on by unique wire C-clips, where today's door handles are screwed on.

95

Aprons are those engine compartment side pieces to which fenders and splash shields are attached. In a front end collision, these units may become dented or buckled. A jack-like Mechanical Body Puller Tool, Porto-Power or even a slide hammer will, many times, work to pull out aprons and flatten dents or buckles. Additional hammer and dolly work is all that may be required to finish off a repair.

Sheet metal is flattened in much the same way as dings and dents on outer body skins. The difference between outer skins and inner supports may simply be variations in the size of metal used for a part's design. Heavier metals require more pulling power than that needed for thinner pieces of sheet metal.

Hydraulic or pneumatic tools, like a Porto-Power, are frequently used by autobody technicians to straighten pillars, aprons, floor pans and other strong units. Should you find that a repair will progress more smoothly with a hydraulic or pneumatic power tool pushing or pulling against an assembly, locate one at a rental yard and rent it until your repair is complete.

To straighten heavier support assemblies, use equipment to reverse the force of impact suffered by the damaged unit. If an apron has been crumpled from the front, maneuver a Porto-Power or other tool so that force pulls the apron toward the front, like pulling an accordion apart. As pressure is applied, direct blows from a body hammer to crowns in an effort to reduce stress on buckles or dents. Apply a little more power to your pulling tool and then repeat hammer blows. A dolly may be useful on the opposite side of hammer hits as a support.

Access to both sides of dented panels is usually necessary. For fenders, you may have to remove a splash shield. Doors are accessed by removing interior panels. Quarter panels can be reached from inside trunk spaces on four door sedans. Rear seat

The top ledge on this interior door panel simply snaps over the door's metal edge. Notice the white clips just under the technician's fingers which are pushed into receptacles that hold the unit on tight to the door. The small square hole in the panel is where the interior door handle goes. It attaches to linkage arms that activate the latching mechanism. Door panels with courtesy lights, power windows or door locks will have wires attached to them. Don't forget to unsnap them before pulling the panel away.

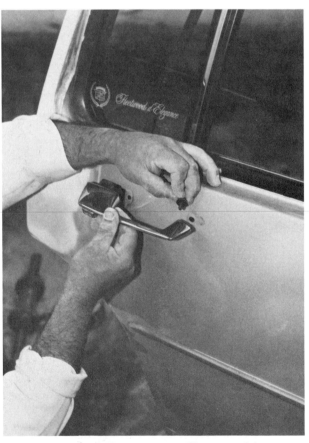

Exterior door handles are generally secured by screws from inside the outer door skin. You will have to remove interior door panels to reach them. Be sure that pads on the base parts of door handles are not lost or misplaced after handles have been removed. They cushion the space between handle and door skin to prevent paint scratching and metal-to-metal contact.

side panels will have to be removed to allow quarter panel access on two door coupes.

Spoons are metal hand tools sometimes used like dollies in extra tight spaces and at other times, to spread out the force of hammer blows. Since doors present repair persons with such tight inner working spaces, spoons are useful in reaching spots between outer door skins and Nader Bars, window tracks and their operating mechanisms. As outer door skin edge perimeters taper down to tight corners next to doorjambs, a spoon can slip into the space to provide a supporting base for hammer hits. Be creative in your use of available tools. There are no clear-cut rules for metal straightening when it comes to being resourceful in tight situations.

Alignment Requirements

Doors, hoods, hatchbacks and deck lids have to be aligned correctly if they are expected to open and close freely. Each of these units has some form of an adjustment mechanism, usually by way of elongated

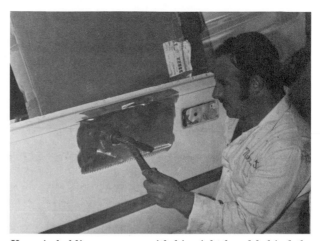

Kane is holding a spoon with his right hand behind the outer door skin. It is being employed as a support base for hammer blows issued on this side of the door to assist in flattening a high spot. Spoons are great for fitting into tight spaces where dollies cannot possibly fit. Inner door areas present technicians with many spots too tight for dolly use. In the way are Nader Bars, latch linkages, lock mechanisms and, of course, window operating levers and bars.

After the first coat of body filler was applied to a dent repair on this door, Kane felt a slight high spot. Instead of smacking that spot with a hammer head, he chose to spread the concussion over a wider area by using a spoon. This method is commonly used by professional technicians to flatten out spots into a wider area than a hammer head alone can accomplish.

Light reflection on this Cadillac door edge makes it look like it is pockmarked with a hundred dents. In reality, metal has been flattened quite well. It is the sanding disc scratches that make it look marred. Hammer and dolly work on the door edge straightened out a sharp bend that was caused when the door opened while the vehicle was backing up. It hit an immovable object and was bent before the driver could stop. Luckily, glass was not broken and the door not sprung out of alignment.

The wide gap between the cowling and hood on this Volvo is an indication that the hood is out of alignment. A collision could have tweaked the structural supports upon which hood hinges are mounted or just knocked the hood off its normal hinged position. In either case, adjustments have to be made so the unit can sit squarely as it was designed.

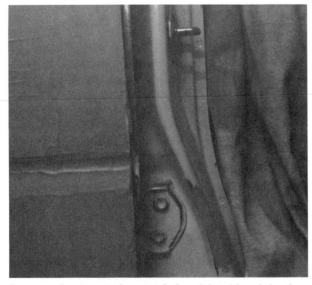

Seam sealer is noted around the right side of the door hinge. Close inspection reveals that it is a bit more forward than the hinge. This is an indication that some type of movement occurred. After all adjustments and alignments are made, this old seam sealer will be removed (scraped off) and new sealer applied. When it has cured, it will be painted. Adjustments to pillars are not simple operations. Technicians have to be aware of what they are doing to avoid damage to other structures. Problems with tweaked pillars should be handled by professionals.

bolt holes. When they have to be removed, mark the location of bolts as they sit on hinge plates. This can be done with a pencil, scribe or other marker. When the part is placed back in position, secure bolts according to their marks to be assured that alignment is at least close.

If a hood, deck lid or hatchback has been jarred out of place, you may need to loosen hinge bolts just enough so the unit can be moved back. Lay the piece down gently, reposition as necessary and then tighten bolts. Close the assembly gently and check the fit. If it is still off, loosen hinge bolts again until they are just barely snug. Move the unit as indicated and then tighten bolts. Continue this operation until the piece opens and closes as expected.

When assemblies like doors and hoods are involved in collision damage, their hinges or other supports are sometimes knocked out of alignment. In extreme cases, you must seek professional assistance from a reputable autobody repair facility.

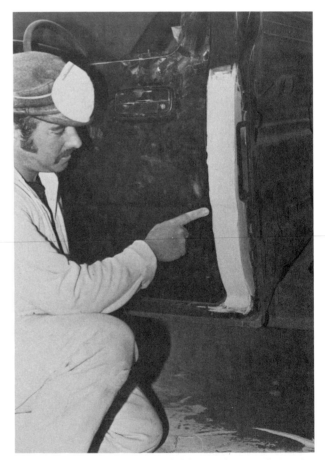

The body ridge on the side of this truck must be maintained if the filler application is to look professional. The new door shell was installed before metal straightening efforts were started on this pillar so that the gap between the door and jamb could be maintained the same as the gap between the front of the door and fender. With that accomplished, filler was applied and now must be sanded so that the ridge maintains the same contour as the door.

In cases of minor misalignment, you may be able to remove light gauge hinges, flatten them with a hammer and put them back with no problems.

Door hinges are very stout. Before bending, they will generally break or cause buckling damage to pillars. Minor door misalignments are frequently corrected by grasping a rear door edge and forcing the unit up or down to reposition it back where it was. You can tell if a door is too high or too low by looking at the latch as it closes against the solid latch pin. When a latch on the door edge sits too high next to a pin, the door must be forced down. If it is too low, upward force must be applied.

This endeavor needs to be completed firmly and uniformly. Jerking actions will not accomplish much. If a few attempts fail to correct the problem, your car may have been subjected to more damage than realized. Minor door alignment problems are generally corrected with just one to three attempts. If they fail, let a professional handle the alignment repair, as the supporting pillar could have been knocked out of place or tweaked.

Other assemblies, like front end units, grilles and bumpers, may also provide wide bolt holes that allow for minor adjustments. With bolts or screws lightly snug, maneuver pieces until they fit as required, then tighten. Check for fit again after all screws, nuts and bolts have been secured. This trial and error method works better than anything else.

Matching Ridges, Seams and Gaps

Autobody repair work can visually be thrown off when ridges, seams or joints do not match. Such obvious defects are clues that bodywork has been done, indicating the vehicle has been involved in some type of collision. These defects not only look bad, but make selling the vehicle to a knowledgeable potential buyer more difficult.

Ridges are those body lines that curve up to a sharply rounded arc and then curve back down. These are often seen on fenders, quarter panels and along the sides of cars. Dents on them are flattened

A squeegee was used to apply filler material to the repair and also used on the jamb side corner to shape the angle. More than one coat of filler has been applied as evidenced by the amount of sanding dust on the floor. Intricate shaping maneuvers like this are better accomplished with two or three light applications of filler rather than one extra heavy layer. In the first place, filler put on too thick may crack because underlying material cannot dry properly. Secondly, attempts to sand off a thick layer of filler are more difficult than slowly and methodically shaping one to three thin layers.

To help determine the starting point of a ridge, masking tape is placed along an established line, as seen here along the door. This gives a technician a line of sight as to where to begin an outward sanding maneuver to conform to the established contour. As sanding continues, the door will be opened and closed in order to get a better perspective of how the shape is coming along.

Kane uses a small sanding block to shape the ridge. Notice he is wearing a dust mask and see how much sanding dust has already accumulated on the floor. The nose of the sanding block is used as needed to help establish the ridge. This is a time-consuming chore, so don't rush. Perfection is what you want and that will take time and patience.

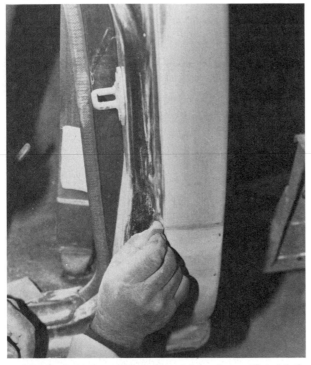

A folded edge of sandpaper is used to clean off and help shape the corner of the repair. See how the ridge shape is coming along? There are three spots on the right side of the ridge that show that filler has been sanded down to metal. This is all right as long as the area feels flat, smooth and even. Basically, it tells a technician that the job is sanded well and feathered into the surrounding area.

in much the same way as flat panels. Try to shape metal back to as close to normal as possible with dent puller, hammer and dolly work. Then sand the applied filler in such a way that the curve and arc once again join with adjacent shapes to look like nothing had ever happened.

Use masking tape as a guide to mark upper and lower limits along ridges. Do this by running a line of tape from the front to the back of a panel, or panels, so that the tape's placement is in line with an entire ridge. This gives an accurate mark for the repair section. Sand with a small hand block first to remove the big stuff. Then use a curved sanding block. An old paint roller wrapped with duct tape is an excellent sanding block for this work. Place at least one full wrap of sandpaper around the roller to keep it secure.

Sand carefully with frequent stops to feel the area for smoothness and contour. Tape will not tell

A dual action sander can be used on operations like this as long as the operator has some experience with its use. DA sanders will remove a lot of material in a hurry. Novice technicians using these power sanders for the first time are amazed at how quickly they can go through a complete layer of filler material. Here Kane uses a low speed by just slightly pushing on the trigger. The machine is used to knock down filler bulk, while hand sanding is employed for final, intricate work.

100

ing his or her own time and complete this repair project at a fraction of the adjuster's estimate.

Assessing damage for a project like this has to be done systematically. If not, you will likely overlook small items like trim, weather stripping, clips, fasteners, emblems, reflectors, lamp bulbs and the like. A good way to obtain a detailed list of needed parts is to divide a vehicle into separate segments, such as driver's side front fender, front passenger door, and rear driver's side door. Use a separate sheet of paper for each segment and jot down every unrepairable part needed for its complete restoration, including screws, nuts, washers and clips. This detailed list will serve as an accurate guide during your visit to a wrecking yard and will let you be assured that all replacement parts will be on hand when repair operations begin.

If you decide to order new parts in lieu of obtaining used ones, be sure to allow enough time for the parts department to acquire them. The parts may have to be ordered from a supplier, which could take a week for delivery. Parts delivery from some mail order companies may take as long as two weeks. You might want to ask about delivery schedules when ordering parts so that you can plan your work activities accordingly.

Planning the Work

Novice autobody technicians sometimes go through tiring, exhausting, waste-of-time activities. Instead of starting a repair operation at the beginning, working through the middle and finishing in a controlled and systematic fashion at the end, they start haphazardly on one panel, do a little work, move on to another segment, take off a few parts and then move on to something else while never really finishing any work on anything. Besides getting nothing done, they end up with an assortment of unrelated parts scattered all over, and a restoration project that will be a nightmare to organize, much less complete.

If repairs to a vehicle with multiple panel problems are made in an orderly, systematic and organized way, the entire project will flow smoothly and present the technician with small accomplishments at the end of each day's work. Parts could be stowed according to whatever segmentation method was derived to be easily retrieved and accounted for reassembly. As new parts arrive or are dismantled from a parts car, they can be stored next to boxes of similar parts so that all pieces of a particular assembly are together.

Begin a project with damage assessment and part dismantling. These operations go hand in hand,

This damaged door has been taken off the car and is now being dismantled so parts can be transferred to the new door shell. A trim removal tool is used to pop loose a C-shaped retainer clip that holds the window crank in place. While undertaking a similar operation, be sure to note any broken or damaged parts so replacements can be ordered.

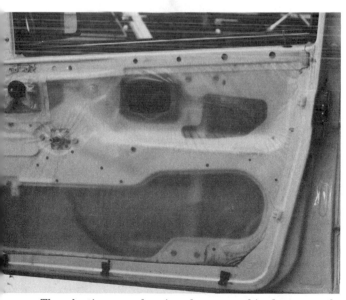

The plastic vapor barrier shown on this door must be maintained. Adhesive holds it in place around the edges. Gently, you can lift it away from the door and fold it up out of the way. Vapor barriers on doors keep moisture from entering the passenger compartment.

as some parts will have to be removed in order to gain access to inspect underlying areas. Have a clipboard or notebook handy to list needed replacement parts and log what kinds of repair work are called for in the area. A box should be nearby to hold dismantled parts. Have a specific spot cleared out in your garage or work area for the storage of large parts, like fenders, doors and wheels.

Start at the top of your car and work down. If a roof is dented, the headliner will have to be pulled down. Make sure that all associated screws and clips are kept together in a separate container so they do not get mixed in with other fasteners as dismantling continues. Note any broken headliner or interior panel pieces and thoroughly examine all damage to the roof and adjacent pillar assemblies. Make sure that headliner material is securely tied or taped into a position that will not hamper repair operations nor lend itself to accidental rips or breaks. Solid head-

Mike Link uses a handy cordless screwdriver to remove large Phillips head screws from the armrest on this interior door panel. Because so many different elements are involved with doors, it is best to have a new door shell ready to accept parts as they come off the old door. If that is not possible, at least make notes as to which items are supposed to be put on first and exactly how they are positioned.

110

liners should be removed from an interior and stored.

Next, concentrate efforts on front end damage. Remove parts as necessary and log all pertinent information on your sheet designated for front end replacement parts and required work. You can start with the hood, then bumper, grille, lights and spoiler. Check the engine compartment for damage to mechanical parts, aprons, radiator or its supports, cruise control unit and any other item that may have been affected by the collision.

Fenders are next. If they are mangled in such a way that access for inspection to adjacent parts is blocked, use a pry bar as necessary or just take them off. Be sure to note any damage to wires, grommets, splash shields, shock absorbers, wheels, tires, wheel covers, brake lines, light reflectors, side lamps, turn signals, emblems, decals and other small parts. In addition, designate the appropriate driver or passenger side fender when listing needed replacement parts.

Move along your vehicle to either front door. If it has been severely smashed, make a note to purchase another one from a wrecking yard. Write down what kind of exterior trim and handle is featured and which interior panel parts need replacing. Check hinges for signs of damage by looking for obvious metal damage, cracked seam sealer or peeling paint. Examine weather stripping, glass, key lock and moldings. Unless in your way, do not remove doors until you are ready to work on them or an adjacent section. They are heavy, awkward objects and the less you have to move them around, the better.

Give rear doors the same attention focused on front doors. Note any damage to seats, seat belt mechanisms or floor pan. If you suspect floor pan damage, move carpet and pad to visually inspect the area. Look for buckled metal, cracked seam sealer or peeling paint.

Quarter panels are quite easy to evaluate. But look behind them carefully to see if any damage has been sustained by the fuel tank filler, fuel tank, panel supports, shock absorbers, wheels, or other parts.

Rear deck lids, hatchbacks and rear body panels all require the same attention to detail. Like grille sections, rear body panels include lamp assemblies and wiring. Emblems, badges, decals and trim must be accounted for.

A special page in your set of notes might be used to designate a certain order for repairs. Tasks could be broken down into daily goals or hour increments. Multiple panel repair operations are time consuming. Do not expect to systematically remove all damaged parts in the morning and complete metal repairs and part replacement in the afternoon. A more realistic expectation might be part dismantling and cleaning one day, metalwork the next, followed by a day applying and sanding filler, with a final day or two scheduled for part replacement.

Removing Salvageable Parts

Salvageable parts are items that made it through a collision without suffering any damage or those that can be easily repaired to look new. If care is not taken during a dismantling operation, otherwise salvageable parts could be mistakenly ruined.

For nuts, bolts and screws located in open areas subjected to water, dirt and road grime, spray threads with a penetrating lubricant and allow it to soak in before loosening. WD-40 and Liquid Wrench are two such products that are readily available at most auto parts stores.

Always use a correct size wrench or socket. Almost all foreign cars are manufactured with metric nut and bolt heads and you would be surprised at the amount of metric fasteners used on American cars, including Suburbans and pickup trucks. Stripping out nuts or bolts will add to your overall work load. If you do not own a set of metric wrenches, don't attempt to dismantle anything off foreign cars and be wary of work on American cars.

Around grille sections, you may notice star-shaped Torx screw heads. These items require a special Torx tool for removal. You can purchase individual or sets of star-headed Torx screwdrivers at most tool houses and auto parts stores. Do not try to remove odd-shaped screws with regular slot or Phillips screwdrivers; you will only strip out their heads. Take note of these items when planning your job so that the proper tools will be at your disposal when needed.

Before banging away at a piece of mangled sheet metal, look around it to see if any undamaged part is in line with your hammer blow. Should a salvageable reflector, lamp or piece of trim be vulnerable, take it off first or protect it with a piece of wood or heavy wad of towels. Envision every part of your car as if it had a dollar sign on it. Each time you salvage one, you put money in your pocket by not having to replace it. This might help you dismantle with a little less eagerness and a lot more scrutiny.

Be keenly aware of glass and its position when swinging a hammer, operating a pry bar or tugging on crimped parts. Although professional glass installers have resorted to banging on windows with their hands to pop them out of stressed openings, you are not afforded their level of expertise or luck,

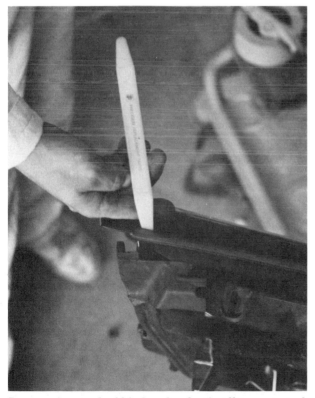

Burrous is proud of his handy plastic all-purpose tool. Since it is made of soft plastic, he can use it to loosen and slide off belt moldings and other rubber and plastic parts without scratching paint. These tools are familiar items around auto glass shops.

Burrous is installing door glass into a Corvette driver's door. If a full frame surrounded the top part of the window, glass would be removed and installed on the interior side of the door. First, belt moldings and side channels would have to be removed and the glass loosened from its channel between the inner and outer door skins. Caution must be exercised whenever working with glass, as it could shatter to cause injury.

and will probably break glass with the slightest tap from a mishandled part or unfortunate adjacent hammer hit. Remove fixed glass before starting metal repair work near it.

If you are not sure how to do this, have a professional glass installer complete the task. Many auto glass businesses provide mobile services. The small fees charged by these companies to remove and install fixed glass safely and correctly is nothing when compared to the cost of new glass, which can run as high as $1,200 per unit.

Completely dismantling doors is not a quick and simple chore. In the first place, many doors only feature a few access holes on their inner side. You have to feel around to locate nuts and bolts. Use a flashlight to improve visibility into the insides of door units. It is always best to take parts off old doors and immediately replace them on new doors because so many little parts must go on in just the right sequence or other mechanisms may not be accessible.

Glass is usually pulled up through the door toward the inside of window frames. Be very careful while removing glass. Twisting or forcing it ever so slightly could cause it to shatter. As a safety measure, consider applying multiple strips of heavy tape across windows. This way, should they shatter, tape will hold them in essentially one piece.

Moldings that surround window frames are removed by loosening screws hidden under weather stripping or by dislodging clips along visible frame members. Determine which methods were used on your car as many makes and models feature various means.

No matter how hard you try, expect to break a few plastic clips as dismantling continues. Not all of these items are designed to be removed and replaced. Plastic rivets are featured on some front end pieces that cannot be salvaged. Other plastic fasteners work like Molly Bolts. They include a center pin that, when inserted into the fastener body, causes fingers to expand and fill the surrounding void. These items are popular around cowling sections on some Asian imports.

Mycon has relied on 3M's Rust Fighter-I to prevent future rust problems on interior body panels. It comes in a handy spray can and should be used on any interior metal part that has received bodywork. When putting a car back together, you must seriously consider rust inhibiting application of material like this for interior sections and other products, like Rust Fighter-E, for exterior applications.

Project cars may have parts stored for extended periods of time until paint work can begin. Pieces that have been stripped of paint should be covered with a coat or two of epoxy primer. This material, used with a catalyst, will prevent moisture from adversely affecting bare metal parts to cause rust and corrosion. Follow label instructions for proper application.

Parts Storage

Cans with plastic lids make ideal storage containers for nuts, bolts, screws, clips and other small parts. Make labels out of masking tape and attach to lids for quick reference. You can also make containers out of empty antifreeze containers by cutting one side out of them. These are good while working under cars because they are flat, their opening is close to the ground and their low center of gravity prevents them from tipping over.

With such a wide assortment of different parts that have to come off some front end assemblies, it is a good idea to tag each item separately. Make tags out of masking tape strips. If yours is a project car and you are not sure when parts will be put back on, go a step further and make actual cards for each part. On these, you can write down any specific instructions you think may be helpful when the time comes to put them back in place.

Another tip for project car rebuilders pertains to parts that have been repaired but must wait in storage a lengthy time before painting. Apply the recommended amount of epoxy primer coats to bare metal parts before storing to avoid rust or corrosion formation. Each epoxy primer container label includes mixing and application instructions. In addition, autobody paint and supply stores provide free guidelines for their specific brands of epoxy primer products.

You must provide a suitable storage area for large parts that are removed for repairs. Items like hoods and deck lids will require a fair amount of room. Long trim pieces are easily bent or twisted and should be stored flat. Interior door panels could remain in a back seat area if no work needs to be performed there. Be inventive. A few large nails attached to a wall could hold long trim pieces and glass might be safe if it were wrapped in a heavy tarp and secured with a rope tied to eyebolts screwed into an unused and uncrowded remote wall area.

Wheels are commonly damaged in side-swipe accidents. This one will have to be polished to look new again. When wheels are removed for whatever reason, be sure the vehicle is safely secured on heavy-duty jack stands. Wheels that have been taken off and need to be stored for a while should be placed out of the way to avoid accidental damage.

Too much stress cannot be put on the subject of personal safety when it comes to work on heavily damaged automobiles. Cutting operations create sparks that could ignite nearby containers of lacquer thinner or gasoline. Without protection like gloves and full face shields, technicians take chances on securing eye injuries or deep abrasive cuts. Use caution when working with equipment like this. Note that a tarp protects the interior of this Bronco II while Kane works to cut out mangled metal in preparation for installation of a new quarter panel.

Cardboard boxes work well to store small- to medium-size parts. Use a felt marker to label boxes and list all contents. Whatever organized inventory system you can develop for your autobody project parts will help the overall project run smoother. At the end of a dismantling procedure, take a little extra time to clean parts before stowing them away in boxes. This helps to reduce moisture absorption during storage and also to make the job of putting them back on your car cleaner and more satisfying.

Cutting Out Damaged Sections

Before tackling a project that involves metal cutting and welding operations, you must have at least some experience with the processes. This can come from a metalworking class or from practice sessions with your equipment and a few sections of scrap sheet metal. Never attempt cutting or weld-ing on your car if you have not done this type of work before.

Safety is a major concern during cutting and welding. High-speed die grinders with cutting discs can quickly sever fingers or cause large, traumatic wounds. Face shields and heavy leather gloves must be worn at all times to prevent hot metal chips from injuring eyes or burning skin. A small slip while using a high-speed, 20,000-rpm abrasive cutting tool will ruin a piece of sheet metal or make repairs more labor intensive.

Air chisels are safer to use than some other metal cutting tools. The only drawback is that their cuts are not always clean and smooth. Practice with this tool is also required. It would be foolish to use any power tool for the first time on a car that you are trying to repair. You have to practice first so that you can get a feel for the tool and for the easiest and most effective means by which to make it operate the way you expect. Scrap doors, hoods and other assemblies can be located at wrecking yards, scrap metal dealers and possibly from a local autobody shop.

Small metal cutting operations can be done by hand with tools like The Eastwood Company's Mini Nibbler. This unit does a great job of cutting metal

Cutting out this quarter panel section was no easy task. Along with having to remove interior panels and head-liner, seats, carpet and pad had to be removed. Spot welds were located and drilled out and an air chisel used to cut stitch welds. The floorboard had to be straightened before the quarter panel was removed so that the new panel would fit as expected. Before any cuts were made, a comparison was made between the old and new quarter panels to be sure that too much metal was not removed. Comparisons continued throughout the project until the old panel was removed.

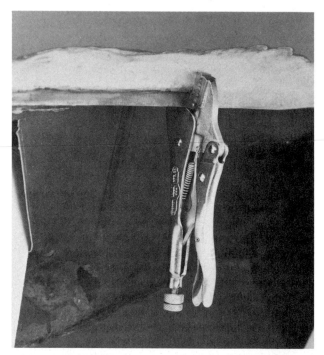

This is a Panel Flanger. The jaws have been outfitted to shape sheet metal edges as you see in preparation for accepting a new panel next to it. The flat edge of a new panel will butt up against the lip on a flanged edge for a tight fit. Spot welds or stitch welds will hold the units together. This way, technicians do not have to try and butt two bare edges together end to end, nor do they have to contend with a bulge on one side or the other. Patch panels can be achieved smoothly and evenly. The Eastwood Company

straight and without warping panel edges. All that is needed is a clean edge to start or a ¼ in. hole. Air powered nibblers are available as well as nibblers that attach to a drill motor. These units easily cut up to 18 gauge (.050) steel or aluminum.

Cutting out sections of bad sheet metal requires planning and a systematic approach. Although professional autobody specialists seldom hesitate to cut out entire roof sections or quarter panels, you must understand that they have had years of experience and lots of practice. Cut out sections of an old fender and then weld in new ones. Continue practicing until you feel confident enough with your work to attempt similar operations on your car.

Before cutting out any sheet metal, Kane has a new panel or patch already prepared. In the case of new panels, there are generally spot welded seams in old panels that can be drilled out so that the new panel will just slip into place. Barring that, measurements must be taken to determine how much bad metal has to come off and how much of the new patch will be used. Once measurements have been scribed on the old panel, masking tape is laid along the line to act as a cutting guide.

Many technicians use a utility cut-off tool that features a high-speed, 20,000-rpm motor and an abrasive disc for cutting flat sheet metal panels. A masking tape guide and a controlled approach help them to make straight cuts every time. A face shield, gloves and long sleeves are always worn. An air powered nibbler would also work quite well.

Caution must always be exercised when cutting sheet metal. You have to investigate what is behind a panel before starting. Check for fuel lines, brake hoses, wiring, and so on. Since abrasive discs shower areas with sparks, make certain that all flammable and combustible materials are out of the way. Have a fire extinguisher available at all times.

Novice autobody technicians may be best off using a nibbler tool. This unit provides an accurate means to cut metal straight without warping edges. It does not spray out a curtain of sparks and is easy to control. Use a line of masking tape as a guide for its use too.

Patch Panels

New and old metal is designed to overlap. This gives patches or new panels support. Special crimp-

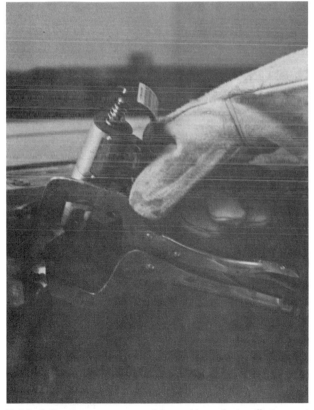

Behind the clamp, a spot weld gun is ready to effect a spot weld along a panel. After every five to six welds, the position of panels is checked for accuracy. Sometimes, welding causes panels to twist out of shape. Moving clamps closer together or to different locations will help to reduce those problems.

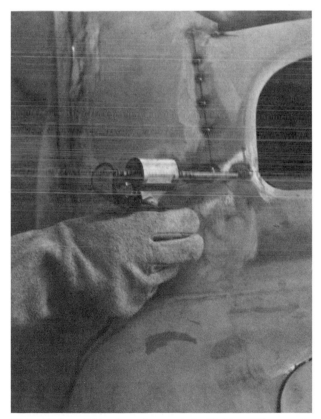

This stitch weld tool works great for light welding needs on thin sheet metal panels. The welding rod actually moves up and down to help users make perfect welds. Always wear heavy leather gloves and a face shield when welding. Be sure the face shield is equipped with a dark lens of the proper grade.

ing tools, called panel flangers, are available from The Eastwood Company and autobody paint and supply stores. They crimp a stepped flange on the end of sheet metal panels so that other panels will fit over the flange and butt against the step. Spot welds are made every 1 to 1½ in. Stitch welds could also be negotiated along metal edges. Pieces are held together with clamps or special panel holding rivets until welding has been completed.

Welding on sheet metal poses problems of metal warping and burn-throughs. Thin metal cannot stand up to a lot of extended heat. Use a low amperage welder and weld short sections at a time, a process called stitch welding. As opposed to completely welding a gap between two sheet metal panel edges, welds are only about 1 to 1½ in. long. Start welding at the center point of a panel and then alternate welds on both sides; e.g., a stitch weld to the right

of the center weld and then on the left side, and back and forth until complete.

After each weld, a water soaked towel is immediately laid on top of the red hot weld to help shrink metal and prevent it from warping or stretching. An alternate method of cooling the metal is to apply compressed air to hot welds. This process allows the technician to control shrinkage because metal is always in view, not covered with a wet towel; although a wet towel placed about 2 in. from the welding area will absorb a lot of welding heat.

These are time-consuming processes but absolutely necessary when working with thin sheet metal panels. When welding on a small spot, stop three or four times to cool the area with a sopping wet towel before completing the job. Continued welding for over a few seconds will either burn through host metal or cause warps. Once again, about the only way you will get a firsthand look and feel at how this process works is to practice.

Spot welds look exactly like their names. As opposed to a using a welding rod or a wire feed welder,

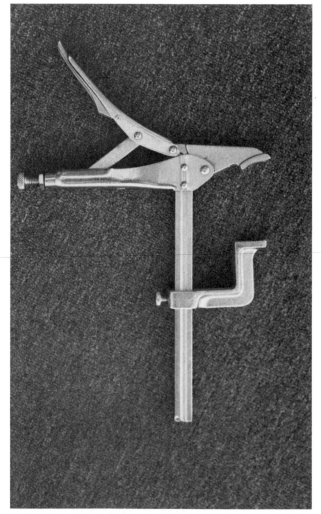

Clamps of all kinds can be found at autobody paint and supply stores. This special tool can be extended to hold wide pieces in place. You will need to clamp patch panels every foot or so to keep them in position while welding. Vise Grip locking pliers work well, as do other brands.

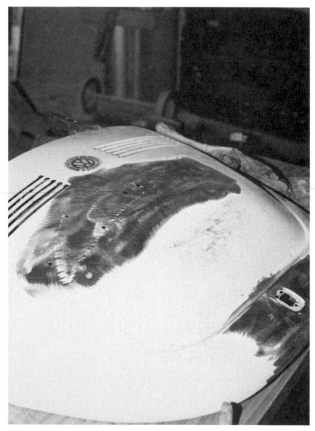

Found at a wrecking yard, this VW Bug engine lid will be used to replace a severely damaged unit. The holes seen in the middle of the lid will be covered with small patch panels. Low amperage wire feed welding will be employed so as to not warp the piece. Afterward, metal will be ground smooth and then covered with a coat of body filler and sanded.

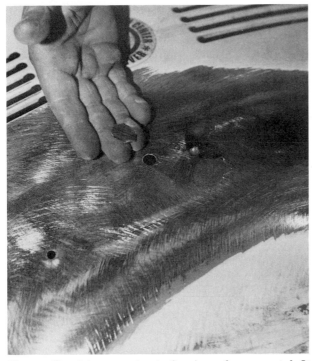

The small patch was cut out of a piece of scrap metal. It is larger than the hole and will be attached from the underside. Just to the right, notice a patch in place from below, covering a slightly larger hole. These pieces will be propped up with a noncombustible item while welding is underway.

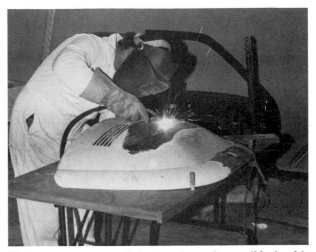

Welding requires a solid ground, made possible in this case by the grounding clamp being attached to a section of bare metal to the right of the photo. Heavy-duty leather gloves must be worn along with a face shield equipped with a suitable dark lens. The lens should be dark enough that you cannot see through it unless you look at a bright welding arc. Lenses of varying darkness are available. Bystanders must not look at welding operations. The intense bright light will injure eyes permanently.

Both patches are secured on the bottom of their respective holes. Low amperage welding will be done on one side and then switched to the other. A sopping wet towel will be placed over the red hot metal to cool and shrink it, and a weld will be put along the top and then bottom, then another application with a wet towel. After that, the middle will be filled in and cooled off. This process will prevent burn throughs at the welds and also reduce the chances of panel warping.

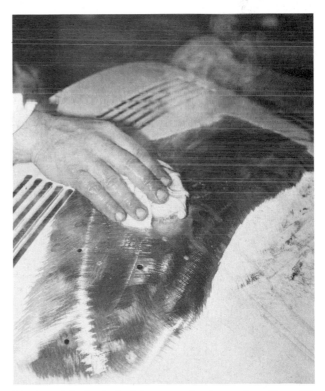

Most autobody technicians prefer to cool welds with towels sopping wet with cool water. Here you can see steam rising from the towel. Be aware that the panel will be hot. Other technicians have had good results blowing cool compressed air on welds to quickly cool them and prevent warping. Whichever method you use, be sure to cool welds as quickly as possible.

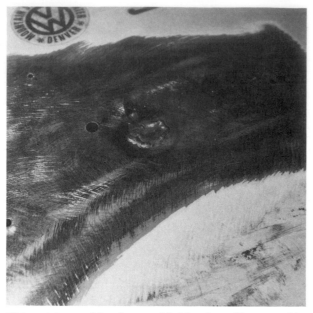

This patch panel has been welded in place. Because of its size, there was no need to completely fill in the middle with welds. Notice that there is no warping or burn throughs. The ridge of welding material will be ground down flush with adjacent metal. Final coats of filler will make this lid look like it had never been worked on.

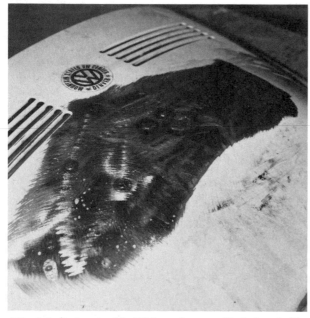

All of the holes on this lid have been welded closed. The smallest ones did not require patches; they were simply filled with welding material. The process took a while to complete because welding had to stop often while wet towels were applied to red hot welding spots. Before tackling this type of operation on your car, be sure to practice first with a piece of scrap metal of equal thickness. Low amperage welding is a must. Practice with different amperage settings, starting out at forty and gradually increasing until a comfortable limit is reached for you.

spot welds utilize special rods that are held in place by a spot weld gun for about five seconds. The Spot Weld gun from The Eastwood Company runs right off regular welders set at 50 amps or less. A trigger is used to touch an electrode to sheet metal. It establishes an arc and raises the electrode while a molten puddle of metal is formed. Their unit will weld eighteen to twenty-six gauge steel and only costs around $40.

Patches can be made out of sheet metal sections from scrap doors or other assemblies and cut to fit small patch panels as needed for your car. You will first have to shape a patch panel into the pattern that will fit into whatever hole you cut out of your car body. A number of metalworking tools are available through autobody supply stores and restoration equipment outlets like The Eastwood Company that are specifically designed to shape sheet metal. Other than that, small pieces could possibly be shaped using a body hammer and dolly or a sandbag as a base.

Caution: Before welding on any car, be sure to disconnect both leads to the battery. Electrical

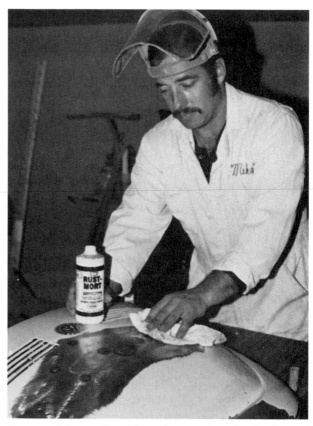

Because this panel is old, has been stripped to bare metal and was exposed to high heat, Kane applies liberal coats of Rust-Mort to kill any rust that may have gotten a start anywhere along the line. This material is supposed to kill rust deposits on contact. It is a good idea to treat older car panels with products designed to kill rust, especially for restorers.

charges from welders have been known to pass through car bodies and into their electrical system. This can be a costly error, because computers or other electronic equipment might be destroyed. Disconnect the positive lead first and then the negative. When installing batteries, connect the negative first and then the postive.

Installing New Pieces

The installation of trim, lights, grille pieces and other assemblies cannot begin until after a repaired body has been painted. If you intend to paint the vehicle yourself, certain paint procedures should be done to some parts before they are put back on the car. Doorjambs, for example, are easier to paint off a car than on it. This way, when jambs have already been painted, doors can remain shut while the rest of the car gets a new coat of paint. The same technique is used for hatchbacks, quarter panels, fenders, hoods and deck lids. At the least, paint the undersides and edges of these units before installing them on your car.

When putting on new parts, have a few large pieces of cardboard on hand. Place parts on these to

This is what the patch panel looked like after it was ground smooth with a 24 grit disc on a high-speed sander. The slight low spot in the center will be filled with body putty.

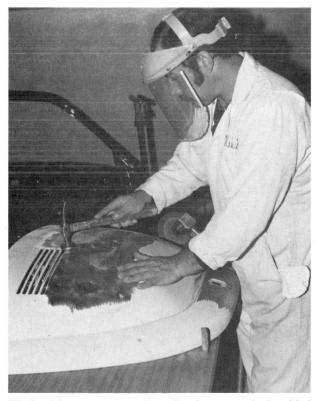

Work with a 24 grit sanding disc has smoothed welded spots. Some work with a body hammer will flatten slight high spots. At this point, the panel is being treated for any surface imperfections, just like any dinged or dented panel. Once again, the repair area is frequently felt with a bare hand to sense any abnormalities on the surface. Hammer and dolly work is employed as needed.

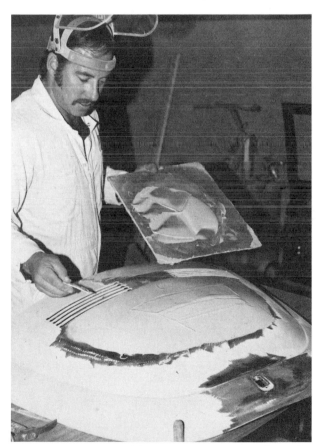

A regular mix of body filler is applied with a medium-size squeegee. Care is exercised around the louvers so they are not plugged with filler material. It takes a little practice to apply an even coat of filler on a rounded panel. Don't get discouraged if your first few attempts do not turn out as nice as this. Just keep practicing.

prevent scratches and have them near the job. Large clean shop towels are handy as cushions when resting large items, like doors, on crates for support while inserting hinge bolts. They also help to protect hood corners and deck lids while they are placed in position.

If your storage system is organized, you should know exactly where to look for nuts, bolts, other fasteners and parts. Assembly should be easy with no part forced into place. If an unusual amount of pressure is required to fit a part into its respective spot, pull it out and investigate why. Chances are, something is not lined up correctly and excessive force will only cause something to break.

Brand new doors should have their inner sides and all four edges painted before being outfitted with glass, latch and other mechanisms. As mentioned earlier, do not strip an old door until you can put all the parts directly into your new one. Have each door sitting side by side so as one part comes off, it immediately goes onto the new unit. The mechanisms and linkages inside doors are not easy

to reach or maneuver. Patience is really necessary for these intricate assembly operations.

When the time comes to install all of the other pieces taken off for body and paint work, remember to take your time and think things through before hastily putting on parts. Carefully install lamp housings and other items on top of new paint. Just a little slip could cause a scratch. Gaskets around lamp assemblies must be positioned correctly or moisture will enter the unit to short out bulbs and corrode reflector shields.

Bumpers are heavy and you should consider using a helper to assist you in supporting these and other heavy items, like hoods, deck lids and hatchbacks, while bolts are fitted into their designated positions. Acknowledge that certain assemblies include a number of alignment points. Instead of tightening every bolt as it is inserted, run it up to a lightly snug position so that the unit can be adjusted into position. Then tighten bolts in a systematic fashion from one corner to the next, top then bottom, side to side so that alignment is not affected.

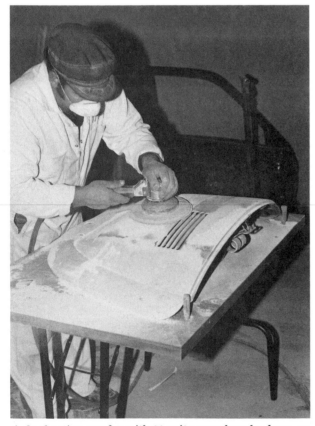

A dual action sander with 80 grit paper knocks down excess filler. A good feel for this tool is needed to effect good sanding maneuvers on unusually shaped panels. Always keep these sanders moving so gouges or ripples are not created. Wear a dust mask and be aware that a lot of dust will be created. Is your garage or shop set up to handle this much dust? If not, you might consider sectioning off a part of it with sheets of plastic.

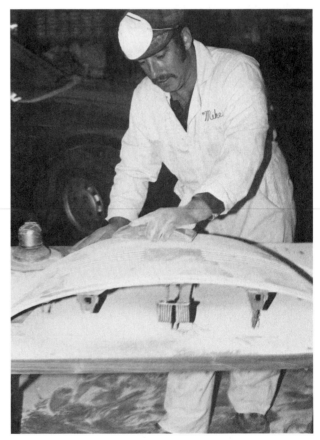

Final sanding is done by hand with a block; 100 to 120 grit paper works great. Be sure to feel the panel often in an effort to locate any high or low spots. If they do crop up, be sure to flatten them with appropriate hammer and spoon work. Take your time and work methodically by always being aware of what you are doing and the ultimate goal you are trying to achieve.

9

Major Collision Damage Considerations

Major automobile collision damage generally involves some frame, suspension, drive train or other structurally critical elements. Seldom does a heavy hit render these kinds of assemblies unscathed. Although in some instances extensive shallow body damage with broken glass results in extremely high repair costs, reflecting heavy hits from a cost standpoint, most knowledgeable auto people take for granted that major damage refers to much more than mere panel destruction.

From a novice autobody technician's viewpoint, major damage could be just about anything that surpasses his or her range of repair capabilities. A clear understanding of basic automotive assemblies and primary manipulative skills with tools and equipment is necessary to effect any autobody repair.

The door skin was opened up with a die grinder to allow visual inspection of internal door parts to see if damage had occurred. Mycon and an insurance adjuster had to determine the degree of damage so an accurate estimate of repairs could be agreed upon. Electric window and door lock mechanisms were inspected and found to be operable. If you have to replace a door, consider cutting a large section out of the old door to help you understand how window and latch mechanisms are positioned and secured.

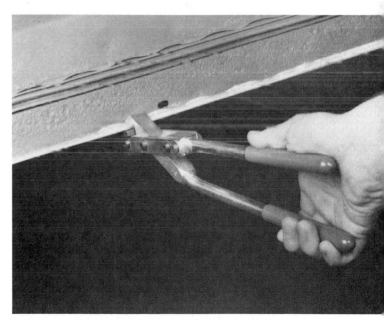

New door skins can be installed on doors when just that part of the assembly has been destroyed, saving the cost of a brand new door. Using a grinder, carefully cut through the outer skin material along the door's edge, then grind off the remaining strip attached to the flat part of the door frame. Once a new skin is positioned, use a door skin installer, like this one, to fold the door skin edge over the frame. Spot welds along each side will keep a skin secure. Cover all edges with seam sealer. The Eastwood Company

In lieu of handing over an entire autobody repair project to a professional body shop or completely forsaking a do-it-yourself restoration project, consider a cooperative effort between you and a technician of choice. Through clear and concise communications, you may be able to have a professional complete repairs to structural components and those assemblies beyond your capabilities. Then you can complete remaining jobs yourself. Not only might you save money, you could also gain personal satisfaction by having had a hand in the overall repair effort.

Because of rising professional body shop labor fees and part replacement costs, many vehicles that present slight hints of major collision damage problems are written off as totals by insurance adjusters. If your totaled car was really special to you, for whatever reason, you might be able to buy it back from an insurance company for a reasonable price.

Depending on the degree of actual direct and indirect damage, you might be able to repair it at a fraction of an adjuster's estimated cost. This can be accomplished by purchasing used parts at a wrecking yard for prices far less than brand new units, hiring a body shop to repair frame, suspension and integral body structures beyond your knowledge limitations and then completing the rest of the work yourself. This may not be feasible for every car, but a possibility for those vehicles of classic, vintage or intrinsically valuable status.

Do It Yourself or Hire It Out

Any sort of frame or suspension damage must be corrected by qualified repair people only. There are no exceptions. Do-it-yourselfers with little or no experience working on these assemblies have no idea of the serious complications that could arise when less than perfect repair work has been performed on them.

Besides minor problems with unusual tire wear, uncomfortable ride or difficult steering, faulty frame or suspension repairs could lead to part failure dur-

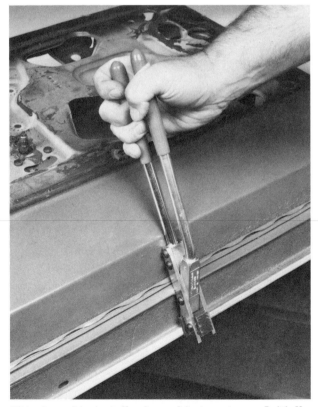

This door skin installer is used in two stages. Initially, door skin edges are folded to a thirty degree angle. Then the tool is reversed to further flatten edges to complete the operation, as illustrated. Nylon pads on the tool prevent scratches to metal skin surfaces. Replacing door skins is not a complex repair. You can achieve the procedure with minimal equipment and a systematic approach. If you have little experience working with metal, strongly consider practicing with a scrap door before attempting work on your vehicle. The Eastwood Company

A side impact collision resulted in quarter panel, door, B-pillar rocker panel and floorboard damage to this Bronco II. A new door, rocker panel and quarter panel were installed. This required a lot of skilled work with special equipment. Before anything was dismantled, the floorboard was pulled out to its normal position. This gave technicians a base to work with for new panel installation maneuvers.

122

ing vehicle operation to cause a complete lack of vehicle control, possibly resulting in a serious, fatal or near fatal accident. Knowledgeable auto enthusiasts trust frame or suspension repairs only to proven professionals.

Full-time autobody technicians prefer to work on major collision projects from the beginning. This way, they can easily determine what damage was actually caused by a crash and from that investigation, through their years of experience, know what kinds of related problems to look for.

If, for example, you attempted repairs to a crunched unibody frame rail segment that you were unable to complete and, in frustration, turned the job over to a professional to finish, they may not be able to totally decipher the degree of direct or indirect damage that had occurred, thereby missing some critical repairs.

Problems may surface later when the majority of work has been done and final alignments or adjustments fail to provide satisfactory results. Should this happen, they will have to start back at square one, rectify anything you inadvertently botched up and might even have to repeat and refinish all of the work that had been completed up to that point. This will cost you a lot of extra money.

"Trying to fix autobody damage that some inexperienced repair person has butchered is always twice as hard and more expensive that if I could have done it from start to finish," says Kane. This is because he not only has to correct problems caused by the other person, but also correctly repair whatever damage existed initially.

Whether you want a body shop to complete all of the bodywork to your car or just portions of it, always communicate openly with the estimator about your intentions. Should you strongly desire a cooperative effort, be frank and up front. Decide together what chores you are capable of and what procedures you will expect him or her to complete. By all means, let a body shop technician inspect your car before dismantling or attempting repairs of any kind.

Unibody Frames

Unibody frames cannot be repaired without the use of special equipment operated by qualified technicians in accordance with strict standards as set by both equipment and auto manufacturers.

Besides autobody shops, companies that specialize in frame repairs may be listed under the heading of "Automobile Frame Repairs" in the automobile section of your telephone book's yellow pages.

Special unibody frame straightening machines suspend cars off the ground. Predetermined points around the underbody are secured with chains and other devices. According to the type of frame damage at hand, technicians follow a specific set of guidelines to pull out crushed areas in accordance with recommended pressure and stress calibrations. Visual alignment gauges and markers are employed to guarantee straight results.

Full Frames

Although their significance in vehicle operation and performance is just as critical as unibody frames, full frames are far less complicated to straighten. Made of heavy steel channels, full frames support a vehicle's body, as opposed to a body being incorporated into a frame structure on a unibody model.

Pickup trucks generally feature full frame designs. Their entire body can be lifted off a frame in order to complete work on it. In addition, should a frame and drive train be in excellent condition and a body totally destroyed, a new body could be placed on the old frame with few problems.

This quarter panel came off a Bronco II. Its full frame chassis made work less complex than if the panel had to be removed and replaced on a unibody vehicle. Work like this cannot be taken lightly. Although dismantling mangled sections of sheet metal is not that difficult, making sure that all remaining parts are aligned properly to accept new parts is critical. If dimensions are off the slightest bit, doors will not fit as expected nor will any other assemblies located in the affected area. You must seriously consider your autobody repair limitations before tackling a major repair like this.

Although do-it-yourself auto enthusiasts have attempted full frame straightening using chains and come-a-longs secured to utility poles and trees, I recommend that all full frame repairs be completed by experienced professionals. They are keenly aware of handling and performance complications derived from improper repairs and the possibility of frame failure should stress cracks or metal fatigue go unnoticed and uncorrected.

Exposing frames to extreme heat from arc welding or torch operations can severely weaken them. Procedures enlisting high heat usage must be done in just the right way to prevent any loss of tensile strength and to reduce the chances of metal becoming brittle. Should you want to learn how to fix and align damaged frames, attend an autobody class at a local community college or vocational school.

Suspension

A suspension system is an ensemble of parts such as leaf springs, coil springs, shock absorbers, struts and steering mechanisms that all play impor-

At a taillight location, spot welds secure a quarter panel edge and rear body panel together. Spot welds are pointed out as round impressions. Thick material seemingly painted over the metal edge is seam sealer. Spot welds on the finished body section were accomplished from the other side or ground smooth, filled, sanded and painted. Many clamps are needed for this kind of work to keep panels in a secure position while welding. Check a panel's position frequently, as welding can cause metal to slightly twist out of position.

tant roles in the overall performance of any vehicle. A failure of one part or one assembly will cause handling problems. These can range from a broken rear shock and a bumpy ride, to a severed tie rod and total loss of vehicle control. Suspension systems are not to be taken lightly.

Shock absorbers are easy to remove and replace. They are relatively inexpensive parts that help to cushion bumps. During your evaluation of collision damage near wheels, check shock absorbers for bent connecting rods, leaking fluid and smashed housings or lower connection supports.

Rear wheel assemblies should be thoroughly inspected when vehicles have been involved in rear end collisions. Look for leaking brake or fuel lines, evidence of differential fluid loss, wheel or tire damage and signs that rear axles have scooted along leaf springs. This is recognized when clean spots appear on top of leaf springs, evidence that the axle has moved from its original location. Tightly secured, dirt is not able to build up under axles. However, front and rear areas around axles will exhibit definite signs of dirt and debris accumulations.

Should this axle adjustment be overlooked, a vehicle will travel down roads in a sideways motion. You may not notice this while driving, except in extreme cases when you look in your side mirror and see that the rear wheel is on the road's center line while the front of your car appears to be a distance away. This condition is unsafe and will cause tires to wear quickly and abnormally.

Leaf spring supported axles can be adjusted front to back by maintaining an identical distance from right front wheel to right rear wheel equal to that for left side wheels. Use a tape measure or string to measure the distance from the center of the right front hub to the center of the right rear axle and compare it to the same spots on left side wheels.

If one is shorter than the other, it may have been knocked forward, while the wheelbase showing more distance may have had its rear wheel knocked backward. You may have to crawl under the car to see for sure, but pay attention to the direction of impact. If the right rear was smashed from the rear, it would stand to reason that the right rear wheel was knocked forward and vice versa.

Support the car *body*, not just axles or differential, on jack stands. Loosen bolts securing the axle to leaf springs and adjust as necessary. A helper may be needed to hold one side as you push or pull the other. Continue adjusting until measurements on both sides are equal. While working in the area, make sure no brake or fuel lines are located along the axle in such a way that axle movement would damage them.

Front end steering and suspension assemblies are much more complicated than rear wheel drive axles. Along with tie rods, A-arms and king pins, other parts work together to provide a comfortable ride and steering capability. Failure of any part in this area could cause disastrous results. Damage to front end suspension or steering mechanisms must be repaired by a qualified front end specialist.

In the case of front wheel drive cars, front end damage presents even more problems. Along with suspension and steering mechanisms, these vehicles feature power train assemblies that directly connect to the engine. Should extensive front end damage occur on a front wheel drive automobile, the engine and transaxle will have to be thoroughly inspected and serviced by a qualified mechanic.

Front suspension, steering and drive line damage should be repaired by a professional, not a novice autobody technician. These assemblies, like unibody frames, are intricate. It is not just a matter of part removal and replacement. Specific calibrations, alignments and adjustments must be maintained or the system will not perform as expected.

Panel Replacement

Automobile bodies consist of many large and small parts, panels and assemblies. Most parts are secured in place by nuts, bolts and other fasteners. Body panels are generally spot welded into place. Spot welds are nothing more than small, single, circular welds used to attach 1 in. sections of two separate sheet metal panels together. These welds appear as obvious ¼ in. dots outlining the perimeter of a sheet metal panel.

Most spot weld unions are covered by seam sealer, a bead of weather stripping or trim molding. About the only place you will see them uncovered, except for paint, is along sheet metal seams on pickup truck beds. Panel replacements are not simple operations easily completed by novice autobody technicians. If you have never done anything like this before, try to acquire actual hands on training through an autobody shop class at a community college or vocational school.

To remove a panel intact, drill out all spot welds securing it. Special drill bits are made for this job

Kane stands through the window opening to maintain a comfortable and balanced position while drilling out spot welds for removal of a quarter panel. A special spot weld removing drill bit is used. He dips the drill bit into cutting oil after each use to prolong the bit's cutting life. Notice that he is wearing a full face shield and has all the tools needed for the job handy on a rolling cart next to the rig. Before this operation got under way, structurally integral components (floorboard, pillar and roof) were already pulled back out to their normal positions.

Drilled holes indicate where spot welds were removed. Unless you maintain complete control over the drilling endeavor, holes can be drilled through the bottom section of sheet metal along with the top. Occasionally this happens. When it does, simply plan to effect a new spot weld from the inside part of a panel instead of the outside. Or disregard that hole for a future spot weld and put new ones on each side.

that drill through an outer sheet metal panel around the outer perimeter of spot welds to section off welds and separate the two metal pieces.

Replacing a rocker panel, quarter panel, roof section, floor pan or fender apron takes a lot of work and finesse. You cannot just start out by drilling spot welds and expect a new panel to slip into place. Consideration must be given to damage beyond the outer panel to those assemblies inside to which the panel attaches. If they have been buckled or dented in any way, a new panel will not fit as expected.

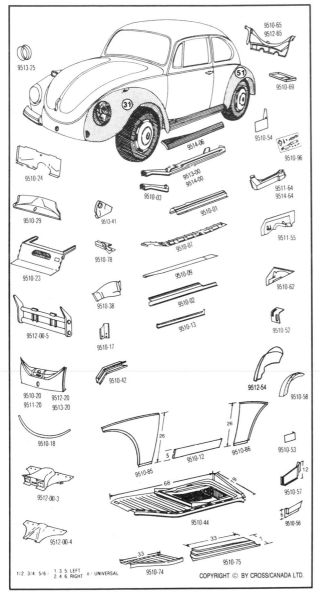

All sorts of new panels can be installed on vehicles. This multi-panel illustration shows how many panel parts can be ordered just for VW Bug bodies. Similar parts can also be purchased for all other car makes and models. In the case of VW bugs, rear fenders are actually real parts. The sheet metal located in front and behind rear fenders is quarter panels. Sherman & Associates, Inc.

Before sheet metal is removed from a vehicle, special equipment is used to pull out damage to floor pans and other structural members so that they return to their original position. When this has occurred, damaged sheet metal can be removed. Then, work with hammers and dollies will finish off inner sections to flatten creases and small dents.

Again, before installing new panels, be certain that those assemblies to which they will be spot welded are in precisely the correct position to accept the new panel. This point cannot be stressed strongly enough. Say, for example, a quarter panel replacement was called for on your two door coupe. If the new panel is installed with floorboard or B-pillar irregularities, there is a good chance that after it has been spot welded in place, the door will not open or close correctly. What will you do then, cut down the door edges?

Panel replacements require more expertise than simply the ability to drill out and replace spot welds.

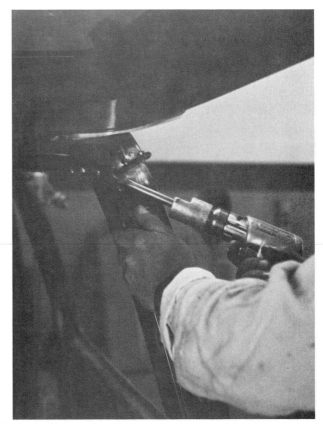

Kane uses an air chisel to separate a C-pillar from its roof connection. Drilled spot welds will not always immediately cause panels to disconnect. Tools like this are frequently needed during extensive repair work on heavily damaged body sections. Careful attention to air chisel work is required so that unnecessary damage does not occur to host panels. Haphazard removal of damaged body panels can ruin host panels causing technicians a lot of extra work that could have been avoided if more time was taken to thoroughly plan and execute the work.

First, you have to know where to look for spot weld connections. On the outer body, they may be filled, sanded and painted over to give the impression that a quarter panel, pillar and roof are all one piece.

In reality, though, there is a separation point. You can generally locate it by removing interior side panels and headliner. Once located, judge the joint's outer location and grind or sandblast the area to remove paint and seam sealer to reveal the seam. Spot welds are usually removed from the outer sides of vehicles so welding does not have to be done inside.

When undertaking such a major operation, always have the replacement panel on hand. This way, you can compare perimeter features of the new panel with actual supports and reinforcements on the existing panel to make sure you do not cut off anything that will be needed for installation of the new panel. Constant comparison is made to ensure what comes off the vehicle matches what will go on.

After a panel is removed, floor pan, pillar or roof edges are flattened. The new panel is placed in position to test for fit. As indicated by measurement and closeness of fit, additional hammer and dolly work, or Porto-Power pulling and stretching, is initiated and completed. After that, the panel is test fitted again. Should all perimeters match and dimensions correspond to expected arrangements, the panel is removed. At that time, outer edges and interior sections are painted to match whatever color is designated.

The outer surface is not painted; this will be done after the entire body has been repaired so that the complete exterior can receive a paint job in one session. The inner sections and perimeter edge sections are painted before panel installation because masking and painting efforts after installation would be too confined and would cause severe paint overspray problems throughout the vehicle's interior.

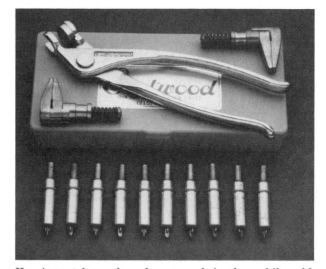

Keeping patch panels and new panels in place while welding requires lots of clamps and special body equipment like this Panel Holding System. Blind Holders are inserted in ⅛ in. holes drilled through sheet metal panels to hold new material in place while welds are completed. The aircraft industry uses items like this to secure airplane skins while riveting. Holes must be welded closed when holders are removed. The Eastwood Company

Air chisel work caused some disfigurement along the edge of this roof section where it was disconnected from a C-pillar. Hammer and dolly work will straighten edges while careful stitch welding can fill in where host metal has been torn off. Unexpected metal damage like this has to be expected during large scale body repair operations. Experienced autobody technicians prove their worth when they are able to fix problems like this.

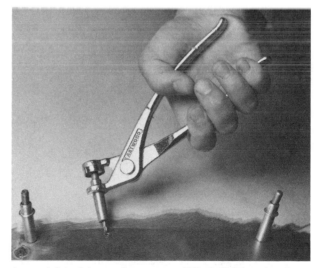

A special tool is used to secure Blind Holders in place, which in turn are used to hold new panels in their respective position while welds are made elsewhere on panel edges. One-eighth inch holes are drilled into sheetmetal panels for the insertion of holders. A set of ten holders, two side grips and the special pliers cost around $30. The Eastwood Company

Installation of body panels requires vise grips or other clamps be placed every foot or so around the perimeter to securely hold it in position. Adjustments of clamps may have to be made periodically as heat from spot welding operations, although at low amperage, can cause slight metal twisting or warping. To be on the safe side, check the position of new panels after every fifth or sixth spot weld. Make sure that lower sections have not pulled up or side edges have twisted outward.

As with any procedure that requires a heat source, be aware of possible fire hazards. While welding in the interior section of your car, consider spreading a heavy tarp or fireproof blanket over all exposed upholstery or plastic. If need be, strip the car's interior completely of all seats, upholstery, headliner and side panels. Also, have a fire extinguisher close at hand at all times.

Some stitch welding may be required on certain panel replacements. Where gaps are featured along seams, welds are needed to add support to the two sheet metal panels. Because these panels consist of such thin sheet metal, a prolonged weld intended to fill an entire gap would be impractical. Instead, rely on stitch welds to secure and seam sealer to close the gap to prevent water and dust seepage.

Stitch welds are similar to normal arc welds except they only extend for about 1–1½ in. Their short length adds strength and support to joints and, at the same time, prevents excessive heat from burning through or warping panels. Again, low amperage welding is necessary.

Partial or complete panel replacement will require welding and may include some metal cutting or shaping work. If you have no experience in this area, I highly recommend you take at least a few classes on welding for autobody operations. The actual practice and hands on instruction will be invaluable.

Where to Find Help

The degree to which you dive into an autobody repair project of major proportions should be directly related to what your car means to you and how it is used. If it is the only source of transportation for your family, can you really afford to practice newly acquired autobody repair techniques to it, or should you have a professional repair it within a minimal time? On the other hand, if it is a project car, you should certainly be able to work on it at a leisurely rate and practice new skills without missing its usefulness until repairs have been completed.

As much as auto enthusiasts tackle autobody repair jobs for pleasure or hobby, a lot of novice auto-

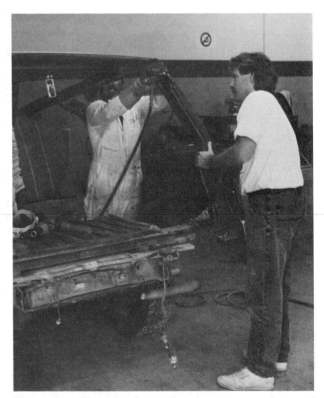

Mycon and Kane work together to remove a damaged Bronco II quarter panel. Even though spot welds were drilled out, some lingering pieces of sheet metal still remain attached and are separated with an air chisel. Help is needed to support and lift off heavy panels. Do not try to do all the work yourself. You could injure yourself or cause damage to nearby body parts. Gloves should be worn to prevent cuts from sharp metal edges. In this instance, mechanical body pullers could be adjusted to secure roof sections at the B- and C-pillars.

This Resistance Spot Welder uses the same technique employed by welding machines at auto factories. Plugged into a 110v AC outlet, it works by electrical resistance to produce intense heat in very small areas. Optional tongs of different sizes and shapes are used for jobs requiring their maneuverability. Serious restorers or autobody technicians may consider equipment like this to produce factory type spot welds on metal up to ⅛ in. thick. This unit sells for around $370. The Eastwood Company

body technicians attempt repairs because they lack the necessary funds needed to have a professional shop complete the work. In both cases, you should be able to find help for a nominal cost or for free.

As mentioned before, most community colleges and vocational schools offer classes in autobody repairs. These classes are usually inexpensive. You might find an amiable body shop owner who would let you hang around to watch technicians in action, but that may prove to be time consuming.

A good option could be car clubs. You would be surprised at the amount of autobody repair talent, knowledge and expertise that is available through members of organized car clubs. In more instances than you can imagine, members of clubs have become noted experts on certain makes and models of automobiles. Who could love a car more or absorb more information about a particular model than an avid auto enthusiast?

George Ridderbusch is such an example. For more years than he can remember, he has had a deep appreciation for Porsche automobiles. Through the years, he has read just about every book, parts manual and periodical printed that contained anything about Porsches. This dedication has led him to be a consistent concours d'elegance winner for years as well as an expert on just about every facet related to these cars.

Just like thousands of people like him, he belongs to a car club—in his case, of course, a Porsche organization. Because of his vast experience and knowledge, he is frequently asked to conduct restoration and repair classes. He does this gladly and the members of his club are privy to a wealth of information.

Through car clubs with members like Ridderbusch, you too can learn what you need about autobody repair, panel replacement and a host of other things. Talk to fellow car enthusiasts and attend auto shows and rallies in hopes of meeting guys like Ridderbusch with a common passion for cars like yours. Who knows, through the years, you might end up like Ridderbusch teaching other members how to fix their cars. After all, someone had to teach Ridderbusch the basics, didn't they?

Overview

Major collision damage repairs are nothing to be taken lightly. All kinds of seemingly unrelated problems can crop up to make restoration efforts difficult, time consuming and downright frustrating. Unless you have the time for practice, the patience to learn and the understanding that trial and effort labors will eventually pan out to satisfactory repairs, you should definitely consider having a professional complete your repair project for you.

Fixing major collision damage problems on cars requires welding expertise. You can get it at school or work through it by practice on old scrap panels.

To maintain a high degree of quality repairs, many technicians prefer to spray new panel edges with weldable corrosion resistant coatings. Burrous has had good results using 3M's Weld-Thru Coating. Welding endeavors burn off primers and other coatings used to protect metal from rust and corrosion. By spraying metal parts with products like this, concealed inner metal edges are still protected after welds have been completed.

Cold Galvanizing Compound is painted on areas of concealed metal to protect them against rust and corrosion. This product has weld-thru capability that will not interfere with spot welds. It can also be used to touch up other galvanized parts, like brackets, clamps or mufflers. The contents include 95 percent pure powdered zinc and 5 percent epoxy. A one quart container costs about $25. Serious consideration must be given to the use of products like this when restoring cars that have undergone a lot of metal stripping work.

You must understand that the vast majority of autobody projects deal directly with sheet metal. You can't expect to fix it unless you know how to work with it.

A lot of options are available for those who choose to pursue them. You can seek a cooperative effort with a local body shop to have them do the intricate stuff and you the finish work. Classes are open at certain schools that offer guidance, support and technical skill instruction in all phases of autobody repair techniques.

Car clubs offer a wide array of talented, knowledgeable and helpful members, eager to assist and teach new members all they know about their favorite automobile make and model. All you have to do is locate the club nearest you that holds a special interest for the same make and model car you own.

Read auto-related magazines and ask at auto parts stores, autobody paint and supply stores, body shops, mechanics garages and anywhere else where automobiles form a business base. Chances are, whatever auto-related problems you are faced with, someone in the club has already dealt with and successfully handled something almost identical.

Finally, when you have come up against an autobody problem you just can't seem to understand, ask someone. Autobody professionals are not in their line of work because they can't find anything else to do. With few exceptions, they just like cars. Seldom will you find professional autobody people who do not like to talk about cars. After all, cars are their life for at least forty hours a week.

Never be afraid to ask a question, no matter how insignificant you think it may be. The only people autobody professionals prefer to ignore are those who think they know it all already. If you are honest and up front, you will get up-front and honest answers.

10

Autobody Repair Extras

Primary autobody repair will usually focus on metal straightening, like taking out dings and dents. Advanced repairs include multiple panel repairs and replacements. Except for flattening a minor ding in the middle of a panel, most of these kinds of bodywork will include some sort of extra work to items associated with panels, doors, fenders, and so on.

Careful inspection of almost any automobile body will reveal a multitude of various attachments. Some are mandatory, such as lights, weather stripping, handles and key locks. Others serve as adornments to dress up a vehicle's appearance, like window trim, body side molding, emblems and bumper guards.

Total completion of any autobody repair mandates that damaged add-on and integral pieces be properly fixed and installed to complement the bodywork that has been accomplished. Although many of these items cannot be attached to a body until paint work has been done, some may require the same paint coverage as body panels (e.g., certain splash shields, flexible bumper parts and painted lamp assemblies). They will be painted at the same time the car is sprayed but separately, as they rest on a table or hang from a wire in a spray booth.

Be sure to allot adequate time for the repair attention needed to fix all of the extra parts that were damaged in a collision. Order replacement parts early, so they will be on hand when you are ready to work on your car. Most importantly, make sure you don't skip over anything that has sustained even the slightest blemish. After all of the paint work is done and all parts installed, you can spend a day detailing your finished rig to make it look clean and crisp with all associated parts and adornments blended together for that like-new appearance.

Bumper Dismantling

Chrome bumpers are easy to remove from most older cars and pickup trucks. Just a few heavy-duty carriage bolts secure bumpers to their brackets and only four more hold brackets firmly in place along frames. Today, a lot of front and rear bumpers are incorporated into entire front nose or rear tail assemblies. Their removal is not nearly as quick and easy as those older styles. Some flexible kinds may present as many as twenty-three individual bolts that all have an effect on the complete assembly's overall adjustment and alignment positioning.

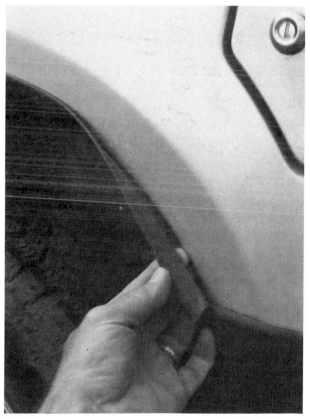

This rear wheel opening trim piece does a great job of protecting metal against nicks and dings, especially from inconsiderate parking lot door slammers. Spray adhesive is used to secure items like this. If allowed to hang loose, wind will sooner or later tear them off. Be sure to spray new adhesive to loosened sections as soon as they are noticed.

In order to comfortably work near a front fender corner and along the hood, this nose section was removed from a Dodge Daytona in one piece. This view shows the amount of separate pieces that combine to make one assembly. Damage to one area on units like this may only present a few damaged pieces. Instead of buying a complete nose in those circumstances, you could save a lot of money by just purchasing replacement items for those individual parts that are not reparable.

Dismantling a large component like this requires much patience and forethought. Consider taking a few pictures of the unit before and during dismantling efforts so you will have an accurate guide to follow when reassembling. Any number of screws, bolts or nuts may have to be loosened in order to take off a damaged piece and replace it with a new one. Pay strict attention to the order in which parts are assembled while dismantling so it can be accurately reversed when putting it all back together.

So-called regular bumpers that are not combined with an entire nose or tail may actually be comprised of many separate parts. Therefore, even a slightly dented bumper may reflect a series of non-repairable damaged pieces that will have to be replaced. Along with a bumper cover, units may include a horizontal pad, face bar, stone deflector, guards, trim, impact absorbers and various support brackets. Before buying a complete bumper unit at a wrecking yard, or ordering a complete bumper as-

A damaged bumper face bar is on the right and a new one on the left. Attached to units like these are foam pads, covers, guard brackets and rubber guards. The mounting support in the bottom right corner of this photo has been bent out of position. In addition, surrounding metal has been pushed in and cracked. Since extensive work would have been necessary to repair the damaged bumper piece, a new one was ordered and installed. All of the other parts were in good condition and did not need replacing. Notice that these main bumper pieces are not solid chunks of steel, like bumpers on cars built years ago. Instead, they are manufactured using pieces of heavy sheet metal molded and welded together to form a strong body part.

The urethane face bar cover and foam pad are seen here after being removed from their face bar support. Many new style bumpers are built this way. The foam pad absorbs a lot of impact before metal face bars are bent out of shape. Pads fit snugly inside covers, which are then secured to face bars with a number of small bolts along the bottom edge. Some designs incorporate bolts on the top edge while others feature snap in protrusions.

sembly set, dismantle the damaged unit to see just exactly what has been destroyed. You may be surprised to learn that only one part needs replacing because the rest have flexed with impact and will easily spring back into their original shape.

Bumper Repair

A lot of bumpers feature one metal main section surrounded by flexible covers and guards attached with thin metal brackets. Heavy-duty foam-like pads inside units absorb shock in efforts to reduce damage to metal segments. Many times, metal brackets and supports can be straightened with hammers and dollies. Once this is accomplished, remaining flexible parts are assembled around the repaired bumper frame, resulting in a perfectly shaped unit.

Heavy hammers may be needed to straighten out main brackets or solid metal supports. As long as stress cracks, broken welds or other significant metal fatigue problems do not appear, straightening efforts should render a metal bumper frame fully operational. However, should structurally significant damage present itself, you will have to substitute that piece with a new replacement.

Scratches and scuffs on urethane bumper guards and covers can sometimes be repaired. Auto parts and autobody paint and supply stores generally stock bumper repair kits. Instructions are included with all kits to clearly explain how to repair various kinds of damage. They work quite well to make abused urethane pieces look new. Be realistic in their expected use. Large avulsions or long tears may be too extensive for a bumper repair kit's abilities and will require part replacement.

License plate frames, lights and supports should also be considered when repairing bumpers. If they

When flexible bumper covers suffer abrasion damage, kits like this are available for their repair. Read the application instructions and intended use of these products before expecting them to fix the damage incurred by your bumper. Severe tears or avulsions might require part replacement, as that kind of damage could easily exceed the capability of repair kit materials.

Chem-Weld is another type of urethane repair material. Although some rips are reparable, most technicians prefer to replace such damaged urethane pieces with new ones. Products like this are available at autobody paint and supply stores. If you are not sure if your damaged part is reparable, ask a jobber for his or her recommendation. They are familiar with the products on their stores' shelves and receive a lot of input from professional autobody technicians as to the quality and implied repair characteristics of those products they have experience using. Since shelf space is limited, these stores generally carry only those items that technicians use on a frequent basis that have proved to work as expected.

Link uses a small dual action sander with a 320 grit adhesive backed sandpaper disc to smooth abrasion damage to this flexible painted bumper part. Masking tape protects grille sections above the work surface and black urethane trim below. When sanding has accomplished a smooth surface, the part will be sprayed with primer, sealer and then paint. A flexible additive will be mixed with paint products that will help them adhere to the material and prevent paint cracks.

are damaged, can hammer and dolly work repair them? If so, great. If not, replace them.

Don't overlook towing bars and their supports. Pickup trucks, Bronco IIs and many other vehicles feature towing mechanisms as part of stock or optional packages. Should damage occur to their assemblies, repairs must be considered and made.

Lots of minor dents and bends in solid metal chrome bumpers can be pounded out and straightened. This is especially important to those who are restoring older cars where stock chrome bumper replacements may not be easily located. Work of this sort usually requires the expertise of a professional using heavy-duty tools and special equipment.

To find a shop that specializes in solid metal bumper reconditioning, look in the yellow pages of your telephone book under "Plating." In addition to bumper straightening services, these facilities normally provide rechrome capabilities. In essence, they are a one stop outlet for complete solid metal chrome bumper restoration.

Grille and Brightwork

Especially for the restorers of vintage or classic cars, plating shops are a valuable resource for the reconditioning of chrome grilles and other related metal pieces. Many times, rust or corrosion may have destroyed the outer beauty of a hood orna-

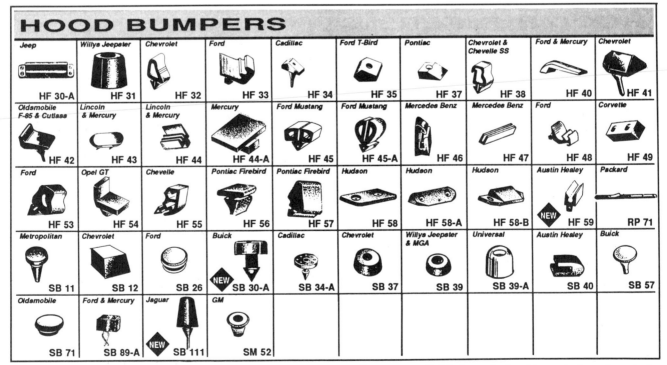

All sorts of little parts are included on fenders, hoods, trunk lids and doors. Molded rubber parts cushion body parts and protect them against metal-to-metal contact. To guarantee a first class repair job, be sure that all of these items are replaced and adjusted correctly. Items like these are available from dealership parts departments for newer cars and from specialty automotive parts outlets for older ones, as depicted in this illustration. Metro Molded Parts, Inc.

134

ment, grille or trim piece. Since replacements could be hard to find or exceptionally expensive to purchase, repair efforts by a plating specialist may prove very worthwhile and cost effective.

These days, plastic seems to be the mainstay for newer automobile grilles and brightwork. This implementation has been done, in part, to help cut manufacturing costs and assist in efforts to meet specific vehicle weight limitations for fuel economy. Newer technology has allowed manufacturers to develop plastics and plastic coatings that make grille and brightwork look just like the real chrome assemblies of yesteryear.

Repairs for these components basically entail replacement with new pieces since plastic seems to rarely hold together with glue. There are instances where a short piece can be glued back together but this piece must not have to support much weight or withstand stress. Check with an autobody paint and supply store for an appropriate glue designed for use on the type of plastic you are mending.

Grille and brightwork are attached to car bodies by a combination of screws, bolts and clips. Patience must be exercised when dismantling and assembling these units. Modern technology seems to have an affinity for hiding fasteners in awkward places. Refrain from tugging or pulling on parts to loosen them. Chances are good that another screw or clip is still holding pieces together. Carefully inspect each piece to see whether it is one solid unit or multiple pieces coupled together. Replace only those parts that are broken.

Parking lamps are also part of a grille assembly. Sometimes glue can be used to successfully repair cracked or broken lenses. Since their cost is minimal, however, replacements are generally easier and quicker to install. Be sure that gaskets are seated correctly or water will enter the lamp housing to cause corrosion on the reflector and around the light bulb socket. Replace burned-out bulbs.

Headlight Adjustment

Too many times, novice autobody technicians forget to adjust headlights after repairs to adjacent sheet metal. In a misaligned position, headlights will shine too far to the left, right, up or down to make them grossly ineffective, possibly to a point where they are beamed directly into oncoming traffic to cause safety problems.

Special headlight adjusting equipment is used to position headlights according to recommended specifications. Although a number of backyard mechanics have had moderate success adjusting headlight beams to match those of another car while both sets shine at a garage door, this is in no way truly accurate. Body shops and repair garages usually have the equipment necessary to adjust headlights, and the cost is nominal.

Basically, a box is attached to headlights by way of suction cups. Bubble levels on each box indicate vertical and horizonal light positions. Headlights feature two adjusting screws with one generally located at the bottom and the other on a side of the unit. Each screw is inserted over a spring so that inward or outward pressure can be applied to a headlight's frame piece. These screws are turned in or out until their appropriate bubble levels on the alignment box indicate perfect positioning.

Side Lights and Reflectors

Most newer cars are required to have side marking lamps or reflectors. In a side body collision, these items are vulnerable to damage. Cracked lenses, bent trim rings and fractured housings are not uncommon.

Bodywork procedures close to side light or reflector locations will require their removal. Make certain they are conveniently stored with other items from that part of the car and not misplaced under a workbench.

Kane's index fingers point to the two headlight adjustment screws on this Toyota pickup truck. They are indicative of most headlight adjustment mechanisms. The screw on the right side is turned in or out to angle the headlight's horizontal plane. The screw on the bottom adjusts vertical positions. After working on this part of your car, be sure to have headlights properly adjusted. For a nominal fee, like $10 to $20, an autobody technician or mechanic will attach a special headlight adjusting unit to headlights and adjust them according to bubble level indicators.

Damage to these items usually calls for replacement with new parts. Only a couple of screws hold lenses in place for easy dismantling. Gaskets placed between lamp lenses and bodies have to be set correctly to prevent moisture build-up inside the assembly. Protective pads located behind reflectors must also be positioned correctly to prevent scratches to paint underneath.

Used parts should be easy to find at wrecking or salvage yards. When trim rings exhibit signs of damage, be sure to inspect adjacent spots along housing edges. Should a gap between a housing and gasket persist, water will seep into the unit to cause corrosion and operational problems.

Body Side Moldings

These trim pieces are secured by screws, clips, adhesives or two-way tape. Decide how they are attached to your car by carefully lifting a corner and looking behind them. Use a special trim removal tool, or plug puller, with a cushion of thin wood or stout cardboard laid between it and the car body surface to prevent scratches.

Thin metal body side trim is delicate, as it can bend easily to form permanent creases. Be extra careful during its removal and installation. Have someone help you by supporting its length while you work to remove or install it. Minor scratches on metal pieces might be erased using fine chrome polish. Painted sections are touched up with an appropriate paint color by using the clean end of a paper matchstick or a fine artist's paintbrush.

It is imperative that all metallic trim pieces be attached to car bodies using proper spacers and designated clips as recommended by the manufacturer. If not, problems with rust and corrosion could develop in a short time.

Some dissimilar metals are not compatible, like steel and aluminum. When they are allowed to touch, corrosion always follows close behind. This commonly occurs when aluminum clip mechanisms are improperly installed along window and/or body side trim sections. As a vehicle vibrates and twists during normal driving, improperly installed clips can often tend to scratch paint and end up touching bare metal. The results of that, combined with rainwater and any other moisture, are corrosion and rust.

If you are not familiar with the installation techniques required for trim placement on your car, seek

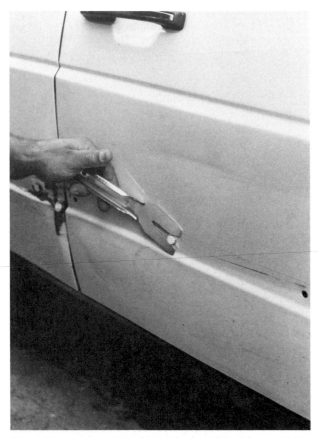

Special trim removal tools are designed just for reaching into tight spaces and popping out trim pins. Since this door will receive metalwork including paint removal, there is little concern over the tool creating a minor scratch. However, when removing trim from sections that present good paint and will not receive bodywork, you should lay a thin piece of stout cardboard or wood down under the tool to prevent scratches or minor metal blemishes. In this case, the tool could be maneuvered in an outward motion to pop out the plastic trim pin. Tool courtesy of The Eastwood Company.

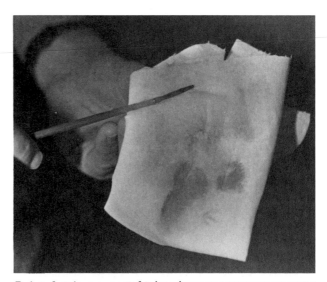

Painted stripes on metal trim pieces are common on some automobiles. When paint chips and touch-up are required, you can use the clean end of a paper matchstick to dab on new paint to tiny nicks. Better yet, use a fine artist's paintbrush to apply touch-up paint to nicks and larger chips. If paint on trim pieces presents multiple chips or peeling characteristics, consider sanding the piece clean and applying an entirely new coat of paint.

help from a local body shop, auto trim installer or dealership service department.

Drip Rails

Repairs to bent drip rails require work with an appropriate body hammer and spoon; dollies are usually too wide to be of any help. Severely displaced rails may have to be pounded back into position with a heavy hammer and then gently shaped with a lightweight body hammer. Be careful, because too much force could cause cracks along drip rail edges. In those cases, welding will have to be implemented to seal gaps.

Some drip rails are adorned with chrome-like covers that just snap on. Ends may be secured with small caps that also snap in place. Removal is accomplished by first pulling off end caps, where used, and

Trim removal operations may entail loosening the adhesive used to hold them in place. Hot air from a blow dryer or heat gun can loosen such adhesives to allow trim pieces to be pulled off safely. In addition, autobody supply stores carry assortments of chemical adhesive removers. Information on labels indicates exactly what the products' intended functions are and how they are to be applied. With using hot air, you may still need one of these products to remove residual glue.

This is a photo of the passsenger side rear window corner on a station wagon. The tire is sitting in back of the interior compartment. Heavy rust deposits are clear signs that either galvanic or poultice corrosion has occurred. Since equally spaced spots of rust are evident along the entire lower window trim piece, it might be safe to conclude that trim clips of a material not compatible with steel have made contact with the steel body to create a galvanic (dissimilar metals) corrosion condition. When installing trim back on cars, be sure clip insulators are positioned correctly and that paint chips are not caused by sloppy work.

The fiberglass fender flair on this car has been ripped apart. Repairs to the unit could make it look presentable but the unit's stability after repair efforts is questioned. In this case, a new flair is in order. Notice that a small chunk is still in place at the bottom of the fender's wheel opening. When installing new flairs, be sure to properly adjust and secure gaskets or beads between them and the car body.

then gently prying up one end off the drip rail base. Continue pulling off just small sections at a time until the entire length has been lifted off.

Although they are lightweight, long sections of loosened drip rail trim covers could tend to droop as they extend over the side of their base. This could cause pieces to sharply bend at a fulcrum point where another spot is just starting to break loose. Have a helper assist you by supporting the free end.

Fender Flairs

Fender flairs come in a wide variety of sizes and shapes. Some are made out of flexible urethane materials and others of stout fiberglass. While one vehicle will feature flairs that were obviously screwed on, another may sport flairs that look like they are an integral part of the fender or quarter panel.

Severely torn or avulsed fender flairs are not likely to support repair endeavors easily or with much longevity. You are better off, in these cases, to buy new flairs. Small blemishes on urethane items might be fixed, while fiberglass repairs are generally successful for minor cracks, stars and other light dents. Fix damaged fiberglass flairs using the same techniques explained earlier for fiberglass repairs.

Add-on ground effects employing fender flairs are usually installed with screws and special glue. Removing them from a car might cause paint to peel off with glue. Before new ground effects can be in-

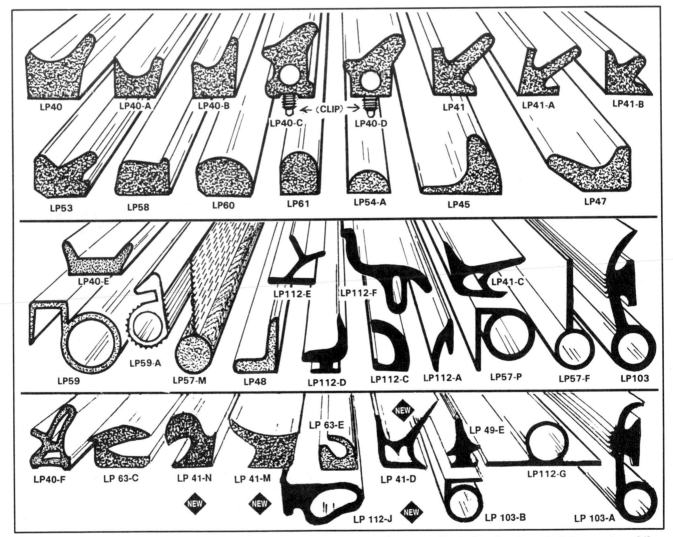

Door side seals, more commonly referred to as weather stripping, are important body parts. Without them, doors can rattle, leak water and allow road dust to easily enter the passenger compartment. Correct replacements for newer cars can be found at dealership parts departments. Generic shapes and sizes may also be located at autobody supply stores. Parts for classic and vintage automobiles, like these, may have to be ordered from specialty parts outlets. Check listings in periodicals such as Hemmings Motor News *for companies that offer replacement parts for older vehicles. Metro Molded Parts, Inc.*

stalled, make certain that peeled paint problems have been corrected with appropriate primer, sealer and paint products.

Flairs that have been custom fitted to look like they are part of a fender or quarter panel were screwed in place, possibly welded if metal, with seams covered and smoothed over with body filler. Taking them off will definitely cause paint problems around wheel openings. Before installing a new flair, all lingering filler will have to be sanded off to expose a clean working surface. Secure flairs with appropriate screws, adhesive, rivets or welds. If gaskets are provided, place them according to installation instructions included with the flair package.

Windows

New replacement windows are available through automotive glass companies. Used ones can be found at a wrecking yard. Compare glass replacement costs between various companies and wrecking yards. The difference may not be worth the hassle of removing windows from a junked car.

Wing window frames are normally secured by two screws from the top under weather stripping and two from underneath inside the inner door area. These small glass windows hang from frames by a hinged mechanism on the side and a support at the bottom. When replacing a wing window with a used unit, be sure all affiliated parts are intact.

To remove door windows, you must first dismantle the interior door panels. Holes on the interior part of doors allow minimal access to window supports, brackets and operating mechanisms. You will need a portable light to illuminate this enclosed area and careful attention to detail in order to determine just what has to be done to get glass out. With the window in a down position, the grooved window support going up each side and along the bottom of the door's window frame must be pulled out.

Pay attention to which parts come off first so that an exact reverse order can be followed when putting new glass in. Be extremely careful of cracked glass, as it could shatter at any time. Once all of the fasteners have been loosened and supports removed, maneuver the glass through the window slot on the interior side of the door. To replace glass, simply reverse the procedure.

Windshields are secured by clips or thick rubber moldings, or sealed in position with extra strong glue-like sealers. Any means might be employed, depending on your type of car, although most newer cars feature the sealer method.

To break seals between windshields and bases, a special tool is used. Basically, the tool consists of a wire with handles at both ends. Two people are needed for the procedure. As one operates a handle on the outside, another works inside. The wire is pulled around the windshield perimeter to cut sealer and break the bond between glass and base. Again,

great care must be exercised to prevent damaged glass from shattering.

Installing leakproof windshields requires more than just inserting a piece of glass into a hole. Even the slightest gap between glass and base can result in leaks. You can certainly install windshields yourself by securing clips, maneuvering rubber moldings or laying down a bead of sealer, but you take the chance of missing minor details that professional automotive glass installers take for granted. Many professional autobody technicians opt for the services of a professional to guarantee a leakproof windshield.

Emblems and Badges

Not much can be done to repair a mangled, cracked or shattered emblem or badge. Replacements will have to be purchased new or found at a

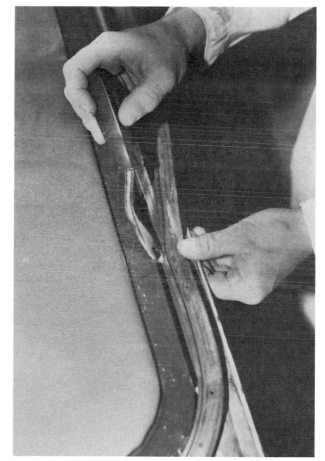

Some weather stripping materials are attached with adhesives. Others, like this section, are secured with plastic pins. A plug puller tool is gently slipped behind weather stripping and slid to the side until it meets resistance. At that point, slight downward pressure on the plug puller handle should easily pop pins out of their receptacles, loosening that section of weather stripping. Take your time while doing this work to avoid accidental tears to the material or scratches on painted panels.

wrecking yard. These items are usually fastened to car bodies with pins inserted through panels and then secured by flat metal clips.

If only small blemishes mar the surface of emblems or badges, delicate filing or sanding may smooth surfaces to a satisfactory finish. Chrome pieces could be rechromed to perfection at a plating shop. Painted segments are repainted with an artist's fine bristled paintbrush.

New car emblems and badges are available at dealership parts departments. You can also find replacement decals, like those on the inside of trunk lids, that show how spare tires and jacking equipment are stowed. To locate new or used emblems and badges for older, vintage and classic cars, peruse issues of *Hemmings Motor News* and other auto-related magazines. Auto swap meets and vintage car clubs also serve as valuable sources for attaining information about hard-to-find auto parts.

Weather Stripping

To keep doors, trunk lids and hatchbacks water and dust tight, weather stripping is installed around their perimeters to ensure tight seals. This soft material is either glued in place or attached with clips. Replacement is warranted when tears or gouges are found or when a section becomes flat and hard.

Damaged weather stripping that is glued on is simply pulled off for removal. After bodywork in the area has been complete, residual glue is wiped off using an adhesive remover product. New weather stripping is installed with new glue designed for such use.

Adhesives and rolls of bulk weather stripping material are available at autobody paint and supply stores. Be sure to bring a section of the old weather stripping with you to the store so you can quickly match the size and style needed. Accurate measurement of the perimeters to be weather stripped will also help to ensure enough material is purchased.

Another type of weather stripping features holes along its base for the insertion of small plastic pins. These wide topped pins fit into the slots and are then inserted into holes located around the perimeters of doors, trunk lids and hatchbacks. Glue is not necessary.

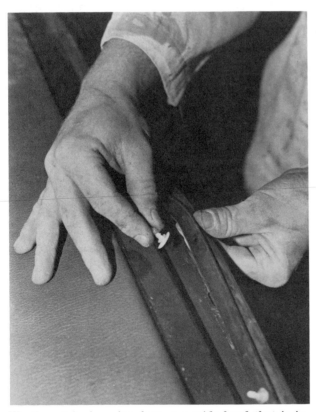

Weather stripping pins feature a wide head that is inserted into holes molded into sections of material. In order to fit into such tight holes, heads are commonly shaped in long, thin, oval patterns instead of being round. When you insert pins into place on weather stripping, try to twist them so that the elongated part of the pin head fits along the length of the strip. This ensures maximum holding strength.

Needle nose pliers with their tips bent at a ninety degree angle are used to remove and insert weather stripping pins. The tool works great, as you can force pins loose by applying direct outward force instead of having to pry against an assembly's metal face. Tools like this are available at autobody supply stores and some auto parts houses.

Overview

Along with the items covered in this section, many other automotive accessories have to be repaired, serviced or replaced when damaged by a collision. Items such as wheels, tires, vinyl striping and lettering, pinstriping, bent seat frames, and radio antennas all have to be fixed or replaced when broken or disfigured.

Vinyl tops might have to be loosened or completely removed to repair roof dents. Have a professional put them back on, however. The process involved in securing vinyl tops is tricky. Not only does the material have to be spread tight, it has to be steadfastly secured. A loose edge will become a large flap in no time after exposure to wind velocities experienced during highway driving.

Ragtop, headliner and upholstery repairs also fall into much the same category as vinyl tops. Unless you have experience in the trade, you might hire a professional to mend and replace torn material.

All in all, unless yours is a project car and you have the time and are bound and determined to learn by trial and error how to fix everything that is broken, remember that the cost for a professional to amend your mistakes and then make needed repairs will cost you more than if he or she were allowed to tackle the job right from the start.

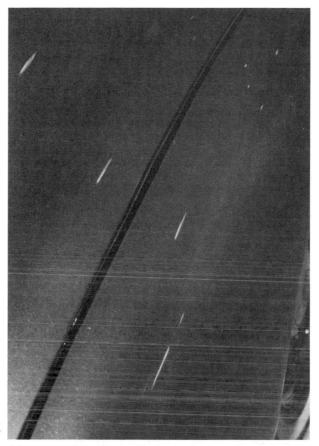

Most newer cars do not have rear fenders. Instead, quarter panels are shaped to include fender areas. Older cars frequently feature rear fenders, of which most include a bead of material that cushions the area between fender and car body as seen here. It is imperative that beads like these are properly placed and adjusted before fenders are cinched up against the car body. Improper placement will not only cause the piece to look bad, it might adversely affect its ability to prevent scratches and wear-throughs from the direct rubbing together of fender and body metals.

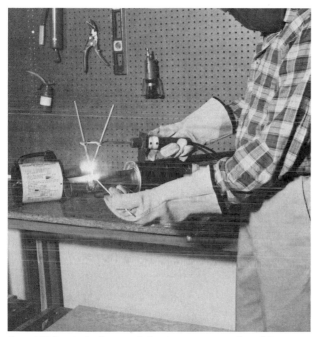

In addition to body panel damage, many other things can be broken on cars as a result of accidental collisions. Mufflers and tail pipes are no exceptions. Sometimes minor torch welding repairs are all that is needed to repair such items. Here a carbon arc torch is used to weld a section of exhaust pipe to a muffler. A unit like this connects to an arc welder's leads and is operated at 75 amps or less. The Eastwood Company

11

Preparing for Paint

All of your autobody work efforts will be marred if paint preparation operations are not done correctly. Large sand scratches, pinholes and other surface blemishes will show through paint to look tacky and amateurish. If incompatible primers, sealers or primer-surfacers are used, paint might peel, crack, blister or orange peel.

It is of utmost importance you use only one brand's complete paint system whenever spraying any paint related product on a car body. Just because one company's primer is priced less than another's is not reason enough to mix and match

products. DuPont, PPG, Glasurit and the others have individually combined research and technology into one complete system for each of their paint products. A paint system includes thinner or reducer, epoxy primer, sealer, primer-surfacer, base coats, color coats and clear coats.

Improper paint preparations caused the repaint coat on this car to easily flake off. Tedious work with a putty knife and air pressure removes that layer so proper paint preparations can be made for a new paint job. Besides the use of paint products that are clearly not compatible (e.g., different product brands), failure to use a paint sealer can be enough to ruin an otherwise perfect paint finish. Consult the jobber at an autobody paint and supply store before purchasing body filler, glazing putty, sealer, primer-surfacer and paint products to be certain that all of them will work together uniformly.

Almost all of the body and paint products you need to use have applicable information sheets available at autobody paint and supply stores. Guides, like these on display at Wesco Autobody Supply, are supplied by product manufacturers and are free for the asking. They include mixing instructions, curing times and other pertinent information about various products.

142

Purchase all of your body filler, glazing putty, resin and hardeners from the same autobody paint and supply store you intend to purchase paint products from. This way, the store can provide you with a completely compatible system, from filler to paint. If you plan to have a professional paint your car, be sure to purchase only those filler, primer and sealer products he or she recommends, so that they will be compatible with the paint products used in the spray booth.

Sanding

A major share (25 percent) of an autobody technician's time is routinely spent sanding. Old paint has to be ground off, filler sanded to produce a flat even surface and glazing putty sanded to a smooth, scratch free finish before basic paint preparation procedures can begin.

Before a painter can spray on sealer or primer-surfacer, surface finishes must be extra smooth with no evidence of sand scratches or tiny pinholes.

Should these blemishes present themselves, apply a new skim coat of glazing putty and additional sanding maneuvers. If, on the other hand, you paint over small sand scratches or pinholes, their outline and texture will be enhanced to stick out like a sore thumb.

Sanding operations must not be taken lightly. You will have to continually feel an autobody's surface with your hand to be assured that the finish is smooth and conforms to the overall shape of panels, ridges or curves. Place a soft cloth between your hand and the car's body to accentuate your hand's sensitivity. Look down the sides and up from the bottom for signs of deep scratches, wobbles or imperfections of any kind.

Should dishes appear, be sure to lightly hammer down high ridges and then refill low spots with filler, including a 3 in. wide area around the perimeter. This way, low spots will be filled and their edges feathered to smoothly blend with adjacent areas. The same procedure must be applied to deep scratches. Refill and sand smooth.

Too much attention cannot be given to sanding operations. After all, you are essentially sculpting a

Terry Vanhee carefully uses a small dual action sander to smooth and feather paint edges along the perimeter of a body repair. Tape along the door edge, handle and key lock protects surfaces from sand scratches. Before color coats are sprayed on, 320 to 400 grit paper is used to smooth primer-surfacer to a fine finish. Meticulous work in getting panels "nib" free pays off when paint finishes glisten to perfection.

Dark spots on top of this hood repair area represent a "Guide Coat" finish. Basically, guide coats are mixes of a compatible primer that spurts out dark splotches on a surface. Finish sanding removes those dark spots to reveal that surfaces have been sanded perfectly even and flat. Sanding with a block continues until all dark sections are gone to guarantee all high spots have been feathered into the general area.

143

new part to a damaged panel. Be alert to use appropriately sized sanding blocks: long boards for work on wide panels and short blocks on small jobs. Gradually work your way to finer sandpaper as results indicate that excessive filler has been knocked down, presenting a need for finish work to smooth lingering raised spots and feather edges.

Filling Pinholes

Which product you use is of little significance as long as the results produce a smooth, scratch and pinhole free finish. You must follow mixing and application instructions carefully. Putting in too much hardener will cause creamy mixtures to set prematurely making smooth applications almost impossible. Instead of laying down an evenly textured coat of putty, you will be fighting with a clay-like substance that curls behind your squeegee and refuses to adhere. In those cases, you have to discard the mix and start over.

Tiny pinholes are covered with a very light skim coat of glazing putty. Mix a small batch as needed according to directions and apply with a clean squeegee. Allow the material to cure and then sand as necessary with 180 grit or finer sandpaper using a sanding block or board. Continue to sand and periodically feel the area with your hand until you are satisfied it is as flat, even and smooth as you want it to be.

Make sure that edges expose an even feathering of bare metal, primer and paint layers between good paint and the area just repaired. This allows for the buildup of new paint products to match those existing on the car body, as primer-surfacer will be sanded flush with 400 to 500 grit paper to blend the repair area with the existing finish.

Masking

Minimal masking is required for the application of sealer and primer-surfacer. Overspray is not much of a problem because of the products' heavy solids content. Additionally, these finishes will be sanded with 400 to 500 grit paper to effect an exceptionally smooth finish with blended edges all around.

Because newspaper is so thin and porous, do *not* use it for masking. Use only paper that is specifically intended for automotive painting use. Actual auto masking paper is thick and will not absorb paint products. If you have to use newspaper, make sure that each section is two to three pages thick.

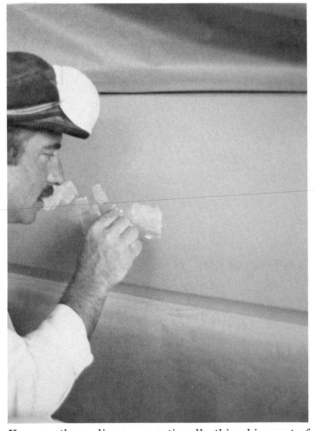

Kane gently applies an exceptionally thin skim coat of glazing putty over tiny pinholes found by Vanhee on a repaired door panel. Because the pinholes were so few and so small, need for a complete putty coat was unwarranted. Cautious work with a razor blade filled in pinholes and did not scratch the surface. Vanhee sanded the area with 400 grit paper to ensure a smooth, flat finish.

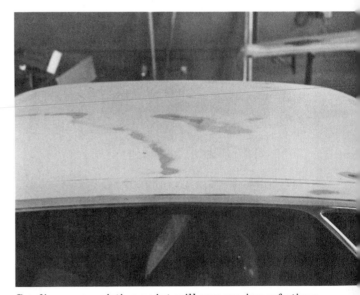

Sanding over existing paint will remove imperfections and dead paint. This roof was sanded with a dual action sander and 320 grit paper. Primer-surfacer will go on next and also be sanded to perfection. Before color coats are sprayed on, a sealer (adhesion promoter) will be applied. Before putting anything on the finish, though, all dust and dirt must be thoroughly cleaned off. Professionals use wax and grease remover to get the big stuff off, followed with glass cleaner to really get surfaces clean. Just before painting, they wipe all surfaces with a tack cloth to remove any traces of lingering dust.

Masking tape designed for automotive use will not leave glue residue when it is pulled off a car body. Cheap masking tape found in discount stores is not made the same. It can absorb paint products, leave an adhesive residue when removed and may allow paint to creep under edges because it does not seal as well as automotive paint masking tape. Spare yourself frustration and spend the extra few dollars it takes to buy quality materials.

Since primered areas will be finish sanded, do not mask off any more than the surfaces that received filler and sanding work. Generally, Vanhee masks a square or rectangular space surrounding feathered perimeters to within an inch or so of the edge. There is no special reason for this, except that squares and rectangles are easiest and quickest to apply. He stays about an inch away from feathered edges at the closest point, as this leaves plenty of room to feather in new primer-surfacer coats.

The top rear driver's side corner of this mini van received body repair work and has been primed. A piece of cardboard was placed in the gap between the top of the hatchback door and roof. Its snug fit worked great for masking that area for primer and guide coat applications. Final sanding with 400 to 500 grit paper will smooth this area to a point where it will be ready for paint.

This Corvette fender has been repaired and shot with primer-surfacer. Because primer-surfacer products are so heavily laden with solids, overspray problems are not as great as with other paint products. Therefore, masking can be held to just the immediate area instead of extending to cover an entire vehicle. Although the fender looks smooth, primer-surfacers need to be sanded to remove any trace of underlying sand scratches or other blemishes. For masking, rely on heavy paper designed for automotive masking purposes. Newspaper is thin and porous and can allow paint products to bleed through.

Vanhee cleans the rear roof area of a mini van in preparation for paint. All of the preliminaries have been completed; that is, bodywork, filler and glazing applications, sanding, primer-surfacer and finish sanding. He is using glass cleaner with ammonia and a Scotch Brite scouring pad to clean the area and roughen up the finish on existing paint at the same time. Existing paint should be scoured to remove its gloss before spraying sealer and color coats to help materials adhere their best.

Epoxy Primer

Before any paint product can be sprayed onto a repaired surface, it must be clean. Air pressure from a compressor works great to blow off sanding dust from body surfaces and behind hidden areas between doorjambs, seams, cracks and the like. Use a clean cloth dabbed with wax and grease remover to clean the masked area and remove lingering traces of wax, grease, vinyl dressing and other contaminants. Then, just before spraying primer, wipe the area off with a tack cloth to remove tiny specks of sanding dust or other minute debris.

Bare metal must be covered to prevent oxidation from corrosion and rust. One of the best products to use for this is epoxy primer such as PPG's DP 40. Application directions and other needed information, clearly printed on container labels and application guide sheets, are readily available at autobody paint and supply stores.

Plastic body filler can be applied directly to bare metal, but some autobody specialists working in areas of high humidity with lots of moisture problems prefer to coat bare metal with DP 40 and then apply filler. After filler and glazing putty have been sanded to perfection, another coat of DP 40 epoxy primer is applied to ensure filler and bare metal are adequately protected against moisture induced corrosion and rust problems. Check with an autobody paint and supply jobber for his or her recommendation.

For project cars, you should definitely consider coating repaired bare metal parts with an epoxy primer, like DP 40, before putting them in storage where they will sit for months until you are ready to start painting. This coating will protect bare metal against moisture contact and prevent rust from getting a start.

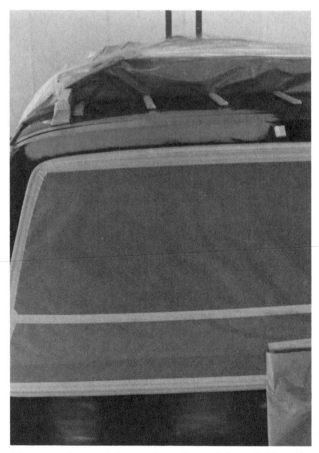

More precise masking is done for paint work than for primer-surfacer and guide coat applications. In addition to needing more definitive masking to protect against relatively thin paint applications and overspray, a wide area of the roof will also receive a coat of clear paint to help the repair match the surrounding paint finish. This is done because the existing paint system included a clear coat. When all of it has cured, it will be wet sanded to further blend the feathered clear coat edges.

Masking is under way in preparation for application of primer-surfacer to this front body panel. After all of the priming chores have been completed, this masking paper and tape will be removed and fresh materials put on. Because air pressure will blow out along with paint during the spraying process, dried primer-surfacer could be dislodged from masking paper to fall on newly applied paint coats. Vehicles must be clean and present no opportunity for dust or dirt to blow off of them while paint is being sprayed. Should this happen, imperfections in the paint finish will occur.

146

Primer-Surfacer

Primer-surfacers are used to fill in tiny sand scratches and other minute surface blemishes. Some novice autobody technicians believe they can fill in low spots with repeated coats of primer-surfacer and thus refrain from having to use any plastic filler. This is a big mistake. A coat of primer-surfacer 1/16 in. thick will shrink a lot more than a ¼ in. layer of plastic filler.

Primer-surfacers must be mixed with a solvent according to instructions on the label. As part of an overall paint system, this product and the solvent used to thin it must be compatible with all additional paint products that will be applied later. The autobody paint and supply jobber will be able to recommend a suitable paint system compatible with your car's existing paint.

A number of primer-surfacer coats must be applied to repaired areas until sufficiently built up to fill in feathered edges. Remember, it will be sanded again so excess primer-surfacer is better than not

A light guide coat adorns the quarter panel on this Toyota coupe. Block sanding until all of the dark marks disappear shows a technician that the panel has been sanded flat and even. If you were to sand with your hand instead of a flat bottomed block, contours along the palm side of your fingers' knuckles could cause slight grooves that would remove guide coat from low spots, giving you a false impression that the surface was flat.

enough. Too little material will not fill as expected to allow sand scratches a chance to show through paint. Be sure to follow mixing directions, drying times and recoat procedures carefully. Applying coats too dry or too wet will cause problems as will recoat applications made before solvents from preceding coats have had time to evaporate.

Once an adequate layer of primer-surfacer has been applied, use a 400 grit sanding disc or a small DA sander or a piece of 400 to 500 grit paper on a sanding block to smooth the surface and feather edges. Take your time to ensure a perfectly smooth, blemish free finish.

Paint Sealer

Sealers accomplish two goals. First, they form a barrier between primer-surfacers and other paint products so that primer-surfacers do not absorb sol-

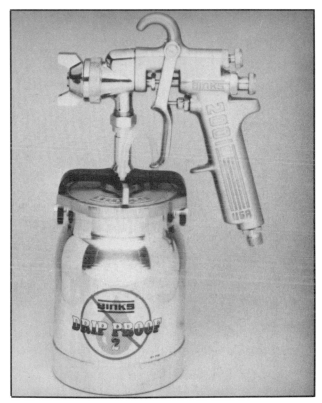

The equipment you use to spray paint products can have an effect on how well the finish on your car turns out. Professional painters do not skimp when it comes to painting tools or equipment. Binks is a well-known brand of spray paint gun throughout automotive circles. Other brands are also good. Cheap spray guns have been known to easily clog during spray sessions and fail to give expected patterns. Replacement parts have been hard to find. Most experienced auto painters advise novices to pay a little more for quality, well-machined spray guns with easy to locate reconditioning kits. After every paint spray session, always take the necessary time to clean spray guns to the point where absolutely no paint is left anywhere on them. The Eastwood Company

vents or any other materials contained in successive paint coats. Second, they provide an excellent paint base for maximum adhesion. In fact, some sealers are commonly referred to as adhesion promoters.

Dennis Laursen, sales rep for Bel-Tech Auto Paint and twenty year veteran painter, strongly recommends the use of a sealer after repaired areas have been sprayed with primer-surfacer. Because you may not know exactly what kind of primer-surfacer was initially used on your car, new paint may react with this primer-surfacer to adversely affect the final color. When you use a sealer, this worry is abated.

A number of sealers are available for different paint applications. Some are strictly designed for enamel products, others for lacquer and urethane based paints. You have to consult an autobody paint jobber to determine exactly the type of sealer required for your specific job and the paint system you have employed.

Except for very light sanding to remove nibs of dirt or debris caught on the surface, there is no need to sand sealers. In fact, sanding sealer material will reduce its overall thickness, which could cause problems if too much were sanded away and primer-surfacer exposed. Paint is sprayed directly onto a sealer application after it has cured according to directions and the surface wiped clean with a tack cloth.

Final Overview

Once a damaged body panel has been metal-worked, filled, coated with glazing putty and finished sanded, the remaining work mainly consists of sealing the repair and then coating it with primer-surfacer to perfect and guarantee the smoothness of an actual surface's finish. Sealer application really is a painter's concern, based on the type of color coats he intends to use.

Although the work of repairing damaged automotive sheet metal sounds rather easy, actual maneuvers can be time consuming and labor intensive. A few minutes operating a long sanding board over a wide panel covered with a layer of plastic filler will quickly prove this point. The use of electric or pneumatic sanding tools will greatly help to has-

Automotive paint products are mixed to arrive at specific color blends. These containers hold various color tints. They are mixed in prescribed amounts to base colors in order to develop specific shades. A microfiche machine is used to look up numeric paint codes that explain exactly how much of which tints are mixed with what bases to come up with specific color shades. Paint codes on identification labels on cars show painters precisely what color was originally sprayed on a vehicle at the factory. Autobody paint and supply stores use the same techniques.

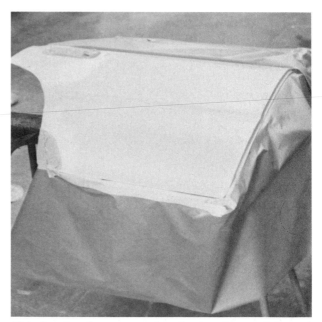

This door has been removed so that its edges and the car's doorjambs could be easily accessed for painting. Because no other part of the vehicle body will be painted in this case, the door will be sprayed alone. If additional parts of the car body were going to be painted, the doors would have been put back on and painted at the same time as the body to ensure a matched spray application. Individual car parts can be painted separately. They are suspended from wires or placed on sawhorses in the paint booth.

ten the process and also lessen one's workload. Caution has to be exercised with their use, as the power they possess can rapidly sand through filler and ruin an otherwise perfect application.

Novice autobody repair technicians must practice the techniques of the trade in order to get a feel for various maneuvers and the use of special tools and equipment.

As much as true blooded auto enthusiast old-timers hate to admit, plastic fillers have become the means by which newer automotive sheet metal panels are repaired. For these cars, old school methods, although tried and true, of brazing and leading in are fast becoming lost arts, saved only by those old car die-hards who have the opportunity to practice their craft on cars of yesteryear that feature an adequate amount of sheet metal to withstand the rigors of repeated heat applications and offer plenty of body to work with.

You can learn more about the techniques used in this profession by attending autobody workshops and welding classes taught at community colleges and vocational schools by skilled, seasoned veterans with years of experience in the autobody repair business. In addition, some autobody experts are among the ranks of car club members all over the country who are eager to share their fountains of information with any fellow auto enthusiast who demonstrates an interest in cars and a sincere desire to learn. People like George Ridderbusch are delighted to teach fellow members various ways to fix cars that they have perfected through years of frustrating trial and error.

More than anything else, though, you have to be serious about the safety factors involved with this type of work. There is no valid reason for anyone in the autobody repair business, either professional or enthusiast, to breathe in dangerous chemical fumes or volumes of body filler sanding dust. Wear respirators or dust masks as recommended.

While working with metal cutting or grinding equipment, always wear gloves and face protection. You might not think twice about buying a special doodad for your car, so why hesitate spending a little bit on yourself for a full face shield and a pair of leather gloves?

Remember to practice with a scrap door, fender, deck lid or hood before attempting actual repairs on your car. Who knows, after making a few repairs, you might discover that you have a real talent for this kind of work and with continued practice and experience you might someday be regarded as a premier autobody repair and customizing genius and be the person others come to for advice and assistance.

There is always more to learn about autobody repair. After all, Kane has been working at it for twenty years and still seems to learn something new every day. But, everybody has to start somewhere and I hope this book has given you the basics you need to at least go out and give it a try.

Certain types of automotive paints are buffed with compound after they have cured according to label instructions. Buffing brings out a deep glossy finish. The work is messy, as seen here. Compound splatters all over and buffing pads distribute a lot of lint.

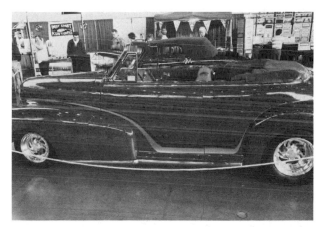

Professional autobody technicians and customizers were not born with the knowledge and experience needed to build cars like this one on display at a major car show. Somewhere along the line, somebody had to teach them one end of a body hammer from the other. Many of their abilities came from trial and error work, painstakingly applied to run-down wrecks that they were allowed to tinker with. Working on cars can be a lot of fun, especially once you learn how to do the things you want to do. So find some old doors and fenders and start practicing. Repair your cars as needed and have a good time. You'll never know the limits of your abilities until you test them. Who knows, as you continue to work and learn, maybe someday the products of your labor will be admired by thousands who attend car shows displaying automobiles with bodywork finished by you.

149

Repairing a Medium Hit — Start to Finish

Body damage consists of a large, shallow dent on the passenger side front door with a crease at the top and a "V" dent at the bottom to indicate that impact started from the front and went toward the rear. The back door has wrinkled metal on the door edge. Body side trim has been ripped loose. Some pins are still in their receptacles, which means the mounting supports on the trim itself could be broken.

A closer look at wrinkled door edge metal on the back door shows that the gap between doors has widened and the plastic mount on trim is completely broken off. Work will entail straightening out the metal and narrowing the gap to equal that to the identical position on the opposite side.

Some door handles are released from operating shafts by way of "C" clip springs. The handle on this Volkswagen Jetta has a hollow interior that is exposed by prying off a cap. A Phillips head screw holds the handle in place.

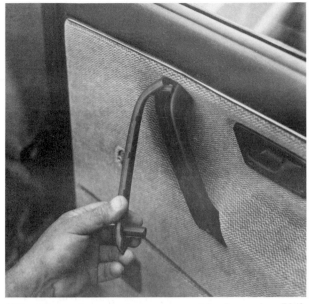

Although most armrests are removed by loosening Phillips head screws directly, the ones on this car are hidden behind a plastic cap. Gently use a small screwdriver to loosen an edge, then pry the cap off to expose fasteners.

In lieu of a hand held screwdriver, cordless units make work progress faster. These are truly luxury tools that work well and have more torque than expected. Various tips fit small to large Phillips and slotted screw heads as well as Allen head and Torx patterns

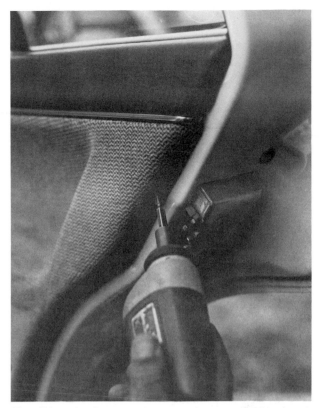

Not all interior door panels come off the same. This Jetta's panels are secured with four Phillips head screws and some plastic clips. The top portion slips over the door frame and has to be lifted up in order to be removed.

Special trim removal tools, like this one from The Eastwood Company, are thin enough to easily fit between door panels and frames, yet stout enough to be able to pry out stubborn pins or clips.

151

Vapor barriers should be replaced after doors have been worked on. This one is set behind plastic fasteners. A sharp razor knife will be used to cut plastic away from the fasteners so it can be folded out of the way. When the repair is complete, the vapor barrier will be put back.

A slide hammer with a ninety degree hook can pull out a lot of metal. Practice with this tool will help you estimate how much force to use when pulling out different kinds of damage.

Kane holds a dolly in his left hand while using a pick head to flatten high points. Sometimes you have to reach a long way to effect repairs. A pick point is used for small, highly arched imperfections.

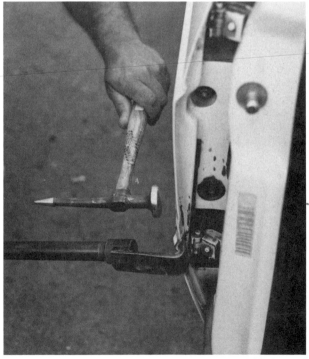

A slide hammer is used to pull out the bulk of folded metal along the rear door edge. While maintaining steady outward pressure on the slide hammer, Kane uses a body hammer to flatten metal.

152

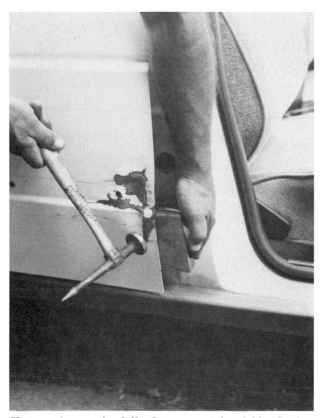

Using a pick hammer from The Eastwood Company, Kane lightly taps down high spots along this ridge. Metal is worked to as close a perfect job as possible, then covered with body filler to hide the repair.

Hammering on the dolly flattens metal quickly. Rather than smack the hammer against metal sharply with a lot of force, it is better to rely on a lot of rapid, light taps.

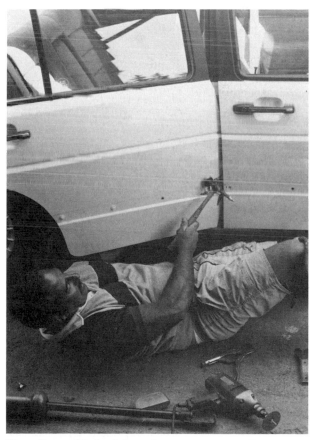

A dent puller from The Eastwood Company has been tightened against the dent. Much of the impression has been pulled out. Outward force is applied to the tool while light hammer hits with a pick end flatten high points.

Kane lies on his back in order to operate a dolly with his left hand and a hammer with his right. Sometimes you have to work in rather uncomfortable positions.

153

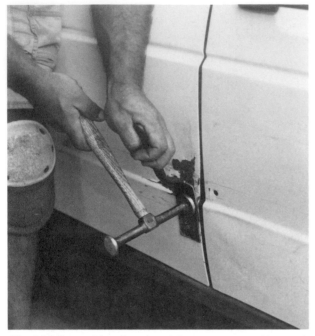

The folded metal has been straightened quite well. In this photo, Kane uses a spoon to spread out blows from a hammer. This is done to flatten a wide area at one time and to push down high spots so they better blend with the surrounding metal.

A slight crease line can be seen on the front door. It will remain, as body filler will remedy the problem. Repairs to the rear door look good at this point.

Although chipped paint makes the area look extra bad, the dent and folded metal repair has progressed nicely. Little holes around the trim hole on the results are left from work with a dent puller.

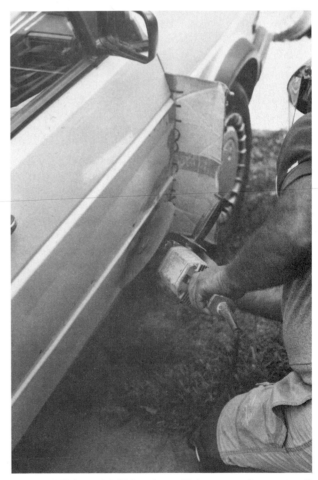

With a full face shield in place, Kane uses a large 24 grit sanding disc to remove paint. The piece of cardboard stuck in the gap between the front door and fender will protect that area from accidental sanding scratches.

A tarp covers the passenger compartment to protect it from sparks and eventual sanding dust. Work with the grinder and 24 grit disc smooths metal slightly while removing paint. Notice the protective cardboard along the bottom door gap.

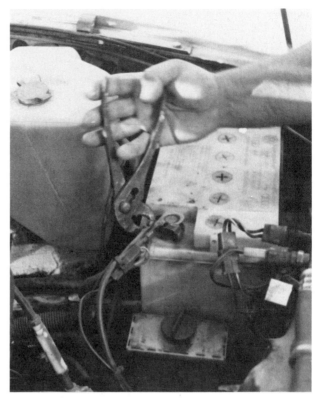

Before doing any electric welding on any vehicle, disconnect the battery. Electricity from welding has been known to travel through car bodies and into electrical systems. A great surge in electrical energy in a car's electrical system can do a lot of damage, like burn out computers.

A piece of coarse sandpaper is folded over and used to get paint and debris out of the small low spots. A small sanding disc with angled corners cut around its circumference would clean these spots quickly.

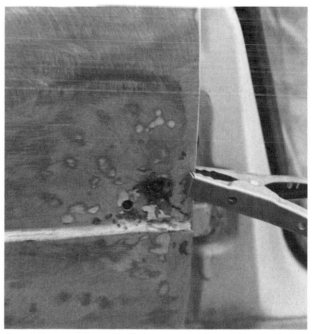

A welding unit's ground clamp must be well grounded to the work. Here the clamp has been secured to bare metal on the door. Fifty amps were used to weld up a spot on the door where a dent puller screw was inserted.

155

This handy little welding unit from The Eastwood Company did an excellent job filling in holes on this thin sheet metal door. Amp levels can be adjusted on this machine and it uses 110 volt household current. Always wear heavy gloves and a welder's helmet when welding. Make sure the dark lens is of an appropriate grade.

Filler covers the back door to extend a few inches past metal repair in all directions. Even though the filler application is not perfectly smooth, enough material is in place to effect repairs.

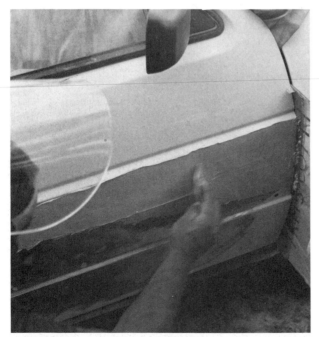

Kane applies the first coat of body filler using a medium-size squeegee. Notice that a wide area is covered with filler, even parts that were not damaged. This is so sanding maneuvers can feather in adjacent areas and make the entire panel flat and even.

An air file is used to initially knock down bulk filler material. Kane always keeps both hands on this machine and never lets it sit idle. The sander is moved up and down or crossways and never left in one place. Notice that Kane is wearing a dust mask.

156

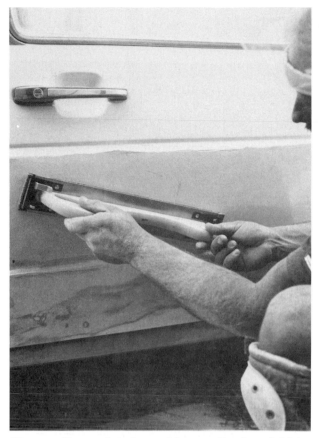

Close sanding work is done with a sanding board. Maintaining firm pressure on the tool guarantees that the flat surface is sanding all areas evenly.

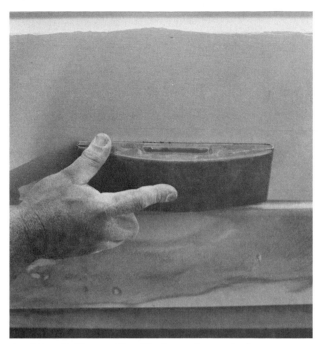

A wide, pliable sanding block can be used along grooves and ridges.

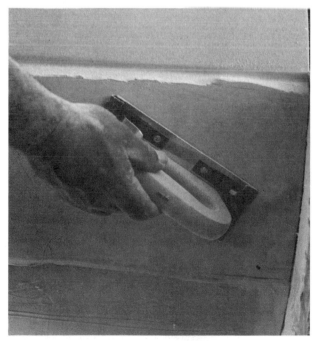

A small sanding board does a good job sanding in tighter spaces next to cardboard and door edges.

A short, pliable sanding block works best for tight areas near grooves, contours and ridges. Here it is used to knock down filler along the top ridge and also material close to the cardboard barrier.

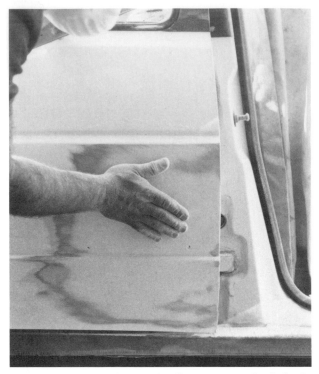

When body filler material had been applied and sanded to perfection, a mixture of glazing putty and hardener was blended together on Kane's mixing board and applied.

Throughout the entire repair, Kane constantly feels the panel with his free hand to sense high and/or low spots. He does this to bare metal, body filler and glazing putty. To increase your hand's sensitivity, lay a cloth between it and the work surface.

These doors have been metalworked, had body filler applied and sanded smooth, a skim coat of glazing putty put on and sanded to perfection.

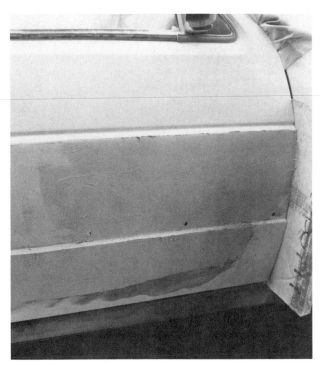

A second coat of body filler was applied because some imperfections persisted after the first. Additional hammer and spoon work was done after the first coat of filler was sanded.

The area was masked off and shot with primer-surfacer. Now it is ready for further paint preparation. One minor mistake has been made—the second trim hole from the front on the rear door was covered over with filler and forgotten. Before painting, it will have to be accessed from the inner side of the door and drilled out.

Bibliography

Because much has been written about autobody repair in many different contexts, it would be foolish to rely on just a few individuals to amass the information needed to write a definitive book on the subject. Therefore, I have listed sources from which I gathered additional material, and included addresses where you may write should you have any questions or comments.

Information and/or material was not necessarily quoted from all sources. In many cases, these books, articles or product guides produced questions that were then answered by professionals like Mycon, Kane, Vanhee, Laursen and Burrous. Therefore, even though you may not have seen actual quotes from some of the companies or individuals, they were helpful nonetheless.

The Eastwood Company
Auto Restoration News
Jim Poluch, Advertising Manager
580 Lancaster Avenue, Box 296
Malvern, PA 19355

BASF Corporation, R-M, Glasurit
George P. Auel, Manager—Marketing Communications
Suite 401 East, 19855 West Outer Drive
Dearborn, MI 48124

PPG Industries, Inc.
Linda Toncray, Advertising Manager
19699 Progress Drive
Strongsville, OH 44136

E. I. DuPont De Nemours & Company
Thomas P. Speakman, Marketing Development and Services
Wilmington, DE 19898

The Key to Metal Bumping, Third Edition
by Frank T. Sargent, available through
The Eastwood Company

Mitchell International
Collision Estimating Guide References
9889 Willow Creek Road
San Diego, CA 92126

Drake Restoration Supplies
4504 "C" Del Amos Boulevard
Torrance, CA 90503

Mustangs Unlimited
185 Adams Street
Manchester, CT 06040

Sherman & Associates, Inc.
28460 Groesbeck
Roseville, MI 48066

Year One, Inc.
Box 2023
Tucker, GA 30085

Metro Molded Parts, Inc.
P.O. Box 33130
Minneapolis, MN 55433

3M Automotive Trades Division
Bldg. 223-6NW, 3M Center
St. Paul, MN 55144

Hemmings Motor News
Box 100
Bennington, VT 05201

Index